W9-BHK-406

NATURAL FOODS SPELL LOVE NOT FAD

What rich party dish made from uncertain packaged contents can match the pure goodness of an untainted, sun-ripened tomato dipped in fresh mayonnaise?—of a plump new radish sparked by butter and pepper instead of salt—or the lingering, nutty taste-joys whole grains contribute to fragrant, honest, home-baked bread?

IT'S EASIER THAN YOU THINK to turn out the Middle East's popular chickpea appetizer, HUMUS, served with Arabic bread—BAY LEAF KEBABS —NOTTINGHAM HOTPOT—BASQUE SHEPHERD'S BREAD—a memorable, luscious chowder —and a creamy frozen dessert from one raw, whole banana in less than ten minutes.

Learn how to add special relish to marvelous soups, hearty stews, casseroles, and a range of international regional delicacies by knowing that every single item you put into them increases food value along with flavor.

THE LOS ANGELES TIMES NATURAL FOODS COOKBOOK

JEANNE VOLTZ, formerly food editor of the *Los Angeles Times,* is now food editor of *Woman's Day* magazine. She is the author of *California Cookbook* and, with Burks Hammer, of *L.A. Gourmet: Favorite Recipes from Famous Los Angeles Restaurants.* Ms. Voltz lives in New York and Miami, Florida.

SIGNET Books of Special Interest

☐ **THE JOY OF COOKING, Volume I by Irma S. Rombauer and Marion Rombauer Becker.** America's all-time, best-selling cookbook is now being published in two convenient-to-use volumes. Volume I of this revised and enlarged edition contains main course recipes that will make all your meals into delicious dining. (#E8625—$2.50)

☐ **THE JOY OF COOKING, Volume II by Irma S. Rombauer and Marion Rombauer Becker.** This volume of America's all-time, basic bestselling cookbook contains recipes for appetizers, desserts and baked goods that will put the finishing touch on any meal you plan. (#E8691—$2.50)

☐ **BAKE YOUR OWN BREAD and be healthier by Floss and Stan Dworkin.** Dozens of easy, delicious recipes for breads that are healthier and cheaper than "store bought" and free of harmful additives. This illustrated, step-by-step guide will take you through each stage of preparation for making and storing a whole breadbasket-full of old favorites and new variations. It's a simple process, easily mastered—try it! (#W7318—$1.50)

☐ **THE EASY WAY TO CHINESE COOKING by Beverly Lee.** In this practical, easy-to-follow guide to authentic Chinese cooking, Beverly Lee shows how to make delicious Chinese dishes—from the simplest to the most festive and elaborate. Included is a list of Chinese stores throughout the U.S. which carry the items listed in the book. (#E8251—$1.75)

☐ **MENU CLASSICS.** A unique guide to the art of gourmet cooking and successful home entertaining. Contains 125 great menus, complete with easy-to-follow recipes for over 900 time-tested and tantalizing dishes. (#E7441—$1.75)

But them at your local bookstore or use this convenient coupon for ordering.

THE NEW AMERICAN LIBRARY, INC.,
P.O. Box 999, Bergenfield, New Jersey 07621

Please send me the SIGNET BOOKS I have checked above. I am enclosing
$_____ (please add 50¢ to this order to cover postage and handling).
Send check or money order—no cash or C.O.D.'s. Prices and numbers are
subject to change without notice.

Name _____

Address _____

City_____ State_____ Zip Code_____
Allow 4-6 weeks for delivery.
This offer is subject to withdrawal without notice.

The Los Angeles Times

NATURAL
FOODS
COOKBOOK

by

Jeanne Voltz

Illustrations by Ellen Friedman

A SIGNET BOOK

NEW AMERICAN LIBRARY

TIMES MIRROR

NAL BOOKS ARE ALSO AVAILABLE AT DISCOUNTS IN BULK
QUANTITY FOR INDUSTRIAL OR SALES-PROMOTIONAL USE.
FOR DETAILS, WRITE TO PREMIUM MARKETING DIVISION,
NEW AMERICAN LIBRARY, INC., 1301 AVENUE OF THE
AMERICAS, NEW YORK, NEW YORK 10019.

Copyright © 1973 by Jeanne Voltz

All rights reserved. This book or parts thereof
must not be reproduced in any form without permission.
For information address G. P. Putnam's Sons,
200 Madison Avenue, New York, New York 10016,
who publish a hardcover edition. A hardcover edition was
published simultaneously in Canada by
Longman Canada Limited, Toronto.

This is an authorized reprint of a hardcover edition
published by G. P. Putnam's Sons.

Ⓢ SIGNET TRADEMARK REG. U.S. PAT. OFF. AND FOREIGN COUNTRIES
REGISTERED TRADEMARK—MARCA REGISTRADA
HECHO EN CHICAGO, U.S.A.

SIGNET, SIGNET CLASSICS, MENTOR, PLUME AND MERIDIAN BOOKS
are published by The New American Library, Inc.,
1301 Avenue of the Americas, New York, New York 10019

First Signet Printing, December, 1975

4 5 6 7 8 9 10 11 12

PRINTED IN THE UNITED STATES OF AMERICA

Table of Contents

Introduction

Natural foods have been eclipsed by a welter of packages, cans, jars and cartons containing foods with little hint of their natural origins.

In the '50s and '60s the housewife who made a fancy party dish with a conglomeration of these packaged foods was regarded with admiration. Since then, there has been a turnabout. The home cook who bakes good honest bread, makes a fragrant soup or stew from scratch or prepares her own homemade pie is regarded as the culinary genius of the 70's.

You can see it in the markets. A supermarket which four years ago dropped brown rice because I was the only customer for it has put it back on the shelves along with a half dozen other whole grain cereals and flours which weren't there before. Health food stores, all claiming to sell natural foods, are springing up in the wildest competition to hit the food industry since franchise chicken.

Some people view the natural foods craze as a youth fad, a movement which will pass when young people find another mode of protest. But a return to simple foods is surfacing in unexpected places—the lunch bag of a businessman escaping the devastation of martini lunches, the fruit dessert instead of cake or pie at family dinner tables, the whole grain sandwich for teen-agers' snacks in place of the gooey candy bar.

We plain food people who have never lost our touch and taste for fresh things hail the revolution. And there are surprising gourmet rewards. One woman expressed home-grown goodness this way: "There's nothing so delicious in all the world as picking a tomato warm from the sun in your grandmother's garden, taking it straight to the kitchen and eating it with fresh homemade mayonnaise."

To paraphrase her nostalgic pleasure, there is nothing more delicious than freshly prepared, lovingly cooked foods using fundamental ingredients. Why, then, is natural food so often equated with coarse, plain, awkwardly seasoned, carelessly cooked foods which taste more like a treatment than a treat?

This book will show how natural foods can be enjoyed in abundance and variety for a health-giving diet.

Natural foods are a modern commitment to a high order of gastronomy which existed two or three generations ago. A crackling crisp apple shaken fresh off an honest-to-goodness apple tree smells and tastes as an apple should—and did in Grandma's day. Honest bread kneaded on an honest board, hot cereal to warm you on a frosty morning, steaming soup to take the chill off a blustery evening, cold crisp salad to refresh you on a torrid summer day all are the pleasures of cooking and eating naturally.

What Is Natural Food?

To the novice, it might seem simple to identify a food as natural or not. Food which comes to you as it comes off the farm is natural, isn't it? Not necessarily. The quest for nature's way runs into vast jungles of controversy and unethical merchandisers who imply that anything they sell is natural, but that anything anybody else sells is "chemically contaminated, unnatural."

Primarily the decision is up to the individual—but, one might hope, an informed individual who can make an intelligent choice. A natural foods advocate must read labels. Ingredients are listed on labels in order of their prominence in the food. Ingredient lists for some so-called foods are shockers. One "orange drink" produced and sold in California listed six ingredients: water, sugar, orange flavor, synthetic vitamin C, vitamin E and food color. A vigilant shopper will find numerous manufactured foods which are essentially water or flour and a complex of additives.

BHT, BHA or propionic acid keeps molds or bacteria from growing in foods. Lecithin, gum arabic or agar-agar emulsify and stabilize the texture of foods; potassium acid tartrate, citric acid or lactic acid controls the alkaline-acid balance of a food. Connoisseurs of the fresh wholesomeness of natural foods choose to avoid as many of these additives as possible, though their functions may be useful to persons who must use processed food.

Foods themselves become additives. There is no known human need for refined sugar except to make other foods more palatable. But how much sugar makes food palatable? Sugar leads the list of ingredients for most presweetened dry cereals. A product called Breakfast Squares, a filled cookie, was introduced in 1971 as an instant substitute for a conventional breakfast. It contained more sugar than any other ingredient; and hydrogenated shortening, the hard type implicated in cardiovascular disease, was the second most predominant ingredient.

At this writing, foods of a certain standard are not required to have an ingredient list on the label, but this may be changed by public demand or by a new U.S. Food and Drug Administration regulation and a few states have passed laws requiring a full list of ingredients on labels of all foods, even those for which a standard has been established.

The new emphasis on natural foods has given rise to a major controversy over the meaning of the word "organic." To some shoppers it means a food grown without manufactured chemicals, such as pesticides or growth enhancers. To some market men it means any food which has no pesticide residues. To others it means food which a grower certifies was not treated with manufactured chemicals while it was growing.

Consumer advocates and organic foods advocates have been clamoring for a government standard on organic foods. At present there is no way an inspector can say that this or that vegetable is not organic, thus violating truth in labeling regulations if it is labeled organic. There is no test to identify food grown without use of manufactured chemicals as there is no laboratory difference between man-made chemicals and chemicals which occur naturally in plants and animals.

The obvious solution to obtaining absolutely natural foods, grown without aid of manufactured chemicals and harvested at their prime, is to grow your own. Home gardening is impossible for most city folk, though even an apartment dweller with a semisunny window can grow a few pots of herbs.

Recipes in this book are designed to adhere to various philosophies concerning natural foods and their origins. There are a few meat recipes, though some natural foods advocates regard all meat as unnaturally grown. We stick to honey and brown sugar as sweeteners. We use mostly whole grain flours.

Recipes call for fresh fruits and vegetables, and freshly made juices. Dried beans, peas and fruits open another doorway to diet variety and receive minimal processing before coming into the market.

But the specific foods you choose depend on your quest for knowledge of where a food came from and how. Some natural foods advocates shop quite comfortably in a supermarkets and supermarkets are stocking an ever increasing variety of natural foods. Others committed to natural foods insist that health food stores are the most reliable places for obtaining high quality natural foods. Some health food stores offer mail order service. Roadside fruit and vegetables stands, especially when operated by the farmer himself, offer good fresh foods. Ethnic stores often supply such goodies as cracked wheat (Armenian or Middle Eastern), buckwheat noodles (Japanese) or fresh snow peas (Chinese).

But even here, the dedicated natural eater must ask questions as to origin and hope for an honest answer. There are unethical operators in this segment of the food industry as in any other.

How to Plan a Menu

Designing a menu takes time, interest and forethought. A good menu is balanced several ways: It must meet sound nutrition standards—offering something from each of the Basic Four Food Groups—milk or other dairy products; legumes, nuts, meat, fish, poultry or eggs; fruits or vegetables; enriched or whole grain bread or cereal. Good nutrition can also be provided in several styles of meals—the conventional meat, potatoes and vegetables menu or such light meals as a peanut butter sandwich on whole wheat bread, fruit and milk.

A good menu is also balanced according to the time and

skill required to prepare it. If you plan a soup that requires peeling three pounds of tomatoes, don't serve fresh green black-eyed peas, which are time-consuming to shell. Serve snap beans instead, and the black-eyed peas another day.

A good menu strikes a balance between heavy and light, a thin soup if the main dish is heavy, a fresh fruit bowl if the main dish is creamy. A good menu also is balanced for taste and eye appeal. Too much spice or herb can destroy good natural flavors. Serve only one highly spiced dish per meal. And vary the colors, a bright green vegetable on a plate with a creamy-colored casserole dish.

Vegetarians have unique problems in menu planning. Substituting legumes for animal foods requires large servings, a cupful for each average serving of meat. The protein of grains complements the protein of legumes, thus improving the nutritional efficiency of both foods when they're served together. Other menu items may carry some of the protein load and supply vitamin B-12, the nutrient most likely deficient in vegetarian diets. Cheese for dessert, for example, can contribute significantly to protein and vitamin B-12 needs. Custard desserts, eggs in dessert, salad or appetizer can boost the nutrient power of the diet.

Simple? Yes, and nourishing and delicious if you cook with the care which high-quality natural foods inspire.

Cooking for Maximum Nutrition

Of course you can cook. But can you prepare food in such a way as to get the maximum nutrition and taste from it? Heat, water, sunlight and air destroy nutrients. Proper cooking and storage techniques preserve nutrients. This means that foods needing refrigeration should be refrigerated immediately after you get them from the market—so don't run another errand or two en route home if you value the nutritive quality, taste and safety of the food you eat.

Thiamin, riboflavin, niacin and ascorbic acid are especially susceptible to heat and oxidation (air damage). The fat-soluble vitamins—A, D, E and K—are somewhat less fragile, but they, too, are damaged by ultraviolet light.

The following techniques will assure maximum nutrients from the foods you buy:

- Do not expose fresh fruits and vegetables to sunlight. Thick-skinned vegetables such as the winter squashes and potatoes and onions should be stored in a cool dry place immediately. This applies to avocados and bananas, too, until they are ripe. Then, they too, should go into the refrigerator and be eaten soon.
- Do not slice, shred, dice or mash fruits or vegetables until just before cooking or serving. The more surfaces exposed to the air and the longer the time, the more nutrients are lost.
- Do not soak cut vegetables before cooking. This wastes valuable nutrients which are lost in the soaking water.
- Cook vegetables in a pan with a tight-fitting lid for as short a time as possible and in as little water as you can —a tablespoon or two, or just the water which clings to tender greens.
- Use the liquid in which vegetables are cooked in soups, sauces, broths and gravies. It generally contains some of the nutrients.
- Use fresh produce at its freshest—minutes after it is gathered if you're lucky enough to grow your own or as soon as you can if you buy it.
- Avoid leftovers of fruits and vegetables, if you can. Each time they're reheated, each hour they wait, even in the refrigerator, they lose nutrients. But if you do have leftovers too good to throw away, use them in salads, or heat and use as soon as possible to preserve as much of the nutritive content as possible.

Better still, purchase what you can eat in one sitting, and shop as often as possible. You'll do better, nutritionally.

Equipping Your Kitchen

Following is what might be considered basic equipment for the cook who has turned her back on the can opener and is cutting, peeling and processing her own foods.

Baking Dishes. A good selection of baking dishes is a

must. Several sizes, deep to shallow, will give you the flexibility you need. Glass or earthenware are both good materials, although enameled ironware can also be used.

Baking Pans. If you're going to be baking breads, cakes and cookies, you'll need an assortment of these. At least two loaf pans 8½ x 4½ x 2½-in., a 10-in. tube pan, a square 8-in. pan and a cookie sheet (stainless steel is more expensive but also more enduring). Loaf pans do lots of jobs; for instance, a cake batter for a 10-in. tube pan can be baked in two loaf pans. If you don't have the pan called for in a recipe try any pan you have, filling it no more than two-thirds full. Reduce the cooking time and learn to tell when bread and cakes are done by testing with a straw or cake tester.

Blender. An indispensable machine for numerous jobs involving natural foods as it will chop as well as puree.

Cast-Iron, Soapstone or Aluminum Griddle. If you make pancakes you'll find them easier to turn on a griddle. And if, between uses, you rub it with salt wrapped in cheesecloth, it will need no greasing. A skillet can be used for baking pancakes, but oil must be used to prevent sticking and the pancakes sometimes tend to be greasy.

Cast-Iron Skillet. Be sure that you have a heavy one that will spread heat evenly and hold it.

Chopping Bowl and Chopper. Since you'll be into all sorts of cutting and chopping, a wooden chopping bowl with semicircular blade chopper is also helpful; it is especially useful for chopping nuts.

Colander. This is essential for rinsing off vegetables and fruit and for straining cooked noodles, macaroni and spaghetti.

Cookware. At least one heavy saucepan with a tight-fitting lid (for rice and other grains, and convertible to any saucepan function); a small one (for boiling eggs, melting butter, or heating a cupful of leftover soup), a large one (for cooking vegetables); a double boiler (for sauce and other foods that need protection from a direct flame); a large kettle (for soups, spaghetti, macaroni, stewing fruits or any job too big for your saucepans).

If the budget allows, and you are purchasing cookware for keeps, buy the heaviest quality aluminum or stainless steel with a heat-conducting core or copper bottom (stainless steel conducts heat poorly and tends to have hot spots which burn food and cause a mess for the kitchen sink). Or even tin-lined copper may be purchased if you have the money and don't mind polishing it.

Cutting Board. A large wooden or plastic cutting board is another kitchen necessity for chopping onions, celery, hard squash or almost anything else that needs cutting. You may also want to knead bread on your chopping board. Wood is the preferred material for easy cutting with a minimum of damage to knife edges. But wood is easily contaminated and difficult to clean. Many people prefer a nonabsorbent plastic, available in restaurant supply houses and some gift shops. Plastic is a little harder on knives, but easier to keep clean and free of flavors.

Dutch Oven. It should be preferably cast iron or another heavy material that spreads heat evenly and holds it. Aside from cooking meat, this pot is also useful for cooking beans.

Glass Jars. You'll need a number of these for cupboard as well as refrigerator storage. Jam jars with tight-fitting lids and other commercial discards can be salvaged for storing food.

Juicer. A electric juicer can be purchased as an attachment to a mixer or can be purchased separately. The human-powered juicers in our kitchen work fine. One is an upside down cone centered in a round strainer. You put it over a measuring cup before you squeeze the juice. For larger quantities of juice, we use a juicer with a strainer basket in which the cut orange, grapefruit or lemon is dropped. A presser blade is whacked down against the fruit and the juice gushes out of a spout. This type is available in restaurant supply shops and hardware stores.

Knives. A good set of knives is as important to the cook as a Stradivarius to the violinist. The best quality you can afford of carbon steel (which corrodes if you don't wipe it off immediately after use) or the new stainless steels which hold an edge, yet are soft enough to be sharpened, are a good investment. Avoid those shiny-bright things which need no rinsing and never hold an edge.

You will need a stone or a good professional knife and blade sharpener to keep knives in tiptop shape. And don't let good knives rattle loose in a cupboard drawer. Store them in a slotted wood case, on a magnet that hangs on the wall, or in any knife case that will protect the blades from knocking against each other.

Long-Handled Kitchen Fork.

Measuring Cups. These should be of heat-proof glass. A two-cup (1 pt.) and a four-cup (1 qt.) are useful to have.

Measuring Spoons.

Meat Grinder. This is essential to the natural foods cook who uses meats, and is helpful in preparing other foods. The heavy metal grinder which clamps to the edge of a table and is powered by hand still works well if it is heavy enough. An electric food grinder is a convenience, but make sure it, too, is sturdy enough to do the jobs you want done.

Mechanical Mixer. The standard type on a stand and/or a smaller electric hand beater. The large mixer mashes potatoes which are pluperfect and is easier to use for cakes and other batters. The smaller hand mixer also works for some of these jobs and has the advantage of being portable to the range top in case you need to smooth out a sauce.

Mixing Bowls. A set of three different sizes should do you. They can double as salad or serving bowls. If they are made of ovenproof glass they can also be used as casseroles.

Shredder. Various types of graters and shredders come in handy for cheese, shredding cabbage or carrots for salads, or cutting potatoes for frying or use in casseroles. The one I use most is made in France and available in gourmet shops and some hardware stores here. It consists of a three-legged frame with a hinged clamp for holding food against the shredding blades. Blades in different sizes are interchangeable. The blade is turned while the food is held tightly against it and, miraculously, you have a bowlful of shredded potatoes or cheese in a few seconds.

Flat graters which rest against a bowl also are useful, especially for lemon and orange peel, and ginger.

Spatulas. A rubber one is indispensable for scraping bowls and coaxing the last bit of food out of a jar; a metal one for use in frying, baking, and various other jobs.

Strainer. Have two of these: a big one for pureeing and

straining larger amounts of food, a smaller one for straining fruit juice or teas.

Swivel Peeler. A must for quick, efficient vegetable peeling.

Tongs. These are indispensable for handling certain hot foods, for deep frying and many other uses.

Wire Whisk. It is useful to have this in two sizes: one for heavy-duty whipping and beating; the other for smaller jobs like beating a single egg.

Wok. This shallow metal vessel is central to Chinese cooking. Its chief advantage to the natural foods cook is that it can be used to fry and sauté foods without using large amounts of oil. Vegetables can be cooked in it quickly in a small amount of oil, thus retaining their crisp freshness as well as their nutritional content.

Wooden Rolling Pin and Pastry Cloth. Get a rolling pin with a stockinette cover, for baking pies. Whole wheat pastries tend to be slightly sticky so the cover and the cloth for rolling are more important than in conventional baking.

Wooden Spoons. Have these in several sizes and you will never again use a metal spoon in cooking. Wooden spoons have many advantages: they are the cook's great contribution to noise abatement; they will not scratch the surface of your pots and pans; they will not bruise, damage, or discolor food, and they don't conduct heat as a metal spoon will.

Good cookware and kitchen gadgetry give you good service, but also demand tender loving care. Here are a few don'ts that will help you preserve them:

- Don't place any pan—cast-iron, enamel, aluminum, porcelain or stainless steel—over high heat.
- Don't heat any pan while it is dry. Such treatment will warp, crackle or even may melt almost any material.
- Don't use harsh scouring powders and steel wool pads on enamels except as a last resort. They can scratch an enamel pan beyond repair.
- Don't fail to dry a cast-iron pan immediately after washing and rinsing or it will rust. Dry it over very low heat on the stove or by putting it in a warm oven for a few minutes.
- Don't throw away the instruction manuals you get with

a piece of equipment. You'll be surprised how many problems aren't problems at all if you read how the blender, mixer or other piece of equipment should be used.

It is understood that all recipes calling for mayonnaise, tomato juice and tomato bouillon, vegetable, chicken and beef broths, cottage cheese and yogurt should be prepared according to the recipes that appear in the book. Consult the Index for page reference. All cheeses should be natural, not processed, and when shredded cheese is called for, it should be freshly shredded; all margarine should be unsaturated; all molasses and dried fruits should be unsulfured, and all pepper freshly ground.

Appetizers
and Snacks

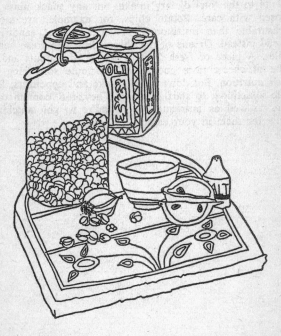

THOUGHTLESS snacking is possibly the major defect in American eating habits. The classic three-square-meals-a-day concept of eating simply doesn't exist any longer. Some families never sit down to a bona fide meal.

If the snacks are well chosen and steer away from worthless or high-fat foods which make up so much of the snack pattern, they aren't necessarily bad.

The snacks and appetizers here are designed to contribute to the total dietary intake, but any snack must be chosen with care. Potato chips, for example, are more pleasurable than nutritional. Try a raisin-nut sandwich spread instead. Or one of the cheese dips with fresh vegetables. A piece of fresh fruit, a couple of walnuts and a cube of cheese taste good and contribute something to one's nutrition. But don't think snacks and appetizers, the little somethings to start, are free. They, too, contain calories as well as nutrients, so if you're weight watching allow for them in your calorie budget.

FRENCH RADISHES

Red radishes
Sweet butter or margarine
Freshly ground pepper

This classic French hors d'oeuvre is a surprise to Americans, who habitually eat radishes with lots of salt, but it is a surprisingly good combination of flavor and texture. Each diner helps himself to radishes, preferably with a plume of greens left on each. A pat of butter and sprinkle of pepper is put on the plate, then the radish is spread with butter and dipped into pepper for each mouthful.

CELERY SICILIAN

1 bunch celery
Cracked ice
½ T fennel or anise seed

Wash celery thoroughly. Use only the most tender portions for this relish. Cut into sticks, leaving some of the leaves intact. Mound cracked ice in a bowl and sprinkle with fennel or anise seed. Bury base ends of celery in ice. Refrigerate until ready to serve. Serve with salt, if wished. The fennel or anise flavors the celery subtly for an unusual and refreshing snack.

COTTAGE CHEESE DIP
(3 cups)

1 pt. cottage cheese
½ cup crumbled blue cheese
½ cup sour cream
2 T freshly grated horse-
radish

1 t salt
Dash cayenne

Combine cottage cheese, blue cheese, sour cream, horseradish, salt and pepper. Process in a blender or beat rapidly by hand or with an automatic mixer until well blended and almost smooth. Chill and serve as a dip for raw vegetables, apple or pear wedges or other fruit.

AVOCADO COTTAGE CHEESE DIP
(1¼ cups)

¼ t crushed dried chiles
1 cup cottage cheese
½ t salt
1 t minced onion
1 T minced celery tops

3 T mayonnaise or sour cream
½ cup soft avocado, optional

Sprinkle crushed chiles over cottage cheese and mix well. Add salt, onion, celery tops, mayonnaise and avocado, which has been peeled and sliced or diced. Beat thoroughly in blender or with automatic mixer. Pile into bowl and serve with cucumber or celery sticks or other raw vegetables. This dip may be varied by adding chopped green onion or green pepper, diced cucumber which has been drained, finely chopped fresh herbs (tarragon is especially good) or seasonings such as mustard or additional dried chiles.

GUACAMOLE
(2 cups)

1 soft avocado
2 t lemon or lime juice
¼ t cayenne or 1 skinned jalapeno chile, minced

1 clove garlic, minced
1 small tomato, peeled and diced

Peel avocado and remove seed. Mash the avocado with lemon or lime juice. Guacamole is not usually perfectly smooth but still keeps a few fine lumps. Add cayenne or chile, garlic and tomato. Mix well. Serve at once with thinly sliced whole wheat bread or tortilla strips, fried until crisp in oil, or as a salad on lettuce.

HUMUS
(Garbanzo Bean Dip)
(2 cups)

3 cups drained cooked
    garbanzo beans
1 clove garlic, minced
1 T wine vinegar

3 T olive oil
1 t salt
¼ t white pepper
Paprika

Place beans in blender with garlic and turn on motor until beans are pureed to a smooth paste. Add a few drops of the bean cooking liquid if needed for moistness. With blender motor running, gradually add vinegar, oil, salt and white pepper. Pile into bowl and sprinkle with paprika. Humus can be served at room temperature or chilled, though flavor is improved if it stands for an hour or two. Serve as a dip with raw vegetables or Arabic bread.

CHEESE PECAN BUTTER
(1 cup)

2 T sauterne
¼ cup butter or margarine,
    softened
1 cup finely shredded
    American cheese

¼ cup coarsely chopped
    pecans
Cooked artichokes

Beat sauterne into butter, then blend in cheese and nuts. Mix thoroughly and pile into a bowl. Serve as a dip or spread for artichoke leaves. Butter can be piled into scooped-out artichoke for a more elaborate presentation.

CEVICHE
(4 to 5 servings)

1 lb. red snapper or sea
    bass fillets
Juice of 4 limes
1 t honey
2 t salt

1 t pepper
⅛ t cayenne
2 T chopped onion
2 cups chopped peeled
    tomato

Remove any skin or dark flesh from fish and cut remaining fish into ½-inch cubes. Place in a glass or ceramic bowl with lime juice, honey, salt, pepper, cayenne and onion. Toss lightly, cover and marinate in refrigerator 3 or 4 hours. Add tomatoes, toss again and pile into cocktail glasses. Or serve in a bowl and let guests pile Ceviche onto small squares of whole wheat toast.

MEXICAN CEVICHE
(6 appetizer servings)

1 lb. fillet of sea bass, rock cod or haddock	¼ to ½ cup diced peeled green chiles
1 cup lime or lemon juice	½ t oregano
1 onion	½ t salt
2 tomatoes	⅛ t pepper
4 T oil	1 avocado
1 T vinegar	

Cut fish in ½-inch cubes, remove skin and place fish in a glass or earthenware bowl. Add lime juice and marinate in refrigerator until fish turns white and opaque, several hours or overnight. Turn fish with a wooden spoon several times while marinating. Dice half the onion very fine and add to fish. Peel tomatoes, dice fine and add to fish. Sprinkle mixture with oil, vinegar, chiles, oregano, salt and pepper. Mix lightly but thoroughly. Cover and refrigerate 3 to 4 hours. Just before serving, peel and seed avocado, then cut into cubes or thin crescents. Serve Ceviche icy cold in stemmed cocktail glasses with cubed or sliced avocado as garnish. Peel and slice remaining onion and arrange over Ceviche.

EGGPLANT CAVIAR
(3 cups)

1 large or 2 small eggplants	2 t lemon juice
3 T olive oil	1 t salt
1 onion, minced	¼ t pepper
1 tomato, peeled and chopped	

Place whole eggplant in boiling water in a large kettle. Cover and boil *20 minutes* or until eggplant is tender when pierced with a fork. When cool enough to handle, peel and chop eggplant fine.

Heat 1 tablespoon oil in a large skillet, add onion and cook until tender but not browned. Add eggplant, tomato and remaining 2 tablespoons oil. Cook until juices running from eggplant and tomato are evaporated. Add lemon juice, salt and pepper. Chill thoroughly. Pile into a chilled bowl and surround with black olives (preferably Greek style) and tomato wedges. Serve as a spread for Greek, Syrian or other crusty bread.

ARTICHOKES À LA GRECQUE
(8 to 12 servings)

2 qt. water	1 bay leaf
1 cup oil (olive oil, if possible)	¼ t dried thyme
Juice of 4 lemons	1 rib celery, cut in 3 or 4 pieces
1½ t ground coriander	2 or 3 dozen tiny artichokes
2 t salt	
½ t whole black peppercorns	

Combine water, oil, lemon juice, coriander, salt, whole peppers, bay leaf, thyme and celery in a large kettle. Bring to a boil. Pull discolored outside leaves off artichokes, trim stems to 1-inch stubs and cut spines off top leaves. As you trim artichokes, drop them into the boiling stock so they will not discolor. After all artichokes are added, cover and boil *8 minutes* or until artichokes are tender. Chill them in stock. Drain and serve in a relish dish or on salad greens as a first course.

NOTE: If tiny artichokes are not available, large artichokes may be cut in halves or quarters, the chokes scooped out with a small spoon, and the prepared artichokes used in the above recipe.

ROQUEFORT WALNUTS
(2 to 3 dozen snacks)

1 3-oz. package cream
    cheese
1 oz. Roquefort cheese

Lemon juice or brandy
4 to 6 dozen walnut halves

Soften cream cheese at room temperature and mash until smooth and fluffy. Crumble Roquefort cheese and blend in well. Add a few drops of lemon juice or brandy to accent flavor. If too thick, thin with a few drops of cream or milk. Roll cheese mixture into small balls and press each ball firmly between walnut halves. Spread on a tray and refrigerate until ready to serve.

NOTE: If some of the filling is left it can be thinned slightly with cream and used as a spread or as a filling for stuffed celery. Or mix in chopped nuts and use as a dip.

BOLLITOS
(About 5 dozen)

2 lb. dried black-eyed peas
4 cloves garlic, peeled
1 T salt

1 t black pepper or 1 small
    chile, minced
Oil for frying

Cover peas generously with water and soak overnight. Remove skins from peas by rolling between palms of hands. Any stubborn bits of skin must be pried off with a sharp knife or fingernail. Combine peas, garlic, salt and pepper and put through a food grinder several times using the finest blade, or puree in a blender. Beat with an automatic mixer until mixture is consistency of a soft batter. This may take *15 minutes* or longer. Refrigerate for an hour or until slightly firmer. Beat again then drop by teaspoonfuls into deep oil heated to 375°. Cook about *5 minutes,* turning once. Drain on absorbent paper and serve hot as a snack. Bollitos are a standard snack in Key West and the Spanish section of Tampa, Florida. They can be prepared in advance and reheated in a moderate oven.

PINEAPPLE-PAPAYA APPETIZERS

Peel and cut pineapple and papayas into bite-size chunks. Dip in soy sauce and thread fruit alternately on wood or bamboo skewers. Broil, using a hibachi, if wished, until lightly browned, turning fruit and basting with more soy sauce. Fruit also may be brushed with honey. Serve hot.

BAKED CARAMEL CORN
(3 quarts)

½ cup butter or margarine
½ cup brown sugar, packed
3 qt. unsalted popped corn

1 cup whole pecans or
mixed nuts

Cream together butter and brown sugar until fluffy. Combine popcorn and pecans in a shallow baking pan. Add the butter mixture by spoonfuls and mix into the popcorn mixture. Bake at 350° stirring two or three times, until crisp, about *8 minutes*.

PEANUT POPCORN
(About 2 quarts)

5 or 6 cups hot freshly
popped corn
2 t salt

2 cups toasted peanuts
¼ cup butter or margarine
1 T peanut butter

Toss popcorn with salt and peanuts. Melt butter over moderate heat and stir in peanut butter. Add to popcorn and toss well.

CHEESE POPCORN
(About 1½ quarts)

5 to 6 cups hot freshly
popped corn
2 t salt

¼ cup butter or margarine
⅓ cup grated Romano or
Parmesan cheese

Toss hot popcorn with salt. Melt butter over moderate heat and mix in cheese. Immediately pour over popcorn and toss well.

TOASTED NUTS

Shelled nuts, preferably per-
    fect halves or whole nuts
    such as cashews and
    almonds

Boiling water, optional
Oil
Salt

If nuts are very dry, drop into boiling water and let stand
for *2 or 3 minutes* to soften slightly. Spread nuts in a
greased shallow baking pan. Roast at 350° until crisp
and lightly browned, about *15 minutes*. Shake pan several
times while roasting to brown evenly. Brush hot nuts
lightly with oil and sprinkle generously with salt.

Nuts may be seasoned by tossing a few pieces of garlic
or crushed dry chile pepper into the pan with them.

SOY NUTS

Soak dry soy beans overnight in water to cover generously. Cook about 10 minutes, until barely beginning to
soften. Drain well, then dry on towels. Heat about 1 in. of
oil in a skillet. Add soy beans a handful at a time and
cook over moderate heat until golden. Drain and sprinkle
with salt. Soy nuts tend to become dry and crumbly when
roasted in the oven.

LIMA SNACK CHIPS
(3 cups)

1½ cups large dry lima
    beans
 ½ cup oil, margarine or
    butter

2 cloves garlic, split
Salt

Rinse lima beans and soak overnight in water to cover
generously. Bring to a boil and simmer *10 minutes*. Drain
well and rinse in cold water. Slip off skins and split beans
in halves. Heat oil or other fat in a large skillet, add garlic
and then beans. Cook over medium heat until crisp and
golden. Drain on towels and sprinkle with salt.

FRESH COCONUT CHIPS

Poke holes in the three eyes in the end of a coconut shell. Drain the coconut water. Place coconut in a baking pan and bake at 250° to 275° for *1 hour*. This helps separate the coconut meat from the shell and makes cracking and shelling it easier. The shell may crack while it is baking.

Cool the coconut slightly, then crack with a hammer. Pry meat from shell. For many uses, the brown skin should be peeled off the meat, but for chips this is not necessary.

With a swivel-blade peeler or a sharp knife, cut coconut meat into paper-thin strips. Spread in a shallow baking pan. Sprinkle lightly with salt and toast in a 300° oven until lightly browned, *20 to 30 minutes*. Coconut should be stirred three or four times while roasting.

Cool and store in airtight containers. Serve as a snack or party tidbit. Coconut chips also can be sprinkled over fruit or ice cream for dessert.

DUTCH SANDWICHES
(6 servings)

6 to 8 oz. Liederkranz or limburger cheese
1 large sweet red onion
Cider or white wine vinegar
12 thin slices pumpernickel or dark whole wheat bread

Butter or margarine, optional
Salt, freshly ground pepper

Let cheese soften at room temperature. Slice onion thin, separate into rings and place in a shallow dish. Sprinkle generously with vinegar, cover and let stand 1 hour. Just before making sandwiches, drain onions well on towels. Spread bread with butter, if wanted. Spread half the slices thickly with cheese and top with onion rings. Sprinkle lightly with salt and pepper and close sandwiches with remaining bread. Cut diagonally and serve with sour pickles and, if wanted, potato salad.

HOMEMADE PEANUT BUTTER
(1½ cups)

2 cups skinned and shelled
    peanuts
1½ t salt

2 T peanut or other oil
Nonfat dry milk

Spread peanuts in a well-greased shallow baking pan and roast at 300° *10 to 15 minutes*, stirring now and then. When golden, remove from oven and cool. Place in blender with salt and oil. Blend at high speed until smooth. The nutritive value of peanut butter can be improved by addition of nonfat dry milk. Blend in 2 or 3 tablespoons of the dry milk.

PEANUT BUTTER PRUNE SANDWICHES
(6 or 7 sandwiches)

1 cup peanut butter
½ cup chopped cooked
    prunes

2 or 3 T mayonnaise
Whole wheat or oatmeal
    bread

Mix peanut butter, prunes and mayonnaise until smooth. Spread on bread.

BEAN FINGERS
(About 1 dozen canapes)

⅔ cup mashed Boston
    Baked Beans (page 82)
2 T mayonnaise
2 T minced onion
Dash cayenne

Boston Brown
    Bread (page 266) or
    other bread, cut into
    fingers or small wedges

Blend mashed beans, mayonnaise, onion and cayenne. Spread on bread fingers. Broil just until bean spread is heated and edges of bread lightly browned. Serve hot.

PARSLEY SANDWICHES
(About 2 to 3 dozen small sandwiches)

1 cup butter or margarine	⅛ t cayenne
½ t dry mustard	1 t onion juice
2 t vinegar	1 cup minced parsley
½ t salt	Thinly sliced bread

Let butter soften at room temperature, then beat until creamy. Blend in mustard, vinegar, salt, cayenne and onion juice, continuing to beat to blend thoroughly. Beat in parsley. Spread on thinly sliced bread, cover with top slices and cut into small squares or triangles.

CALIFORNIA SANDWICH
(1 sandwich)

2 thin slices whole wheat, oatmeal or pumpernickel bread	Salt, pepper
	¼ avocado
Soft butter or margarine	Lemon juice
2 thin slices onion	3 or 4 T alfalfa sprouts

Spread bread with butter or margarine. Place the onion on one slice bread and sprinkle lightly with salt and pepper. Peel avocado and slice into very thin crescents. Arrange in overlapping layer over onion. Sprinkle lightly with lemon juice, salt and pepper. Arrange alfalfa sprouts over avocado. Close sandwich with remaining slice of bread.

Peanut Butter California Sandwich. Spread one slice of bread with smooth peanut butter instead of butter or margarine.

California Gold Sandwich. Mix alfalfa sprouts for sandwich with equal amount of coarsely shredded raw carrot.

Mexicali Sandwich. Instead of avocado and butter, spread bread for California Sandwich with generous layer of Guacamole (page 22). Garnish sandwich with a thin sliver of chile pepper.

ONION CUCUMBER SANDWICH

Thinly sliced oatmeal or
  whole wheat bread
Soft butter or margarine
Thinly sliced peeled
  cucumber

Thinly sliced onion
Salt, coarse pepper

Spread bread with butter. Arrange cucumber in overlapping rows on half the bread slices, covering bread completely, but keeping layer thin. Top with thin, overlapping layer of onion. Sprinkle with salt and pepper and close sandwich with another slice of bread.

EGG SALAD SANDWICH SUPREME
(6 sandwiches)

1 cup chopped hard-cooked
  egg
½ cup diced celery
¼ cup diced walnuts

¼ cup mayonnaise, about
12 slices whole wheat bread
  Soft butter or margarine

Mix chopped egg, celery, walnuts and enough mayonnaise to moisten. Spread bread with butter. Spread filling on half the slices of bread and close sandwiches with remaining bread. Cut diagonally into halves.

PINEAPPLE CELERY SANDWICHES
(3 or 4 sandwiches)

½ cup well drained
  shredded pineapple
¼ cup diced celery

Mayonnaise
Oatmeal or whole wheat
  bread

Mix pineapple and celery. Add just enough mayonnaise to moisten. Spread on oatmeal or whole wheat bread.

CHEESE NUT SANDWICHES
(4 or 5 sandwiches)

1 cup shredded Cheddar
cheese
½ cup chopped pecans or
walnuts

¼ cup minced onion
Mayonnaise
Whole wheat or rye bread

Combine cheese, nuts, onion and enough mayonnaise to moisten. Spread on whole wheat or rye bread.

COTTAGE CHEESE SANDWICHES
(6 or 7 sandwiches)

1 cup cottage cheese
¼ cup butter margarine,
melted
½ t salt
¼ cup finely chopped green
onion

2 T minced parsley
Whole wheat, oatmeal or
rye bread
Sliced radishes, optional

Blend cottage cheese, butter, salt, onion and parsley. Spread on whole wheat, oatmeal or rye bread and arrange radish slices over spread, if wanted.

MARIE'S TEA SANDWICHES
(About 2 dozen small sandwiches)

½ cup raisins
½ cup pecans or other nuts
3 to 4 T sour cream or
milk

Dash salt
Thinly sliced whole
wheat or pumpernickel
bread

Put raisins and nuts through food grinder, using fine blade. Stir in sour cream or milk to moisten well and make spreadable. Add salt and mix again. Spread thinly on bread, close sandwiches with a second slice of bread and cut into fingers, small squares or triangles.

PEANUT BUTTER HOTS
(24 snacks)

¼ cup butter or margarine
¾ cup peanut butter
2 or 3 T honey

6 slices whole wheat or rye
  bread, toasted

Soften butter and blend with peanut butter until smooth. Spread on toast. Cut each slice of toast into four fingers. Place side by side in a greased shallow pan and drizzle with honey. Broil until hot and bubbly.

MINIATURE PIZZAS
(8 servings)

4 English muffins (page
  272)
8 thick slices tomato
½ t salt
⅛ t pepper
⅛ t oregano

1 cup coarsely shredded
  mozzarella cheese
Shreds of jerky or other
  cooked meat, optional
2 T grated Parmesan
  cheese

Split English muffins and arrange on a baking sheet. Top each with a tomato slice and sprinkle with salt, pepper and oregano. Sprinkle mozzarella cheese over pizzas and add a few bits of jerky or other meat. Sprinkle with Parmesan. Broil 10 minutes or until hot and bubbly.

Soups

SOUP is possibly the first thing a cave woman cooked after the first crude pot was shaped to sit at the edge of the open fire. Hearty soups—bean, vegetable and others—still exude a primitive fragrance and flavor that captures honest healthy appetites. Served with a sturdy bread, they make a meal in themselves. Light soups hot or cold start a meal or are sipped as a snack.

VEGETABLE BROTH
(8 cups)

2 carrots, peeled and diced
1 large onion, peeled and
    diced
3 ribs celery, diced
1 turnip, diced
1 tomato, peeled and
    chopped

2 T minced parsley
1 green pepper, chopped
10 cups water
2 t salt
2 t honey
¼ t pepper

Combine carrot, onion, celery, turnip, tomato, parsley and green pepper in a large kettle. Add water, salt, honey and pepper. Cover and simmer *45 minutes* or until vegetables are tender. Strain and refrigerate until ready to use. To serve as a clear soup, add a pat of butter to each cupful of hot soup.

CHICKEN BROTH
(4 cups)

2 lb. chicken wings, backs
    and necks
5 cups cold water
4 whole black peppercorns
1 small onion, peeled

3 whole cloves
1 T minced parsley
1 t salt
1 egg

Place chicken pieces in deep pot with water, whole black peppercorns, onion studded with the cloves, parsley and salt. Cover and simmer *1½ to 2 hours,* until meat is falling off bones. Strain broth, pour into a bowl, cover and refrigerate overnight. Lift off congealed fat and discard or reserve for use in cooking. Start heating stock. Separate the egg, and save the yolk for another purpose. Beat the white lightly and stir in the crushed egg shell. Add the egg white and shell to broth and slowly bring to a boil. Boil *2 or 3 minutes* without stirring. Pour broth through two thicknesses of cheesecloth. Serve hot as soup or use in sauce and as a base for other soups.

BEEF BROTH
(6 cups)

2 lb. beef soup bone,
    cracked
1 lb. boneless beef chuck or
    stew beef
1 carrot, sliced thickly
1 onion, peeled and cut in
    quarters
1 rib celery, sliced

1 turnip, cut in quarters
8 cups cold water
6 whole black peppercorns
1 bay leaf
1 blade mace
1 T minced parsley
1 t salt
1 egg

Place soup bone in shallow pan. Roast at 400° *2 hours.*
Add beef, carrot, onion, celery and turnip. Roast at 400°
1 hour longer or until vegetables are browned but not
scorched. Scrape bones, vegetables and juices into a large
kettle. Rinse roasting pan and add this with cold water,
peppercorns, bay leaf, mace, parsley and salt to bones.

Heat slowly to simmering, skimming off solids which
rise to the top. Cover and simmer *1 hour* or until meat
is very tender. Strain broth, pour into a bowl, cover and
refrigerate overnight. Lift off fat which congeals on top
and pour soup into a large kettle. Separate egg and save
yolk for another purpose. Beat egg white lightly and stir
in crushed egg shell. Stir into broth and bring to a boil.
Boil *2 or 3 minutes.* Strain through 2 layers of cheesecloth.
Serve hot or refrigerate and use in sauces or as a base
for soups.

TOMATO BOUILLON
(6 servings)

1 cup sliced carrots
1 cup sliced turnips
1 cup sliced celery
1 cup sliced onion
1 t salt

¼ t pepper
1 bay leaf, crumbled
3 cups water
3 cups chopped peeled
    tomatoes

Combine carrots, turnips, celery, onion, salt, pepper and
bay leaf in saucepan. Add water, cover and cook *30
minutes* or until vegetables are tender. Strain and return
liquid to pan. Press tomatoes through a fine sieve to re-

move seeds, add to soup and heat. Taste and add more salt and pepper if wanted. Serve hot or chill and serve cold with sour cream and minced chives on top.

FISH STOCK
(6 cups)

1½ lb. fish trimmings
    (heads, bones, tails)
1 small onion, sliced
2 carrots, sliced
1 bay leaf
6 whole black pepper-
    corns

2 whole allspice or cloves
3 or 4 sprigs parsley
1½ t salt
½ lemon
8 cups boiling water

Fish trimmings for chowder may be bought in some good fish markets, or use your own, storing trimmings in the freezer until you accumulate enough to make stock. Place fish pieces in large pot with onion, carrots, a small cheese-cloth bag containing the bay leaf, whole black peppercorns, and allspice, and the parsley, salt and the lemon, which is squeezed over the fish. Add boiling water, cover and sim-mer *30 minutes*. Strain and store in refrigerator or freezer. Use in soups or sauces.

WASHINGTON CHOWDER
(6 to 8 servings)

1 small onion, sliced
1 T oil, butter or
    margarine
2 potatoes, peeled and
    diced
1½ cups water

1 t salt
¼ t pepper
1 cup chopped peeled
    tomatoes
1 cup corn cut off cob
2 cups milk

Cook onion in oil in a saucepan until tender but not browned. Add potatoes, water, salt and pepper. Cover and cook *15 minutes* or until potatoes are soft. Add to-matoes and simmer *5 or 10* minutes longer. Add corn, bring to a boil, then slowly stir in milk. Heat but do not boil. Ladle into hot bowls.

CALIFORNIA CORN CHOWDER
(4 to 6 servings)

¼ cup oil or 4 oz. salt
    pork, diced
1 small onion, diced
½ cup diced celery
1½ cups cubed potatoes
2 cups water
½ t salt
½ t honey
¼ t freshly ground pepper
2 cups milk
2 cups corn cut off cob
Minced parsley or
    paprika

Heat oil or cook salt pork in kettle until lightly browned and crisp. Add onion and celery and cook until tender but not browned. Add potatoes, water, salt, honey and pepper. Cover and simmer until potato is tender. Add milk and corn and bring to a boil. Taste and add more salt if needed. Ladle into warm bowls and sprinkle with parsley or paprika.

CREAM OF FRESH TOMATO SOUP
(6 to 8 servings)

2 cups peeled, chopped
    tomatoes
½ cup chopped celery
2 T chopped onion
Dash basil
2 t honey
4 T butter, margarine or
    oil
4 T whole wheat flour
4 cups milk, scalded
1 t salt
⅛ t white pepper

Combine tomatoes, celery, onion, basil and honey in a saucepan. Blend well and simmer about *15 minutes*. Press mixture through a sieve or puree in a blender and strain to remove seeds. Melt butter in top of double boiler over direct heat. Stir in flour. Add milk and stir and cook until smooth and thickened. Remove from heat. Slowly stir in tomato mixture. Season with salt and pepper. Cook over boiling water, covered, *15 minutes*. Serve at once, topping each serving with a few whole wheat croutons or a spoonful of plain yogurt sprinkled with minced parsley.

CREAM OF POTATO SOUP
(4 to 6 servings)

3 medium-size potatoes
1 medium-size onion
2 t salt
Water

2 cups milk
½ cup heavy or sour cream
Minced parsley

Peel and thinly slice potatoes and onion into a saucepan. Sprinkle with 1 teaspoon salt and add water to barely cover. Cook until soft. Put potatoes and onion through a food mill or colander with liquid. Heat milk and cream together and stir in potatoes. Heat until almost boiling. Add remaining salt. Ladle into warm bowls and sprinkle with parsley.

CREAM OF PUMPKIN SOUP
(4 servings)

1 T oil
2 T minced onion
¼ t ginger
1 cup mashed cooked
   pumpkin

1½ cups chicken broth
1 t salt
1 cup cream
Sour cream
Paprika

Heat oil in a small skillet. Add onion and ginger and cook until onion is tender but not browned. Combine onion mixture with pumpkin, broth and salt in a blender. Blend until smooth. Turn soup into a saucepan, stir in cream and heat to serving temperature. Ladle into hot bowls and top each serving with a spoonful of sour cream and sprinkle with paprika. Or chill thoroughly, thin with more cream as needed, check seasonings and add more salt or ginger and serve in chilled soup cups.

SOPA VERDE
(6 to 8 servings)

1 bunch green onions
(8 or 10)
2 cups shredded lettuce,
packed
4 sprigs parsley, leaves
only

1 T butter or margarine
4 cups water or chicken
broth
¾ t salt
Dash pepper

Wash and drain vegetables, then grind in a blender or food grinder, using fine blade. Melt butter in a saucepan, add greens mixture and cook until slightly thickened. Add the water or stock, season with salt and pepper and simmer *25 minutes*. Ladle into hot bowls and serve with a spoonful of yogurt on top, if wanted.

POTAGE CRÉCY
(Fresh Carrot Soup)
(6 servings)

1 lb. carrots
¼ cup butter or margarine
1 small onion, diced
1½ t salt
¼ t pepper

1 t honey
1 qt. beef broth or water
1 T soy sauce, optional
1 cup cooked brown rice
1 cup cream or milk

Peel carrots and slice them thin. Cook in butter in a large kettle until tinged with brown, add onion, salt, pepper and honey and cook until onion is tender but not browned. Add beef stock or water. Soy sauce is not needed if beef stock is used. Add rice, cover and simmer *1 hour* or until rice is tender. If a smooth soup is wanted, force through a fine sieve or puree, 2 cupfuls at a time, in a blender. Return to heat, add cream or milk and heat. Ladle into hot bowls. Pass whole wheat croutons browned in garlic oil to serve with soup, if wanted.

10-MINUTE SPINACH SOUP
(3 to 4 servings)

2 cups milk
2 T rye flour
2 T butter or margarine
1 t salt
   Dash pepper

⅛ t nutmeg
2 cups raw spinach leaves, packed
1 thin slice onion
½ cup celery leaves, packed

Combine milk, rye flour, butter, salt, pepper, nutmeg, spinach, onion and celery in blender. Cover and blend thoroughly, until spinach pieces are very fine. Pour into saucepan and heat over low heat, stirring now and then. Serve at once.

CREAMY LETTUCE SOUP
(6 servings)

1 large head iceberg lettuce
2 t soy sauce
¾ cup water
2 T lemon juice
1 small onion, thinly sliced
¼ cup butter or margarine
¼ cup whole wheat flour

1 t salt
⅛ t cayenne
   Dash nutmeg
2 cups milk
¼ cup dry white wine, optional

Core, rinse and drain lettuce. Shred enough of it to measure 4 cups, packed. Chill remaining lettuce. Combine shredded lettuce, soy sauce, water and lemon juice in blender and blend until smooth. If necessary, process lettuce in two batches. Or lettuce can be shredded very fine with a sharp knife and combined with water, lemon juice and soy sauce.

Cook onion in butter in large saucepan until tender but not browned. Remove onion from pan with slotted spoon and blend flour, salt, cayenne and nutmeg into pan drippings. Stir in milk and cook and stir until soup comes to a boil and is thickened. Blend in wine, the pureed lettuce mixture and onion. Heat well and serve with additional shredded lettuce as a garnish.

SPRING GREEN SOUP
(6 to 8 servings)

2 qt. water
4 T oil, preferably olive
4 potatoes, peeled and diced

2 t salt
⅛ t cayenne
3 bunches green onions

Combine water, oil and potatoes in a large kettle. Cook over moderate heat *30 minutes* or until potatoes are soft. Remove potatoes from stock with a slotted spoon and puree in a blender or by forcing through a sieve. Return pureed potatoes to stock, add salt and cayenne and bring to a boil. Meanwhile, wash and drain green onions, then chop. Add green onions to soup, cover and simmer *20 to 30 minutes* or until onions are tender. If a smooth soup is wanted, puree it in a blender or force through a sieve, return to kettle and reheat. Taste and add more salt and cayenne, if wanted. Serve hot or chilled. Chilled soup can be thinned with sweet cream, if wished.

MUSHROOM BISQUE
(6 to 8 servings)

1 lb. small mushrooms
4 cups chicken broth
¼ cup butter or margarine
3 T whole wheat flour
¼ t dry mustard
Dash nutmeg

¼ cup dry sherry
½ cup cream or rich milk
Whipped cream or sour cream
Paprika

Rinse mushrooms quickly under cold running water and drain well. Remove stems and chop fine, add to chicken broth and simmer *30 minutes*. Strain this mushroom broth and set aside. Slice mushroom caps. Melt butter in saucepan, add mushroom caps and cook until lightly browned. Sprinkle flour, mustard and nutmeg over mushrooms and blend carefully. Gradually add broth and cook and stir until mixture thickens slightly. Cook over low heat *10 minutes*, stirring two or three times. Stir in sherry and milk or cream. Heat to serving temperature and ladle into hot bowls. Garnish each serving with a spoonful of whipped cream or sour cream and sprinkle with paprika.

DUTCH ONION STEW
(6 servings)

6 onions
6 T butter or margarine
3 cups cold water
3 T whole wheat flour
2 cups scalded milk

1 egg yolk
1 t salt, or to taste
⅛ t cayenne
½ cup shredded Edam
  cheese

Peel and chop onions. Cook in 3 tablespoons of the butter until tender but not browned. Add cold water and simmer *30 minutes*. Press through a food mill or puree half at a time in a blender. Melt remaining 3 tablespoons butter in a saucepan. Blend in whole wheat flour, then slowly stir in milk. Cook and stir until smooth and thickened. Stir a small amount of hot sauce into egg yolk, then stir egg yolk into sauce. Add to onion puree along with salt and cayenne. Heat but do not boil. Ladle into warmed bowls and sprinkle with cheese.

HOT FRUIT SOUP
(6 to 8 servings)

3 cups orange juice
11 to 12 oz. mixed dried
  fruit (prunes, apri-
  cots, apples, pears),
  chopped coarsely
⅛ t cloves

3 T honey
1½ T cornstarch
½ cup dry white wine or 6
  T water and 2 T
  lemon juice
1½ cups orange sections

Reserve 2 tablespoons orange juice. Pour remaining orange juice into a saucepan, add dried fruit, cloves and honey. Bring to a boil, cover, reduce heat and simmer *10 minutes* or until fruit is soft but not mushy. Blend cornstarch to a paste with reserved orange juice. Stir into simmering soup and cook and stir until slightly thickened and clear. Remove from heat and stir in wine and orange sections. Serve in hot bowls.

CURRIED APPLE SOUP
(6 to 8 servings)

2 large sweet onions,
  chopped
¼ cup butter or margarine
2 T curry powder
2 T whole wheat flour
1 qt. chicken or vegetable
  broth
4 egg yolks, slightly beaten

1 cup heavy cream
2 tart apples, peeled and
  diced
Juice of 1 lemon
½ t salt
Dash cayenne
Thin apple slices

Cook onions in butter until tender but not browned. Stir
in curry powder and cook and stir a few seconds. Stir flour
into onion mixture, then add broth. Cook and stir until
smooth and thickened, then bring to a boil, stirring often.
Stir a little of the soup into the egg yolks, then stir the egg
yolks into the soup. Cook and stir about *1 minute*. Stir in
the cream. Remove from heat and add the diced apple.
Puree in a blender or press through a food mill or sieve.
Add lemon juice and salt and cayenne. Reheat but do not
boil, then ladle into hot bowls. Garnish with thin apple
slices.

FILBERT SQUASH SOUP
(6 servings)

1½ cups mashed cooked
    Hubbard or other
    winter squash
1 cup finely chopped
  filberts
1 small onion, minced
1 qt. chicken or vegetable
  broth

1 t salt
⅛ t cayenne
2 T butter or margarine
Whipped cream, sliced
  toasted filberts

Combine squash, chopped filberts, onion and broth in a
saucepan. Bring to a boil, cover and simmer *30 minutes*,
stirring now and then. Stir in salt, cayenne and butter.
Ladle into warm bowls, top with whipped cream and
toasted filberts.

CREAM OF PEANUT SOUP
(10 to 12 servings)

1 medium onion, chopped	2 qt. chicken broth
2 ribs celery, chopped	1 cup creamy peanut butter
¼ cup butter or margarine	2 cups cream or rich milk
1 T whole wheat flour	Chopped roasted peanuts

Cook onion and celery in butter until tender, but not browned. Stir in the flour until well blended. Add chicken broth and stir constantly until soup comes to a boil. Remove from heat and press soup through a strainer. Add peanut butter and cream or milk to soup. Stir until well blended and heat but do not boil. Ladle into soup bowls and garnish with chopped peanuts.

CREAM OF ALMOND SOUP
(5 to 6 servings)

1 cup blanched slivered almonds	⅛ t mace
	⅛ t allspice
2 cups chicken broth	2 T rye flour
2 cups cream or rich milk	1 T butter or margarine
1 lemon twist	Lemon twists, toasted
Salt, pepper	blanched almonds
Dash paprika	

Grind the slivered almonds fine in a food chopper or by processing a few at a time in a blender. Set aside. Combine chicken broth, cream and lemon twist. Bring to a boil, then reduce heat. Add salt and pepper to taste, paprika, mace and allspice. Knead flour with butter until well blended and stir into soup. Simmer soup, stirring often, until slightly thickened. Remove lemon twist and stir in ground almonds. Simmer *5 minutes* longer. Ladle into warm bowls and garnish each with a lemon twist and toasted almonds.

NAVY BEAN CHOWDER
(6 to 8 servings)

1 cup dry navy beans
2 oz. salt pork, thinly
    sliced, or 2 T oil

3 T minced onion
1½ t salt
3 cups milk

Soak beans overnight in water to cover. Drain off water, measure and add water to make 3 cups. Heat this water. Meanwhile, cook salt pork and onion until onion is tender but not browned. Add hot water, beans and salt. Cover and simmer *1 hour* or until beans are tender. Some of the beans may be mashed in kettle with wooden spoon if a thickened soup is preferred. Add milk and heat to scalding. Add more salt and pepper, if wished, and sprinkle with minced parsley.

LIMA GUMBO
(8 to 10 servings)

1 lb. dry lima beans
10 cups water
1 ham hock
3 large onions, diced
12 whole black pepper-
    corns
1 large bay leaf

6 sprigs parsley
1 cup diced carrot
½ cup diced green pepper
2½ cups tomato juice
2 t salt
1½ t lemon juice
Dash cayenne

Combine lima beans and water and let beans soak overnight. Add ham hock and onions to the beans. Tie black peppercorns, bay leaf and parsley in a small square of cheesecloth and add to beans. Cover and simmer *3 hours* or until beans are very soft. Remove about 1½ cups of the beans and the ham and set aside. Force remaining soup through a sieve or puree in a blender, processing in 2-cup batches. Return soup to kettle and add carrot, green pepper, tomato juice, salt, lemon juice and cayenne. Cover and simmer *35 minutes*. Stir in the reserved beans and the ham, which has been removed from the bone and diced. Taste and add more salt or other seasoning, if needed. Serve in warm bowls.

MINESTRONE CALIFORNIAN
(6 to 8 servings)

1 cup dry navy or small
   pea beans
3 T oil
1 clove garlic, minced
1 large onion, chopped
1 cup shredded escarole,
   spinach or Swiss chard
1 large tomato, peeled
   and chopped
1 rib celery, sliced
4 carrots, peeled and
   diced
1 cup diced peeled
   potatoes

6 cups beef broth
2 t salt
½ t pepper
½ t oregano
¼ cup minced parsley
1½ cups shelled fava beans
   or green peas
4 to 6 oz. whole wheat
   spaghetti, broken
   into ½-in. pieces
Grated Parmesan or
   Romano cheese

Soak beans overnight in water to cover generously. Heat oil in a large kettle. Add garlic, onion, escarole or other greens, tomato, celery, carrots and potatoes. Cover and cook over moderate heat *15 minutes*, stirring now and then. Add beans with water in which they were soaked, beef broth, salt, pepper, oregano, and parsley. Cover and simmer until beans are tender, about *1¼ hours*. Add fava beans or green peas and spaghetti. Simmer *15 minutes* longer, stirring now and then. This soup generally is preferred quite thick. If you like a thinner soup, add hot broth or water. Ladle into hot bowls and pass cheese to sprinkle on soup.

SIX-BEAN SOUP
(12 servings)

½ cup dry large white
   beans
½ cup dry red beans
½ cup dry pink beans
½ cup dry pinto beans
½ cup dry garbanzo beans
½ cup dry white beans
   Water
1 T salt
½ t pepper
¼ t crushed red chiles

½ cup olive oil
1 large onion, chopped
2 or 3 cloves garlic,
   minced
3 ribs celery with leaves,
   chopped
½ cup minced parsley
3½ cups chopped peeled
   tomatoes
Grated Romano or Par-
   mesan cheese

Combine all beans in a large pot, add 10 cups of water and soak overnight. Simmer beans in soaking water until soft, about *2 hours*. Add salt, pepper and chiles when beans are almost tender. Meanwhile, heat olive oil in a large kettle. Add onion, garlic, celery and parsley and cook until onion is tender but not browned. Add tomatoes and cook, mashing tomatoes into mixture until most of juice has evaporated. Add bean mixture to sautéed vegetables and simmer *45 minutes* longer. Add 3 or 4 more cups water or enough to thin soup as desired. Heat and serve in hot bowls and pass cheese to sprinkle on soup.

Almost any leftover beans are delicious in this soup: soy, fava, yellow-eye and whole dried peas. Split peas tend to make the soup cloudy and lentils and black beans spoil the color, though they taste good, too. Any vegetables such as sliced broccoli or zucchini, shredded cabbage or sliced carrot may be added toward the end of the cooking.

GARBANZO GREEN SOUP
(4 to 6 servings)

¼ cup olive or other oil
2 leeks, white part only,
    thinly sliced
1 cup shredded lettuce
2 cups drained cooked
    spinach, chopped
1 cup drained cooked
    garbanzo beans
2 cups chicken or vegetable
    broth

⅓ to ½ cup lemon juice
2 T finely chopped fresh
    mint
1 t salt
¼ t pepper
Sour cream, optional
Chopped fresh dill

Heat oil in a saucepan, add leeks and cook until tender, but not browned. Add lettuce, spinach, garbanzo beans and broth. Simmer *10 minutes.* Cool slightly, puree in a blender, blending in two batches. Add lemon juice, mint, salt and pepper. Serve hot with sour cream and garnish with dill. Soup should be thick, but if too thick for your taste thin with a little more broth.

VEGETARIAN PEA SOUP
(8 to 10 servings)

1 lb. dry split peas
2 qt. water
1 bay leaf
3 onions
3 whole cloves
6 ribs celery, sliced
2 carrots, sliced

2 small white turnips,
    diced
1 T salt
½ t pepper
¼ cup butter, margarine or
    oil

Place peas in a large kettle with water. Bring to a boil, cover and simmer *30 minutes.* Add bay leaf, 1 onion studded with cloves, celery, carrots, turnips, salt and pepper. Cover and simmer *30 minutes* longer. Chop remaining onions and cook in butter until tender but not browned. Add to soup and simmer *30 minutes* longer. Serve soup in warm bowls. Float thick slices of whole wheat toast on top, if wished.

COUNTRY TURKEY-CORN SOUP
(6 to 8 servings)

1 turkey carcass, giblets
   and neck
1½ qt. boiling water
1 onion, sliced
3 ribs celery, chopped
1 carrot, sliced

1 T minced parsley
1 T salt
2 cups corn cut off cob,
   including milky liquid
2 hard-cooked eggs,
   chopped

Place turkey carcass, giblets, neck, wing tips and any other scraps in large kettle. Add boiling water, onion, celery, carrot, parsley and salt. Cover and simmer *1½ hours* or until meat almost falls off bones. Check several times while cooking and add more boiling water if needed to provide a generous amount of broth. Remove bones from broth and strip off the meat and cut it into small pieces. Return meat to broth and add corn. Simmer *10 minutes*. Add chopped eggs.

OYSTER STEW
(4 servings)

1 pt. oysters with liquor
¼ cup butter or margarine
¼ cup minced celery leaves
1 qt. rich milk or half milk
   and half cream

½ t salt
Dash cayenne
Paprika

Pick over oysters, removing any bits of shell. Heat butter in saucepan, add celery leaves and oysters with their liquor. Cook just until edges of oysters curl. Add milk and heat until film forms over top. Season with salt and cayenne and serve at once. Sprinkle each serving with paprika.

AUTUMN FISH CHOWDER
(6 servings)

¼ cup diced salt pork, butter, margarine or oil
1 onion, chopped
1 lb. fish fillets (cod, haddock, sea bass, whitefish, etc.)
1 cup fish stock or clam juice
1 cup diced potatoes
½ t salt
⅛ t pepper
2 cups milk
Minced parsley or chives

Fry salt pork until lightly browned, or heat other fat in large pot. Add onion and cook until tender but not browned. Cut fish into 1½-in. chunks. Add to chowder along with fish stock, potatoes, salt and pepper. Cover and simmer *15 minutes* or until potatoes are tender and fish flakes easily with a fork. Add milk and heat thoroughly. Serve in warm bowls and garnish with parsley or chives.

Fresh Clam Chowder. Substitute 1 pt. shucked clams for fish and use clam liquor plus water instead of fish stock.

SHRIMP BISQUE
(6 servings)

1½ lb. shrimp
2 T diced celery
2 T diced onion
¼ cup diced mushrooms
4 T butter or margarine
2 T whole wheat flour
2 cups chicken broth or stock made from shrimp shells
2 cups cream or rich milk
½ t paprika
⅛ t nutmeg
1 t salt
3 T dry sherry (optional)

Shell and devein uncooked shrimp. Set aside a few whole shrimp for garnish and chop remaining shrimp fine. Cook chopped and whole shrimp, celery, onion and mushrooms in butter until onion is tender but not browned. Remove whole shrimp and set aside. Stir flour into remaining shrimp mixture. Add broth or stock, cream, paprika, nutmeg and salt. Cook and stir until smooth and slightly thickened.

Add more salt and nutmeg if needed. Stir in sherry. Serve in a heated tureen or soup bowls and garnish with reserved shrimp, split in halves.

BAKED SHRIMP SOUP
(6 servings)

1½ qt. milk
½ lb. cooked cleaned shrimp
1 rib celery
3 T butter or margarine

½ cup fine dry whole wheat bread crumbs
½ t salt
⅛ t pepper
Dash mace

Scald milk with shrimp, celery and butter. Remove celery. Stir bread crumbs, salt, pepper and mace into soup. Transfer to a shallow baking dish. Brown slowly about 5 in. from broiler heat. Stir top under once or twice. Broil until a golden brown. Serve at once.

MUSHROOM BARLEY SOUP WITH BUTTERMILK
(4 to 6 servings)

1 lb. lamb shanks, meaty bones left from roast lamb or lean beef short ribs
1 cup dried mushrooms, about 2 oz.
6 cups water

2 t salt
¼ t pepper
½ cup pearl or whole barley
2 green onions, sliced
1 T oil
2 cups buttermilk

Put lamb or beef, mushrooms, water, salt and pepper in a large kettle. Cover and simmer *45 minutes* or until meat is almost tender. Cook barley and green onions in oil in skillet until barley is lightly toasted. Add to soup, cover and simmer *1 hour* or until barley is tender. Taste and add more salt and pepper, if needed. If wished, remove bones from soup, cut off meat and return to soup, then discard bones. Slowly stir buttermilk into hot soup. Heat but do not boil. Serve in warm soup bowls.

MULLIGATAWNY
(6 to 8 servings)

1 3-lb. stewing chicken
6 cups water
1 small onion
2 whole cloves
2 carrots, cut in chunks
1 bay leaf
6 whole black peppercorns
2 t salt
  Chicken broth, if needed

2 T butter or margarine
1 large onion, diced
1 tart apple, diced
½ cup diced unpeeled
  eggplant
1 to 2 T curry powder
Hot cooked brown rice
Raisins, toasted nuts,
  shredded coconut

Cut chicken into pieces and put in large kettle with water. Peel small onion, stud with the cloves and add to chicken along with carrots, bay leaf, peppercorns and salt. Cover and simmer *2 hours* or until chicken is tender. Remove chicken from broth and cool until it can be handled. Remove meat from bones and cut into chunks. Discard bones.

Strain broth and add enough additional broth to make 8 cups. Return to kettle and add chicken. Melt butter in a skillet, and add diced onion, apple and eggplant and cook until apple and eggplant are soft. Stir in curry powder. Stir the curry mixture into soup and simmer about *5 minutes*. Taste and add more salt, if needed. Serve over mounds of rice in large bowls. Pass raisins, chopped nuts and shredded coconut to sprinkle over soup.

MEATY PUMPKIN SOUP
(8 to 10 servings)

½ cup dry garbanzo beans
4 qt. water
1 beef soup bone
1½ lb. cubed boneless beef
  or lamb
1 ham hock
¼ t pepper
½ t oregano
1 onion, sliced
1 clove garlic, crushed
1 cup cubed peeled
  pumpkin

½ cup chopped peeled
  tomato
2 medium-size white
  turnips, diced
2 carrots, sliced
3 ears corn, cut in 2-in.
  pieces
Salt
Cilantro or parsley
  sprigs

Combine beans and 2 cups water in a large kettle and soak overnight. Add remaining water, beef bone, meat, ham hock, pepper, oregano, onion and garlic to beans. Bring to a boil, skim as solids rise to the top, cover and simmer *1½ hours* or until meat is tender. Add pumpkin, tomato, turnips and carrots. Simmer covered *20 minutes* longer or until vegetables are tender. Add corn and salt to taste, cover and simmer *10 minutes*. Remove beef and ham bones from soup. Serve soup in warm bowls and garnish each serving with a sprig of cilantro (fresh coriander) or parsley.

BORSCH WITH SHORT RIBS
(6 to 8 servings)

2 to 2½ lb. short ribs
7 cups water
1 onion, peeled
1 carrot, cut in chunks
2 ribs celery, cut in chunks
2 t salt
¼ t pepper
1 bunch beets
¼ cup lemon juice
2 T honey or to taste
Peeled hot boiled
    potatoes

Trim all fat possible off short ribs. Remove bones, leaving meat in large chunks. Combine short ribs, water, onion, carrot, celery, salt and pepper in a large kettle. Cover and simmer *2 hours* or until meat is tender. Remove excess fat with a bulb baster or by passing an ice cube wrapped in cheesecloth over surface of soup. Wash and trim beets, leaving on about 1 in. of stems. Cook in boiling, salted water until tender, *20 to 45 minutes*, depending on size of beets. Peel beets and cut into thin strips. Add beets to soup along with lemon juice and honey. Simmer *10 minutes* longer. Taste and add more salt, if needed. Put one or two potatoes in each soup plate and ladle in hot soup.

CHILLED TOMATO SOUP
(4 to 6 servings)

2 cups diced peeled tomato
1 medium onion, diced
1 clove garlic, crushed
2 T olive oil
1 T vinegar
½ t salt
¼ t cayenne
½ t cumin

1 t honey
1 cucumber, peeled and
    diced
1 rib celery, diced
2 green onions with tops,
    diced
1 small green pepper, diced
Ice cubes

Combine tomato, onion, garlic, oil and vinegar in a blender or bowl. Blend or mash with the back of a spoon until creamy. Season with salt, cayenne, cumin and honey. Chill thoroughly. Divide cucumber, celery, green onions and green pepper among chilled soup bowls. Place an ice cube in each soup bowl and pour in soup. Serve immediately.

GAZPACHO SANTA BARBARA
(4 to 6 servings)

2 or 3 cloves garlic
2 t salt
¼ t cumin
2 T vinegar
4 T olive oil
2 cups tomato juice
2 cucumbers, peeled and
    diced

4 large tomatoes, peeled
1 cup whole wheat
    croutons browned in
    oil
1 sweet red or green
    pepper, diced
2 green onions, chopped

Mash garlic with salt in a bowl with back of spoon until garlic is pulverized. Work in the cumin, vinegar and olive oil. Add tomato juice, one of the cucumbers and three of the tomatoes. Mix well, cover and chill several hours. Just before serving place the remaining cucumber and tomato, the croutons, sweet pepper and green onions in small bowls. Ladle Gazpacho into chilled soup bowls and pass chopped vegetable and croutons to sprinkle on top.

CHILLED SPINACH SOUP
(4 to 6 servings)

2 lb. spinach
3 T butter or margarine
1 T grated onion
2 T finely diced celery
3 T rye flour

¾ t salt
Dash pepper
3½ cups spinach water and
    milk
½ cup cream or rich milk

Wash spinach and cook covered, in the water which clings to it, until tender. Drain well, reserving liquid. Chop spinach fine. Spinach may be pureed in a blender or by forcing through a food mill for a smoother soup. Melt butter. Add onion and celery and cook until tender. Stir in flour, salt and pepper. Combine spinach water and milk to make 3½ cups. Add slowly to onion mixture. Stir in cream gradually. Cook and stir over low heat until slightly thickened. Add spinach puree and mix well. Chill several hours or overnight. Thin with a little more cream or milk if soup is too thick.

CHILLED WATERCRESS SOUP
(6 servings)

2 T butter or margarine
1 small onion, chopped
4 small potatoes, peeled
    and sliced
3 cups chicken broth

1 t salt
1 bunch watercress
    Boiling water
2 cups cream or rich milk

Melt the butter in a large pot and add onion. Cook until onion is tender. Add sliced potatoes, chicken broth and salt. Bring to a boil, reduce heat and simmer *35 to 40 minutes,* until potatoes are soft. Force soup through a fine sieve or puree in a blender, processing in two portions. Meanwhile, cook watercress in boiling salted water *1 to 2 minutes.* Puree by forcing through a sieve or in blender. Add watercress puree and cream or milk to soup and mix well. Chill several hours or overnight. Ladle into chilled soup cups. Garnish with sprigs of fresh watercress.

CACIK
(Yogurt Cucumber Soup)
(6 to 8 servings)

1 large cucumber	1 T chopped mint or dill
1 t salt	1 t oil
2 cups yogurt	1 to 1½ cups water
3 or 4 cloves garlic, crushed	Ice cubes

Peel cucumber and grate into a bowl. Sprinkle with salt. Add yogurt, garlic, mint and oil. Stir gently to blend, then stir in enough water to make soup the consistency of eggnog. Chill and ladle into chilled bowls. Add an ice cube to each serving.

SCANDINAVIAN STYLE YOGURT SOUP
(6 servings)

2 eggs	2 cups yogurt
3 T honey	2 cups buttermilk
2 t grated lemon peel	

Wash eggs and break into a bowl. Beat until thick and light colored. Add honey in a fine stream while continuing to beat. Gradually beat in lemon peel. Stir in yogurt and buttermilk. Chill about *2 hours* and ladle into chilled bowls. Float a lemon slice on each serving, if wished. This soup should be served the day it is prepared.

BUTTERMILK VEGETABLE SOUP
(12 servings)

6 cups buttermilk	2 green onions, chopped
4 hard-cooked eggs, chopped	2 T lemon juice
1 large cucumber, diced	1 t dill weed or 1 T minced fresh dill
1½ cups drained diced cooked beets	1 t salt
	¼ t pepper

Combine buttermilk, chopped eggs, cucumber, beets, green onions, lemon juice, dill, salt and pepper. Chill well. Taste

and add more salt, pepper, onion or lemon juice, if needed.
Ladle into chilled bowls.

CANTALOUPE SUMMER SOUP
(3 to 4 servings)

1 t unflavored gelatin 2 cups diced cantaloupe
2 T cold water ¼ t salt
1 cup orange juice Sour cream, fresh mint
1 T lemon juice

Soak gelatin in cold water about *5 minutes*. Pour orange
and lemon juices into blender, then the gelatin mixture,
then the cantaloupe and salt. Cover and blend until mixture is thoroughly pureed. Pour into a shallow dish and
place in refrigerator for *1 hour* or longer. Blend again
just before serving. Pour into chilled bowls. Top each
serving with a spoonful of sour cream and a sprig of
mint or fine chopped mint leaves, if wanted.

BANANA BISQUE
(4 to 5 servings)

4 or 5 bananas Salt
1 qt. cream Honey, optional
2 T lemon juice Cinnamon

Peel bananas and place in blender with cream, processing
half at a time if blender will not hold entire recipe easily.
Blend until smooth. Add lemon juice and blend a few
seconds longer. Taste and add salt, and honey, if needed.
Chill thoroughly. Thin with a little milk, if too thick.
Pour into chilled bowls and sprinkle lightly with cinnamon.

TOMATO MELON BALL SOUP
(6 servings)

2½ to 3 lb. tomatoes
1 t honey
1 T grated onion
1½ t lemon juice
½ cup sour cream
1 t salt

12 cantaloupe or Persian
   melon balls
12 honeydew or water-
   melon balls
Minced parsley

Peel tomatoes, cut off stem ends and squeeze to remove as much seeds and juice as possible. Puree tomatoes in blender or by forcing through a sieve. There should be 3 cups of puree. Combine tomato puree, honey, onion, lemon juice, sour cream and salt. Beat until smooth. Chill thoroughly. Serve in chilled bowls with two of each kind of melon ball in each serving. Sprinkle with parsley.

Grains

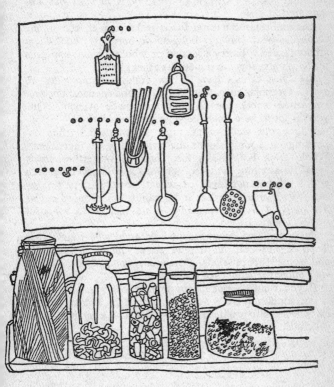

BROWN rice with its mildly nutty flavor, is the rallying cry of the natural foods revolution. Once you've tasted it, you may wonder why until recently it had all but disappeared.

The enthusiastic natural foods seeker can choose among cracked wheat (bulgur, bulghur or burghul), buckwheat groats (kasha), barley (pearled or whole), millet and grits made of corn, soy and sometimes other grains.

Breakfast cereals have a new emphasis among nature eaters. Granola, an oatmeal based, crunchy, naturally presweetened cereal, can be bought or made at home. One version given here lends itself to many variations—including numerous seeds or mixtures of grains and fruits depending on your taste or the availability of ingredients. Whole grain hot cereals have become wintertime treats again. Is anything quite so good on a cold morning than a dish of hot porridge (of wheat, corn, barley, rice or oats), with milk or cream and a handful of chopped dates? To many of us no sweetening is needed, but a spoonful of honey may be used.

Pasta made of buckwheat, whole grain wheat and other flours is available in oriental stores, health food stores and some supermarkets. Some are flavored or colored with pureed artichokes or spinach.

If you want to make your own whole wheat or buckwheat noodles, there is a recipe on page 73. It takes a little extra time, but you'll be surprised at how easy it is—and delicious!

HERBED RICE
(4 servings)

¼ cup butter, margarine or
   oil
1 onion, minced
1 cup brown rice
3 cups chicken broth

¼ t thyme
¼ t marjoram
1 bay leaf, crumbled
1 cup minced parsley

Heat butter in skillet. Add onion and cook until tender but not browned. Add rice and cook until pale golden, stirring often. Add chicken broth, thyme, marjoram, bay leaf and ¾ cup parsley. Cover and simmer *1 hour* or until liquid is absorbed and rice tender. Fluff up with a fork, turn onto hot platter and sprinkle with remaining parsley.

INDONESIAN YELLOW RICE
(4 servings)

1 cup brown rice
3 cups Thin Coconut Cream
   (page 297)

2 T butter or margarine
1 t salt
1 t turmeric

Combine rice, coconut cream, butter and salt in a heavy saucepan. Stir in turmeric. Cover tightly and place over high heat. Bring to a boil, stir once, cover tightly and turn heat as low as possible. Steam until rice is tender and liquid absorbed, about *50 minutes*. Fluff up with a fork and serve.

BROWN RICE CASSEROLE
(4 to 6 servings)

1 cup brown rice
½ onion, minced
¼ cup olive or other oil
1 cup chopped peeled
   tomatoes
1½ cups hot water

1 cup sliced mushrooms
1½ t salt
¼ t pepper
1 cup diced Cheddar
   cheese

Brown rice lightly in oil, stirring often. Add onion and cook until tender but not browned. Add tomatoes, hot water, mushrooms, salt and pepper. Bring to a boil. Stir in cheese. Turn into a greased 1½-qt. casserole. Cover and bake at 325° *1¼ hours,* turning with a fork two or three times after the first half hour of baking.

WEDDING PILAF
(6 servings)

1½ cups brown rice	½ cup raisins
3½ cups boiling water	¼ cup chopped pitted
1½ t salt	dates
½ cup butter or margarine	
½ cup blanched almonds, split	

Add rice to boiling water and sprinkle in salt. Cover tightly, bring again to a boil, turn heat low and simmer until rice is tender and water absorbed, about *50 minutes.* Add ¼ cup butter and toss to mix well. Cover and let stand over very low heat while preparing topping. Melt remaining ¼ cup butter in a skillet, add almonds and cook until they barely turn color. Add raisins and toss to heat well. Add dates and mix well. Remove from heat. Turn rice onto a platter and top with fruit and almond mixture.

NOTE: This is adapted from the Armenian wedding pilaf, though Armenians prize polished white rice and generally wash their rice before cooking it. However, this version has interesting flavor and texture.

RISI E BISI
(6 to 8 servings)

3 T butter or margarine	2 cups brown rice
3 T oil	2 cups shelled green peas
2 onions, chopped	2 t salt
4½ cups chicken or beef broth	2 T grated Parmesan cheese

Heat butter and oil in a Dutch oven or other large heavy pot. Add onion and cook until golden. Add broth and bring to a boil. Add rice, peas and salt. Bring to a boil. Cover and bake at 350° *1 hour*. Stir in cheese and, if needed, more boiling broth. Bake uncovered *10 or 15 minutes*. If rice is not tender, stir in more boiling broth and cook *10 to 15 minutes* longer.

GREEN RICE
(6 servings)

1 cup thinly sliced green
   onion tops
½ cup diced green pepper
2 T oil
1 cup uncooked brown
   rice

¼ cup minced parsley
1 t salt
Dash cayenne
2½ cups boiling chicken or
   vegetable broth

Cook onion tops and green pepper in oil until tender but not brown. Place rice in a greased 2-qt. baking dish. Add the green onion mixture, parsley, salt, cayenne and boiling broth. Stir, cover tightly and bake at 350° *50 to 60 minutes*, until rice is tender and liquid absorbed. Check about *15 minutes* before done and add additional boiling broth if rice is dry.

RICE O'BRIEN
(6 servings)

½ cup chopped onion
½ cup chopped green
   pepper
¼ cup chopped sweet red
   pepper

2 T oil
3 cups hot cooked brown
   rice
1 t salt

Cook onion, green and red pepper in oil until tender but not browned. Add rice and toss lightly. Sprinkle with salt and toss again.

SPICED PILAF
(6 servings)

2 T oil
2 large green onions with
  tops, sliced
1 cup brown rice
2½ to 3 cups vegetable or
  beef broth

½ t ginger, cumin or
  coriander
Salt, pepper
Minced parsley or
  cilantro for garnish

Heat oil in a heavy saucepan. Add green onions and cook until tender. Add rice and cook until translucent in appearance. Add broth, spice and salt or pepper. Amount of salt will depend on saltiness of the broth. Cover tightly, bring to a boil, turn heat low and simmer until rice is tender and liquid absorbed, *50 to 60 minutes*. Stir and let stand over very low heat for a minute or two. Serve with meats, fish or vegetables.

NOTE: Thinly sliced carrot, a few shelled green peas or sliced zucchini may be added to spiced pilaf along with broth and seasonings.

ARROZ HORNO CON ALCACHOFAS
(Baked rice with artichokes)
(8 to 10 servings)

¼ cup olive oil
1 small onion, chopped
2 cloves garlic, minced
½ to 1 cup sliced
  mushrooms
2 cups long-grain rice
3½ cups chicken broth
¼ t powdered saffron or
  bijol

2 cups cooked artichoke
  hearts
½ cup drained cooked or
  canned green peas
1 t salt
½ t hot pepper sauce
½ cup beer or dry white
  wine

Heat oil in skillet, add onion and garlic and cook until tender but not browned. Add mushrooms and rice and cook and stir until rice is translucent and coated with fat. Add chicken broth and stir in saffron until dissolved. Pour into greased casserole or complete in skillet. Arrange artichoke hearts around edge of casserole and add peas, salt and pepper sauce. Cover with waxed paper and bake at 350° *20 minutes* or until liquid is absorbed and rice is tender. Sprinkle beer over rice. Cover again with waxed paper and casserole or pan lid and put back in oven, with heat turned off, for *15 to 20 minutes*. If rice must be held for a longer time, turn oven very low.

BAKED MILLET
(6 to 8 servings)

2 T oil
½ onion, chopped
½ cup chopped mushrooms
1 cup hulled millet

½ t rubbed sage
4 cups chicken broth or
   water
Salt to taste

Heat oil in a large skillet or saucepan. Add onion and mushrooms and cook until mushrooms are lightly browned. Add millet and cook and stir until well coated with oil. Add sage and broth. Bring to a boil. Turn into a greased 2-qt. baking dish. Cover tightly and bake at 300° *1½ hours*. Serve hot with meat, poultry, fish or eggs. This makes a main dish when served with stewed dried beans or peas.

GRITS SOUFFLÉ
(6 to 8 servings)

1½ cups milk
1½ cups water
1 t salt
¾ cup hominy grits, soy,
   barley or rye grits

4 eggs, separated
3 T butter or margarine

Combine milk, water and salt and bring to a boil. Stir in grits slowly. Cover and cook *3 to 5 minutes* or until done. Stir occasionally while cooking. Cool grits slightly. Beat egg whites until stiff. With same beater, beat egg yolks slightly and stir into the warm grits along with butter. Fold in egg whites. Turn into a greased baking dish, preferably a straight-sided soufflé dish, and bake at 350° *45 minutes*, until firm and puffed. Serve immediately.

SIMPLE BULGUR
(8 servings)

2 T minced onion
¼ cup oil, butter or
    margarine
2 cups bulgur

3 cups chicken broth
½ t salt (or to taste)
¼ t pepper

Cook onion in butter in heavy saucepan until tender but
not browned. Add bulgur and stir until lightly browned.
Add the broth, salt and pepper. Cover and simmer *20
to 25 minutes*, until liquid is absorbed and bulgur tender.
Taste and add more salt, if needed. Fluff with a fork and
serve at once.

BULGUR PILAF
(8 servings)

¼ cup butter or margarine
1 cup diced celery
1 large onion, minced
2 cups bulgur
2 cups boiling broth or
    bouillon

2 cups boiling water
1½ t salt
¼ t pepper
1 cup sliced toasted
    almonds or pine nuts

Melt butter in a large skillet, add celery and onion and
cook until tender but not browned. Add bulgur and cook
until lightly toasted. Pour into a greased 2-qt. casserole.
Add boiling broth and water, then salt and pepper. Cover
and bake at 350° *1¼ hours* or 325° *1½ hours*. Uncover
and sprinkle with almonds. Bake uncovered *5 or 10 minutes*
longer.

MUSHROOM WHEAT PILAF
(6 to 8 servings)

¼ cup butter or margarine
2 cups bulgur or
    buckwheat groats
1 T minced onion
4 cups chicken broth
½ t marjoram

½ t salt
Freshly ground pepper
½ t rubbed sage
1 cup sliced mushrooms
    sautéed in butter

Melt butter in large skillet. Add bulgur or groats and onion. Cook slowly until wheat and onion are lightly browned, stirring often to prevent sticking. Add broth, marjoram, salt, pepper and sage. Cover and simmer *15 to 20 minutes*, until wheat is tender. Turn into a greased baking dish and top with mushrooms. Bake at 325° *15 to 20 minutes* or until heated through. If not ready to serve, cover and hold in slow oven for up to *1 hour*, moistening with hot broth, if needed.

FARMER'S PILAF
(6 to 8 servings)

½ cup butter or margarine
2 onions, chopped
2 cups large bulgur
3½ cups hot chicken or
    vegetable broth
1 cup minced parsley
2 large tomatoes, peeled
    and chopped

1 small green pepper,
    chopped
1 t basil
1 t salt
¼ t pepper
½ t cumin
Yogurt (optional)

Melt butter in a large heavy skillet or Dutch oven, and add onions and cook until tender but not browned. Add bulgur and cook and stir for about a minute. Add hot broth and mix well. Add parsley, tomatoes, green pepper, basil, salt, pepper and cumin. Cover tightly and simmer *30 minutes* or until all broth is absorbed. Stir lightly with a fork and let stand in a warm place *15 minutes* before serving. Serve yogurt over pilaf, if wished.

BARLEY CASSEROLE
(6 servings)

2 green onions with tops,
    sliced
6 mushrooms, sliced
2 T oil, butter or margarine
1 cup pearl or whole barley

1 t salt
Dash cayenne
2 cups water
½ cup pine nuts
Minced parsley

Cook onions and mushrooms in oil until tender but not browned. Add barley and cook and stir until it looks translucent. Add salt, cayenne and water. Bring to a boil and turn into a greased 1½-qt. casserole. Cover and bake at 350° *40 minutes* or until water is absorbed. If water evaporates before barley is tender, add additional boiling water. Stir in pine nuts and serve. Dust with parsley.

BARLEY WITH DATES
(6 servings)

5 cups water
1 t salt

1 cup whole or pearl barley
1 cup pitted dates

Bring water to a boil, add salt and stir in barley. Cook and stir about *10 minutes*. Set pan over boiling water, cover tightly and cook *3 or 4 hours*. Snip dates into small pieces and stir into barley. Heat thoroughly. Serve with scrambled eggs, an omelet or meats.

KASHA WITH ONIONS
(4 to 6 servings)

1 cup kasha (buckwheat
groats)
1 egg, slightly beaten
2 cups chicken broth

Salt to taste
3 T butter
1 small onion, thinly sliced

Stir kasha and egg in hot skillet until rather dry in appearance. Meanwhile, bring chicken broth to a boil. Add to kasha. If broth is well seasoned, additional salt may not be necessary. Cover tightly and cook over very low heat until liquid is absorbed, *about 30 minutes*. About 10 minutes before kasha is done, stir in 1 T of the butter. Melt remaining butter in another skillet, add thinly sliced onion and cook, stirring often, until golden. Serve onion and pan drippings over kasha. Or kasha may be served with Mushroom Sauce (page 237).

WHOLE WHEAT OR BUCKWHEAT NOODLES
(4 to 6 servings)

1 egg
½ t salt
¾ to 1 cup whole wheat flour, or use half buckwheat

Beat egg lightly and work in salt and enough flour to make a very stiff dough. Knead on a lightly floured board and roll out paper thin. Cover with a towel and let stand *20 minutes*. Fold sheet of dough over loosely and cut into strips through the two layers of dough. Noodles may be cut fine (½ in. wide) to wide (up to 2 in. wide). Cook in boiling salted water until tender, about *6 minutes*. Drain and proceed with recipe as desired or serve with grated cheese and oil or butter.

NOODLES WITH COTTAGE CHEESE
(4 to 6 servings)

4 oz. thin buckwheat, whole wheat or spinach noodles
1 cup cottage cheese
1 cup sour cream or yogurt
½ t salt
¼ t pepper
1 green onion with top, chopped
2 T butter or margarine, melted
¼ cup wheat germ

Cook noodles in boiling salted water until barely tender. Drain and mix with cottage cheese, sour cream or yogurt, salt, pepper, green onion and butter. Turn into a well-greased baking dish. Top with wheat germ and bake at 350° *1 hour* or until bubbly and lightly browned.

SPAGHETTI MARINARA
(4 servings)

1 lb. whole wheat spaghetti
¼ cup olive or other oil
4 to 6 tomatoes
1 clove garlic, minced
½ t dried basil or 3 fresh leaves, chopped
½ cup grated Parmesan cheese

Cook spaghetti in 4 to 6 quarts rapidly boiling salted water just until tender. Drain well and keep warm. Meanwhile, heat olive oil in a large skillet. Peel and remove cores from tomatoes, but do not seed. Cut tomatoes into wedges into hot oil, add garlic and cook slowly, mashing tomatoes with back of spoon to release juices, though tomato wedges should partially hold their identity. Simmer a minute or two, then add basil. Simmer and stir a minute longer. Sprinkle half the cheese and some of the sauce over spaghetti, toss thoroughly, then pour remaining sauce over spaghetti and top with remaining cheese. Serve at once.

HUNGARIAN NOODLES AND CABBAGE
(4 to 6 servings)

¼ cup butter or margarine	½ t salt
1 onion, chopped	½ t paprika
1 2-lb. head of cabbage	8 oz. whole wheat noodles
⅛ t pepper	

Heat butter in a large skillet, add onion and cook until lightly browned and beginning to shrivel. Meanwhile, shred cabbage coarsely. Add to onion mixture and sprinkle with pepper, salt and paprika. Cover and cook until cabbage is tender, about 20 minutes, shaking pan occasionally to prevent scorching. Meanwhile, cook noodles in 3 or 4 qt. rapidly boiling salted water until tender. Drain, turn out onto platter and top with cabbage. Toss lightly. Sour cream or cottage cheese may be added to this dish for extra heartiness.

WINTER GARDEN MACARONI
(4 servings)

4 oz. whole wheat elbow or shell macaroni	½ cup chopped green onion
1 cup sour cream	½ t salt

Cook macaroni until just tender and drain. Add sour cream and onion and toss lightly to blend. Sprinkle with salt. Serve hot or chill in refrigerator for at least *3 hours*.

GREEN CHEESE SPAGHETTI
(4 to 5 servings)

1 lb. thin whole wheat
    spaghetti
¼ cup butter or margarine
¼ cup olive or other oil
½ cup grated Parmesan
    cheese

½ cup minced parsley
1 clove garlic, minced
Salt to taste
Freshly ground pepper-
    corns

Cook spaghetti in 4 or more qt. boiling salted water until barely tender and drain. Meanwhile place half the butter on a platter or in a shallow bowl suitable for tossing. Place spaghetti over butter in dish and sprinkle with about half the oil, Parmesan cheese, parsley and the garlic. Toss gently but thoroughly, adding more oil, cheese, parsley and the remaining butter from time to time. Toss in salt and pepper to taste, top with parsley and freshly ground pepper. Serve at once.

GRANOLA
(6 to 8 servings)

2 cups uncooked oatmeal,
    quick or old-fashioned
1 cup wheat germ
1 cup chopped walnuts
½ cup sesame seeds

1 cup shredded coconut
½ cup chopped dates
½ cup honey
½ cup oil
½ cup chopped dried apples

There are as many versions of this cereal, a homemade version of Granola, as there are natural foods addicts. It is adaptable to various tastes and resources. Many home cereal makers prefer brown sugar to honey, add other grains, such as flaked barley or cracked wheat or buckwheat, other nuts or raisins or dried apricots in addition to or instead of dates.

To make the cereal, combine the oatmeal, wheat germ,

walnuts, sesame seeds, coconut and dates in a 9 x 9-in. shallow pan. Mix honey and oil in a small saucepan and heat, stirring until mixed. Add to cereal mixture and toss lightly. Bake at 325°, turning from bottom with a spatula every *5 minutes.* Cook until lightly browned, about *20 minutes.* Cool, add chopped apples and store in covered containers in refrigerator or freezer. Serve with milk or cream as a breakfast cereal or as a topping for creamy desserts or fruits.

OVERNIGHT HOT CEREAL

Soak whole grain wheat, buckwheat groats, brown rice or hulled whole barley in water to cover for 8 to 10 hours. Ground grains (cracked wheat, corn and wheat grits, rolled oats, mixed grain cereals) do not require soaking. Place cereal in large, wide-mouthed thermos which has been rinsed with hot water. Add salt and sufficient boiling water to cook cereal—about 4 cups water for each ½ cup ground grain cereal, 3 to 4 cups for each cup of soaked whole grain cereal. Screw cap on thermos and turn it on its side. Let stand overnight.

To serve, uncap thermos and scrape out cereal into bowls with a rubber spatula. Pour milk into thermos, shake to remove any cereal clinging inside and pour over hot cereal.

It is preferable to use a thermos with a plastic liner for this method of cooking cereal to prevent danger of breaking liner with spoon while scooping out cereal.

OATMEAL FLUMMERY
(6 to 8 servings)

1 t salt	¼ cup honey
1½ cups milk	¼ cup orange or other
2 cups water	fruit juice
2 cups uncooked oatmeal,	1 t grated orange peel
quick or old-	Raisins or chopped
fashioned	dates, optional

Add salt to milk and water in saucepan and bring to a boil. Stir in oatmeal and cook and stir *5 minutes*. Stir in honey and orange juice and peel, cover and remove from heat. Let stand *3 or 4 minutes*. Stir in raisins or dates, if wanted. Serve hot with milk and additional honey. This may be served as a simple dessert or breakfast cereal.

HONEY APPLE OATMEAL
(6 servings)

4 cups water	¼ cup honey
1 t salt	1 T lemon juice
2 cups uncooked oatmeal, quick or old-fashioned	2 or 3 apples, thinly sliced
	2 T butter or margarine

Bring water to a boil, add salt and stir in oatmeal. Cook *1 minute* for quick oats or *5 minutes* for old-fashioned oats, stirring now and then. Cover pan, remove from heat and let stand *4 or 5 minutes*. Meanwhile, combine honey and lemon juice in a small shallow saucepan and bring to a boil. Add apples and stir to coat them well. Cover and simmer *3 to 4 minutes*, just until apples are barely tender. Stir in butter. Serve oatmeal in large bowls with apples and syrup over it. Sprinkle with cinnamon, if wanted, and serve with milk or cream.

CORNMEAL MUSH
(6 servings)

1 cup cornmeal	Butter or margarine or milk
½ cup cold water	Honey or molasses
1 t salt	
4 cups milk	

Blend corn meal with cold water until smooth, then blend in salt. Pour milk into the top of a double boiler and bring to a boil over direct heat. Stir in corn meal mixture and cook and stir until slightly thickened and smooth. Place over boiling water, cover and cook until it has reached the consistency of a thick gruel, about *40 minutes*.

Spoon into cereal bowls and serve hot with butter, margarine or milk and honey or molasses.

Fried Mush. Pour hot mush into a well-greased baking pan. Chill until firm. Cut into squares, rectangles or finger shapes, roll in corn meal or wheat germ and brown in hot oil, butter or margarine. Serve hot with molasses or honey.

FRUIT MILLET PORRIDGE
(4 to 6 servings)

1 cup water
1 cup milk
½ cup hulled millet
½ t salt

2 T honey
¼ cup dried figs or apricots
Boiling water

Combine water and milk in top part of a double boiler and bring to a boil over direct heat. Slowly stir in millet and salt. Cook and stir over direct heat *about 5 minutes.* Place over boiling water in double boiler, cover tightly and steam *35 to 40 minutes,* until liquid is absorbed and millet tender. Stir in honey. Meanwhile, soak figs or apricots in boiling water. Cut into small pieces with kitchen shears and add to hot millet. Cover and steam *5 minutes* longer. Serve hot with more milk and honey, if wanted.

Vegetarian
Main Dishes

VEGETARIANISM has been practiced by certain people, usually for religious or ethical reasons, for hundreds of years. Today there is some evidence that less meat and more nonmeat principal dishes may be better for total health.

Regardless of your convictions, why not an occasional non-meat main dish for dinner? Thirty or forty years ago macaroni and cheese served as an entrée was common. Baked beans and brown bread is the classic New England Saturday supper. And millions of the world's people live almost exclusively on vegetable protein.

These main dishes are interesting alternates to the inevitable meat dish on the American table. In some cases, cheese or eggs bolster the vegetable protein. In others, grains and legumes complement each other. You will find additional dishes suitable for vegetarian main dishes in the Eggs and Cheese chapter, the Grains chapter and a few in the Vegetables chapter. A hearty soup or salad also can serve as a vegetarian entrée.

These dishes offer variety to the person choosing to eat no meats. They also have appeal for the family on a budget or who want to cut their meat consumption for health reasons.

Dry Bean and Legume Cookery

Water is removed from beans as they are dried, thus the principal procedure in cooking dry beans, a good source of protein and basic to vegetarian cookery, is to restore water. The beans are soaked to rehydrate them partially, and then cooked in large quantities of water.

Unskinned dried beans which are whole must be soaked before cooking or it is impossible to get them tender. Split peas and lentils, which are small, often are cooked without soaking. There are three methods by which navy beans, dry large white or small white beans, pea beans, pink, pinto or kidney beans, black beans, soy beans or garbanzos may be soaked. Often the choice is personal preference or convenience, but this is how:

Conventional Soak

Cover dry beans with about three times as much water, cover with a cloth and soak overnight at room temperature. If water is absorbed, add more water before cooking or while soaking.

Refrigerator Soak

Cover dry beans with about three times as much water, cover with a cloth and soak 1 to 2 hours at room temperature. Add more water, if needed, cover and soak in refrigerator overnight. In warm weather beans may ferment while soaking at room temperature. This makes the refrigerator soak preferable for superior flavor.

Freezer Soak

Pour dry beans into a freezer container which can be sealed airtight. Cover the beans with about three times as much water, cover with a cloth and soak 1 to 2 hours at room temperature. Add more water, if needed, cover with lid, sealing tight, and freeze. To cook, put unthawed block of frozen beans in a large kettle and cook as usual. Beans can be stored this way for several weeks or months in the freezer. Beans soaked by this method cook more quickly than beans soaked by other methods.

Quick Soak

Pour dry beans into a large saucepan, cover with about three times as much water, bring to a boil, boil 2 minutes and remove from heat. Cover and let beans soak 1 hour. Cook beans as usual.

BOSTON BAKED BEANS
(6 to 8 servings)

2 cups small pea beans,
    yellow eye beans or
    soy beans
1 small onion
2 whole cloves
2 oz. salt pork, scored, or
    lump of butter or
    margarine

½ t salt
½ t dry mustard
¼ cup molasses

Cover beans generously with cold water and soak overnight. Simmer until tender, about *1 hour*. Stud onion with cloves and place in a bean pot or deep casserole. Pour in beans, reserving some of the liquid if beans are soupy. Bury salt pork in beans with rind exposed or drop the lump of butter into beans. Blend salt and mustard in a measuring cup. Add molasses, then hot bean liquid or hot water to make 1 cup. Pour over beans, cover and bake at 275° to 300° *6 to 8 hours*. Add more hot water if needed. Uncover and bake *30 or 40 minutes* longer to brown. Serve hot with Boston Brown Bread, apple sauce and coleslaw.

SOY BEANS COUNTRY STYLE
(8 to 10 servings)

1 lb. dry soy beans	6 T butter or margarine
2 t salt	½ t leaf oregano
½ t pepper	¼ cup minced parsley
1 clove garlic, minced	1 green pepper, chopped
2 medium onions, chopped	3 chopped peeled tomatoes
1 bay leaf	

Cover beans with water and soak overnight. Bring beans to a boil in soaking liquid, reduce heat, cover and simmer *1 hour*. Add salt, pepper, garlic, 1 onion and the bay leaf and simmer *1 hour* longer or until beans are tender. Stir now and then while cooking and add hot water if needed to keep beans covered with liquid.

Meanwhile, heat 4 tablespoons butter in skillet, add remaining onion and cook until tender but not browned. Stir in oregano, parsley, green pepper and tomatoes. Cook and stir until the consistency of a thick sauce. Drain beans and stir in the tomato mixture and remaining 2 tablespoons butter. Serve hot with hot cooked brown rice.

SOY BEAN LOAF
(6 to 8 servings)

1¼ cups dry soy beans	1 cup fine dry whole
1 qt. water	wheat bread crumbs
1½ t salt	3 eggs
1 small onion, minced	1 cup milk
3 T oil	

Combine beans and water and soak overnight. Cover pan, bring beans to a boil, turn heat low and simmer *1 hour*. Add salt and simmer *1 hour* longer or until beans are tender. Drain, saving liquid for soups or sauces. There should be about 1½ cups cooked soy beans. Mash beans well with a potato masher or wooden spoon, or by beating with a mixer. Beans also can be pureed with some of the milk in a blender, but care should be taken not to liquefy them. Combine the mashed or pureed beans with onion, oil, bread crumbs, eggs and milk. Mix well and pack lightly in a well-greased 9 x 5-in. loaf pan. Bake at 375° *1 hour* or until set. Turn out onto platter, slice and serve hot with hot Tomato or Mushroom Sauce (pages 239, 237) if wished.

SOY BEAN CURRY
(6 servings)

½ cup oil
1 cup diced celery
1 clove garlic, minced
1 onion, minced
1 small carrot, thinly sliced
1 large green pepper, chopped

3 cups drained cooked dry soy beans
1½ to 2 t curry powder
1 cup water
2 T minced parsley

Heat oil in a large saucepan, add celery, garlic, onion, carrot and green pepper and cook until onion is tender but not browned. Add beans and stir in curry powder. Add water, cover and simmer *5 to 10 minutes* to blend flavors. Stir in parsley and cook rapidly uncovered for *2 or 3 minutes*, until some of the liquid is evaporated. Serve hot with hot cooked brown rice and condiments such as chutney, minced onion, diced hard-cooked egg and cucumber relish.

FRIJOLES REFRITOS
(Refried Beans)
(6 to 8 servings)

½ lb. pink, pinto or red kidney beans
Water
2 t salt

1 onion, sliced
6 T oil or bacon drippings
½ cup shredded Jack or Cheddar cheese

Cover beans generously with water and soak overnight. Add salt and sliced onion. Cook until beans are very tender, adding more water if needed, but beans should not be soupy. Drain beans of any excess liquid and save for soups or sauces. Heat 3 tablespoons of the oil in a large skillet. Add beans and cook, stirring and mashing with back of spoon to make a paste. Gradually work in remaining oil. Sprinkle with cheese. This dish is usually served with rice.

LOUISIANA RED BEANS AND RICE
(6 to 8 servings)

1 lb. red kidney beans
3 qt. water, or as needed
4 bay leaves, crumbled
1 T salt

2 cloves garlic, crushed
2 or 3 ribs celery, chopped
¼ cup chopped parsley
1 large onion, chopped

Wash and drain beans. Put in large pot with 2 qt. of the water. Cover and let soak overnight or 6 or 8 hours. Add more water if beans become dry. Bring to a boil, turn heat low and add 2 bay leaves and the salt. Cover and simmer *45 minutes* to an hour, until beans are beginning to get tender. Add garlic, celery, parsley, onion and remaining two bay leaves. Cover and simmer *30 minutes* longer. Serve hot on rice. Beans may be sprinkled with vinegar or lemon juice, if wished.

PINTO CASSEROLE
(6 to 8 servings)

2 cups dried pinto beans
5 cups water
2 T oil
2 cups chopped peeled
   tomatoes
1 large onion, coarsely
   chopped

¼ cup chopped green or
   sweet red pepper
1 large clove garlic, minced
2 t salt
½ t crushed rosemary leaves
¼ t crushed marjoram or
   oregano

Soak beans overnight in water. Add oil, bring to a boil, reduce heat and simmer, covered, until beans are tender, about *1½ hours*. Add tomatoes, onion, green or red pepper, garlic, salt, rosemary and marjoram or oregano. Turn into a greased baking dish and bake at 325° *1 hour*.

WHITE BEAN PLAKI
(6 to 8 servings)

1 lb. dry navy beans
2 cloves garlic, minced
2 onions, chopped
½ cup minced parsley
½ cup olive oil

2 cups chopped peeled
  tomato
1½ t salt
¼ t pepper

Soak beans overnight in water to cover generously. Add fresh cold water to cover and garlic, cover and simmer *30 minutes* or until beans are tender. Cook onions and parsley in oil until tender but not browned. Add tomato and cook until saucelike in consistency. Add salt and pepper. Stir into beans and cook *15 minutes* longer. Serve hot with bread and, if wished, cheese.

BEANS ITALIANO
(6 servings)

2 cups dry navy beans
1 bay leaf
2 onions, minced
1 clove garlic, mashed
2 T minced parsley
1 t chopped dill weed
½ cup oil
2 cup chopped peeled
  tomatoes

½ cup chopped green or
  sweet red pepper
1 cup diced celery
Salt, pepper
¼ cup grated Parmesan
  cheese, optional

Soak beans overnight in water to cover generously. Add enough more water to barely cover beans, bay leaf, onions, garlic, parsley and dill. Simmer until beans are tender but not soft, about *1½ hours*. Heat oil in a large skillet, add tomatoes, green pepper and celery and cook until saucelike in consistency. Add to beans along with salt and pepper to taste. Turn into a greased casserole. Cover and bake at 300° *2 hours*. Uncover, sprinkle with cheese and bake *20 minutes* longer.

CREAMED LIMA BEANS
(6 to 8 servings)

2 cups dried lima beans
1 onion, sliced
1 green pepper, chopped
1 T oil, butter or margarine

1 t salt
¼ t pepper
1 cup milk or cream
Minced parsley

Soak beans overnight in water to cover generously. Cover and simmer until almost tender, about *1 hour*. Cook onion and green pepper in oil until tender but not browned. Add to beans along with salt and pepper. Cover and simmer *30 minutes* longer or until beans are tender. Most of the liquid should be absorbed. If not, drain some of the liquid off and reserve for use in soups or sauces. Stir in milk or cream, simmer a minute or two, taste and add more salt and pepper, if needed. Turn into serving dish, sprinkle with parsley and serve with hot cornbread and other vegetables.

DAHL
(4 to 6 servings)

2 cups dried lentils
4 cups water
1 T turmeric
1½ t salt
½ t crushed dried chiles

¼ cup clarified butter or oil
1 large onion, chopped
2 cloves garlic, minced

Combine lentils and water in a large kettle. Add turmeric, salt and dried chiles. Cover and simmer until lentils are tender, *30 to 45 minutes*. Meanwhile, heat clarified butter * (the classic Indian ghee) or oil in a large skillet. Add onion and garlic and sauté until tender but not browned. Drain lentils and pour hot sauce over them. Serve hot or cold with brown rice or wheat pilaf or serve as an accompaniment to curries.

* To clarify butter, melt slowly in a small saucepan and skim off foam which rises to the top. Pour off the clear liquid butter, which is the clarified butter.

SPLIT PEA WHIP
(8 to 10 servings)

1 lb. split peas
4⅔ cups water
¼ cup butter or margarine
1½ t salt
½ small onion, diced
2 small carrots, thinly
  sliced
1 bay leaf

¼ cup brown sugar,
  packed
2 T lemon juice
½ cup cream or rich milk
1 T finely chopped mint
Salted peanuts or soy
  nuts, optional

Wash split peas, drain and combine with water, 1 table-spoon of the butter, salt, onion, carrots and bay leaf in a saucepan. Bring to a boil, reduce heat, cover and simmer until peas are tender and liquid absorbed, *45 to 50 minutes.* Remove bay leaf. Add remaining 3 tablespoons butter, the brown sugar, and lemon juice. Whip with an electric beater or spoon until smooth. Whip in cream and mint. Turn into a warm serving bowl and sprinkle with peanuts or soy nuts, if wished.

TIAN
(8 to 10 servings)

½ lb. dry white beans
Water
Salt
3 T olive oil
4 pattypan squash, diced
4 zucchini, diced
1 or 2 cloves garlic,
  minced

2 lb. spinach or chard
¼ t oregano
Pepper
½ cup grated Parmesan
  cheese

Cover beans with water and soak overnight. Add more water if needed and simmer until tender, about *1 hour.* Add 1 teaspoon salt just before beans are done. Drain beans and sprinkle with 1 tablespoon of the oil. Heat remaining oil in a deep skillet and add the pattypan and zucchini squashes and garlic. Cook, stirring to prevent scorching, until squashes are tender. Transfer to a greased 3- or 4-qt. baking dish. Wash spinach thoroughly and shake off as much water as possible. If using chard, shred it coarsely. Spread spinach or chard over squash. Top with the beans and season to taste with salt and pepper. Crumble oregano over the top and sprinkle with the cheese. Bake at 350° *30 to 40 minutes*. When about half done stir cheese through vegetable mixture. Serve hot or cold as a meat accompaniment or vegetarian main dish.

ARMENIAN LENTIL PATTIES
(6 servings)

1 cup red lentils
1 small onion, minced
3 cups water
1 cup fine bulgur
1½ t salt
1 t paprika
¼ t cayenne or crushed
   red chiles

2 T oil
1 egg
½ cup finely chopped
   green onion with tops
½ cup minced parsley
½ cup finely diced green
   pepper

Combine lentils, onion and water in a saucepan. Bring to a boil, cover and simmer until lentils are tender, *10 to 15 minutes*. Red lentils, which really are a bright orange color, become tan colored while cooking. Add bulgur, salt, paprika and cayenne. Mix well, cover and let stand *10 minutes*. Stir again and cool to lukewarm. Knead in egg and oil with spoon or with hands. With hands moistened in water, shape into about 12 egg-sized patties and roll in mixture of the greens.

NOTE: Red lentils can be obtained at markets which sell Armenian and Middle Eastern foods or an import market in a large city.

BAKED KASHA AND PINE NUTS
(4 servings)

1 cup kasha
1 egg, slightly beaten
2 cups chicken or vegetable
   broth
Salt to taste

¼ cup shelled pine nuts
Yogurt
Minced parsley or
   cilantro (fresh
   coriander)

Stir kasha and egg in hot skillet until rather dry in appearance. Add broth and salt. Bring to a boil and turn into a greased 1-qt. casserole. Cover and bake at 350° *30 minutes* or until liquid is absorbed. Stir in pine nuts and bake uncovered *10 minutes* longer. Add a little more boiling broth if kasha appears too dry. Serve hot with cold yogurt and minced parsley or cilantro.

NOODLE VEGETABLE STEW
(6 to 8 servings)

4 oz. soy bean thread or vermicelli
Boiling water
¼ cup oil
1 cup coarsely shredded carrot

1 medium onion, thinly sliced
½ cup thinly sliced celery
1 cup bean sprouts
2 T sesame seeds
2 to 3 T soy sauce

Drop bean thread into boiling water, let soak *5 minutes* and drain. If vermicelli is used, cook until barely tender and drain. Meanwhile, heat oil in wok or large skillet or Dutch oven. Add carrot and sauté until crisp-tender. Skim out carrot and add to noodles. Cook onion in oil until wilted, skim out and add to noodles. Cook celery and bean sprouts together in oil, add sesame seeds and cook just until lightly toasted. Add noodles with carrot and onion to wok, toss lightly, add soy sauce and stir over low heat *for a few seconds.* Serve hot with cooked brown rice, if wanted, and more soy sauce.

VEGETARIAN CHOP SUEY
(6 servings)

1 large onion, chopped
1 cup sliced celery
½ lb. mushrooms, sliced
2 T oil
6 cups bean sprouts, washed and drained
¼ cup beef, chicken or vegetable broth

1 green pepper, chopped
1 T honey
2 T soy sauce
Salt to taste
Hot cooked brown rice

Cook onion, celery and mushrooms in oil in large kettle or wok until onion is tender but not browned. Add bean sprouts and broth and cook and toss until bean sprouts are cooked crisp-tender. Be careful not to allow vegetables to become soft. Add green pepper, honey, soy sauce and salt. Heat thoroughly and serve with brown rice.

MILLET SAUSAGE
(6 to 8 servings)

2 cups water
½ cup hulled millet
½ t salt
½ t rubbed sage
½ t crushed red pepper, or
    to taste

1 cup finely chopped
    mushrooms
1 T oil
1 cup chopped walnuts
Whole wheat flour
Oil for frying

Bring water to a boil in a heavy saucepan. Slowly stir in millet, salt, sage and crushed pepper. Bring to a boil, stirring constantly, cover, turn heat very low and cook until millet is tender and water is absorbed. Meanwhile cook mushrooms in 1 T oil until browned. Stir mushroom mixture and walnuts into hot millet. Taste and add more seasoning, if wanted. Pack into a greased 8½ by 4½-inch loaf pan. Chill several hours or overnight. Cut into thick slices, dredge in whole wheat flour and cook in a small amount of hot oil, turning to brown both sides. Serve hot as an accompaniment to scrambled eggs or topped with Mushroom or Tomato Sauce (pages 237, 239).

MEDITERRANEAN CASSEROLE
(8 servings)

1 cup bulgur
1 small onion, minced
¼ cup oil
1 cup drained cooked
    lentils
1 cup drained cooked
    garbanzos

¼ cup minced parsley
2 cups liquid drained
    from beans and water
¼ t oregano
1½ t salt
¼ t pepper

Cook bulgur and onion in oil in large skillet, stirring often, until bulgur looks translucent and onion is lightly browned. Add lentils, garbanzos and parsley. Add liquid, oregano, salt and pepper. Bring to a boil and pour into a greased 1½-qt. baking dish. Cover and bake at 350° *45 minutes* or until liquid is absorbed. Fluff up with a fork and return to oven for 2 or 3 minutes.

GHIVETCH WITH CHEESE
(6 servings)

1 cup thinly sliced peeled carrots
1 cup diagonally cut snap beans
½ cup thinly sliced celery
2 medium tomatoes, peeled and cut in quarters
1 yellow summer squash, thinly sliced
1 zucchini, thinly sliced
½ onion, thinly sliced
½ head cauliflower, broken into flowerets
½ sweet red pepper, cut in strips
½ cup shelled green peas
1 cup vegetable or chicken broth
⅓ cup olive oil or other oil
3 cloves garlic, minced
2 t salt or to taste
½ bay leaf, crumbled
½ t savory, crushed
½ t tarragon, crushed
Grated Parmesan cheese
Jack or Swiss cheese, cut in strips

Combine all vegetables in a shallow baking dish. Heat broth and add oil, garlic, salt, bay leaf, savory and tarragon. Bring broth mixture to a boil, pour over vegetables and cover casserole tightly. Bake at 350° *1 hour* to *1 hour and 15 minutes,* or until vegetables are tender. Gently stir up vegetables from bottom twice while cooking. Uncover casserole, sprinkle generously with Parmesan cheese and cover with strips of Jack or Swiss cheese. Broil until bubbly.

VEGETARIAN POLENTA
(6 servings)

4 cups water
1 T salt
2 cups polenta meal or
    yellow cornmeal

¾ cup grated Romano or
    Parmesan cheese
2 cups hot Deluxe Tomato
    Sauce (page 239)

Bring salted water to a boil in a heavy 3-qt. saucepan. Slowly stir in polenta meal (available in Italian markets) or cornmeal. Reduce heat and cook and stir until mush pulls away from the side of the pan and is rather firm. Cover and cook without stirring *15 minutes* longer.

Turn into a warm deep bowl. Sprinkle with half the cheese and top with half the sauce. Serve remaining cheese and sauce on the side.

VEGETARIAN FRIED RICE
(6 servings)

2 cups brown rice
5 to 6 cups water
1½ t salt
    Juice and grated peel of
    ½ lemon
4 T safflower, corn,
    cottonseed or soy oil
¼ lb. mushrooms, sliced
1 large carrot, peeled and
    coarsely shredded
1 small zucchini, sliced
2 ribs celery, sliced
4 green onions with tops,
    sliced

1 small green pepper,
    diced
2 T sesame seeds
¼ cup coarsely chopped
    almonds, walnuts or
    pine nuts
1 T sesame oil
¼ lb. fresh bean sprouts
2 eggs
2 T water
1 T soy sauce or to taste

Combine rice and water in a saucepan (using larger amount of water for long grain rice, less for short grain), bring to a boil, add salt, lemon juice and peel. Cover and cook over very low heat until rice is tender and water absorbed, *40 to 60 minutes*.

Meanwhile, heat 3 tablespoons oil in a skillet, add mushrooms, carrot, zucchini, celery, green onions and green pepper. Cook and stir until onions and pepper are tender but not browned. Skim out vegetables with a slotted spoon and set aside. Add sesame seeds and nuts to oil in skillet and cook until lightly browned. Immediately remove from heat.

Heat remaining tablespoon vegetable oil with sesame oil in a large skillet, Dutch oven or wok. Add cooked rice and vegetables and cook and toss until heated through. Add bean sprouts. Beat eggs with water, pour over rice mixture and cook and toss until egg is set. Add soy sauce, mix lightly and pile onto hot platter. Sprinkle toasted sesame seeds and nuts over top.

CHEESE NUT LOAF
(6 to 8 servings)

1 cup cooked brown rice
1 cup wheat germ
1½ cups chopped walnuts
1 onion, minced
½ cup thinly sliced
   mushrooms

1 lb. sharp Cheddar
   cheese, shredded
1 clove garlic, minced
¼ t salt
⅛ t pepper
4 eggs, beaten

Combine rice, wheat germ, walnuts, onion, mushrooms, cheese, garlic, salt and pepper in a large bowl. Mix well, add eggs and mix thoroughly. Pack mixture into a well-greased 9 x 5-in. loaf pan. Bake at 350° *50 minutes* or until firm. Remove from oven and let stand *10 minutes*, then carefully loosen at sides with narrow spatula or knife and turn out onto a warm platter. Slice and serve plain or with Fresh Mushroom Sauce (p. 237).

BAKED EGGPLANT FRITATTA
(4 to 6 servings)

2 large eggplants	4 eggs
1 cup grated Parmesan or Romano cheese	½ cup milk
	1 t salt
½ cup wheat germ or fine dry whole wheat bread crumbs	⅛ t pepper
	Oil

Prick unpeeled eggplants at intervals with a fork. Broil, turning often, until skin is shriveled. (Or bake eggplants at 450° until skin is shriveled.) Cool eggplant, strip off skin and chop the meat fine. Mix with ¾ cup of the cheese, wheat germ or crumbs, eggs, milk, salt and pepper. Turn into a well-greased 7 x 11-in. baking dish. Sprinkle with remaining cheese and a little oil. Bake at 350° *45 minutes* or until a knife inserted in center comes out clean.

EGGPLANT ROLLS
(6 servings)

2 medium eggplants	1 t salt
3 T oil	¼ t pepper
2 eggs, beaten	1½ cups dry bread crumbs
2 T minced parsley	½ lb. mozzarella cheese, sliced
3 T grated Romano or Parmesan cheese	1 cup Tomato Sauce (page 239)
2 cloves garlic, minced	

Wash and dry eggplants, but do not peel. Cut lengthwise into ½-in. slices. Brush cut surfaces with oil and broil until soft and lightly browned on both sides. Combine eggs, parsley, Romano cheese, garlic, salt, pepper and bread crumbs. Mix well and place a spoonful of the mixture on each eggplant slice. Top with a slice of mozzarella cheese and trim cheese to fit eggplant slice. Roll and fasten with wooden picks. Pour a thin layer of tomato sauce into a greased shallow baking dish. Arrange rolls one layer deep in baking dish and pour remaining sauce over eggplant rolls. Sprinkle with additional Parmesan cheese. Bake at 350° *20 minutes* or until sauce is bubbly.

BREADED EGGPLANT WITH CHEESE SAUCE
(4 servings)

1 large eggplant
1 t salt
2 eggs
2 T milk
1 cup whole wheat flour

2 cups fine dry whole wheat bread crumbs
Oil for frying
Cheese Sauce (page 238)
Minced parsley

Peel eggplant and cut into ½-in. slices. Sprinkle with salt. Beat eggs with milk. Dip eggplant in flour, then in eggs, then in crumbs, coating heavily. If time allows, spread on a tray and refrigerate for *30 minutes* or longer. Pour oil to a depth of about ½ in. in a large skillet and heat. Add eggplant a few slices at a time, making sure slices do not overlap, and fry until golden brown. Drain on absorbent paper. Serve 2 or 3 slices of eggplant with a spoonful of cheese sauce and a sprinkling of parsley for each serving.

EGGPLANT STUFFED WITH EGG
(6 servings)

1 large eggplant
Salted water
2 T oil
1 onion, minced
1 green pepper, chopped
1 clove garlic, minced
2 tomatoes, peeled and chopped

1 t salt
¼ t pepper
1 T lemon juice
3 hard-cooked eggs, chopped fine
Wheat germ or cereal flakes

Wash and dry eggplant, cut in halves lengthwise and scoop out pulp, leaving half shells ½ in. thick. Cover with salted water and let stand while preparing stuffing. Heat oil in large skillet. Add onion, green pepper and garlic and cook until tender but not browned. Add tomatoes and eggplant pulp, which has been chopped fine. Cook until tender, mashing in pan to form a paste. Stir in salt, pepper, lemon juice and eggs. Drain eggplant shells and fill with mixture. Sprinkle with wheat germ. Place in a shallow baking dish. Bake at 350° *25 minutes* or until heated through.

CHEESE-STUFFED PEPPERS
(6 servings)

6 large green peppers
  Boiling salted water
2 cups cooked brown rice
  or kasha
2 cups shredded sharp
  Cheddar cheese
1 T minced onion

1 egg, beaten
1 T melted butter or
  margarine
¼ cup chopped walnuts,
  optional
Water, tomato juice or
  broth

Cut tops off green peppers or cut them lengthwise into halves. Remove seeds and ribs. Cook pepper shells in a small amount of boiling salted water *2 or 3 minutes,* just until they can be pierced with a fork. Drain and arrange in a shallow baking dish. (Cooking liquid can be used for broth for baking peppers or reserved for use in soups.) Mix rice or kasha, 1½ cups cheese, onion, egg, butter and walnuts.

If too dry, mix in water, tomato juice or broth. Pile stuffing lightly into pepper cases. Sprinkle with remaining cheese. Pour ½ in. water, tomato juice or broth around peppers. Cover and bake at 375° *20 minutes.* Uncover and bake *10 minutes* longer, until tops are slightly browned.

VEGETABLES PARMIGIANA
(6 to 8 servings)

1 eggplant
2 zucchini
1 green pepper
2 large onions
2 T oil
2 cups Tomato Sauce
  (page 239)

1 lb. mozzarella cheese
½ t salt
⅛ t pepper
¼ t oregano
2 to 3 T grated Parmesan
  cheese

Cut off ends of eggplant and zucchini and peel eggplant. Slice vegetables crosswise. Cut green pepper into squares. Peel and slice onions. Heat oil in large skillet, add eggplant, zucchini, green pepper and onions and cook until barely tender. Slice mozzarella cheese. Layer vegetables, cheese and sauce into greased baking dish, sprinkling layers with salt, pepper and oregano. Finish with sauce and sprinkle with Parmesan cheese. Bake at 350° *20 to 30 minutes,* until heated through and cheese is melted.

FRANK'S ARTICHOKES
(6 servings)

6 globe artichokes
½ cup finely slivered
    Romano cheese
1 T minced parsley

¼ t freshly ground pepper
    Boiling water
2 T olive oil
1 t salt

Trim artichoke stems to a 1-in. stub and trim off leaf edges about 1 in. from top. Turn each artichoke upside down on board and press down firmly to spread leaves and loosen choke. Scoop out choke with a sharp-edged teaspoon. Mix cheese, parsley and pepper and sprinkle into prepared artichokes so some falls into center and some between leaves. Place artichokes upright in 1½ in. boiling water in a large pot. Sprinkle with olive oil and salt. Cover and boil until artichokes are tender, *25 to 40 minutes,* depending on size. Serve hot. A dipping sauce may be offered but is not necessary with artichokes prepared in this way.

RICE-STUFFED CABBAGE
(4 to 6 servings)

1 medium head cabbage
    Boiling water
2 T oil
4 or 5 green onions, sliced
    thin
½ cup brown rice
½ cup minced parsley
2 tomatoes, peeled and
    diced

1 cup water
1 t salt
½ t cinnamon
½ cup chopped walnuts
4 whole cloves
4 to 6 carrots
    Salt, pepper

Place cabbage in deep pot of rapidly boiling water, cover and blanch for *5 minutes.* Remove cabbage from water, drain well and carefully spread leaves as if opening flower petals. Cut a large piece from center.

Heat oil in skillet, add green onions and cook until tender. Add rice and cook until it appears translucent. Add parsley, tomatoes, water, salt and cinnamon. Cover tightly and cook 25 minutes or until most of liquid is absorbed. (Rice will not be tender at this point.) Chop center portion of cabbage and add to rice along with walnuts. Carefully spoon stuffing into center of cabbage and between leaves. Shape into head again and tie securely with clean string. Place in deep pot. Stud cabbage with whole cloves. Peel carrots, cut into two or three pieces each and place around cabbage. Sprinkle with salt and pepper. Add 1 cup boiling water. Cover and simmer on top of range or in oven at 325° until tender and flavors are well blended, about 2 hours. Cut into wedges to serve.

NUTTED ONION CUPS
(6 servings)

6 large onions	¼ cup minced parsley
Boiling water, salt	2 cups dry whole wheat or
½ cup butter or margarine	rye bread crumbs
1 rib celery, diced	½ cup chopped walnuts
½ t rubbed sage	¼ cup grated Parmesan
1 clove garlic, minced	cheese
Dash pepper	

Peel onions and cut a thin slice from each end. Using a skewer, pierce each onion several times from top through center to prevent them from collapsing while cooking. Stand onions upright in a saucepan in which they fit snugly, cover them with boiling water and sprinkle lightly with salt. Cover pot and bring to a boil. Reduce heat and cook 30 minutes or until onions are tender but not soft. Cool and scoop out centers. Chop centers and set aside.

Meanwhile, melt butter in skillet. Brush onions with some of the butter. Cook celery and onion in remaining butter until celery is tender. Add sage, garlic, pepper, parsley and bread crumbs. Mix well and remove from heat. Stir in nuts and cheese. Spoon mixture into onion cups. Arrange in a greased shallow baking dish and bake at 325° 35 minutes or until heated through.

PEANUT BUTTER ONIONS
(4 servings)

6 medium onions	¾ cup peanut butter
2 T butter or margarine	½ cup fine dry whole wheat
2 T whole wheat flour	bread crumbs or wheat
½ t salt	germ
¾ cup milk	

Peel and slice onions thin. Cover with boiling water and let stand *10 minutes*. Drain onions, reserving ¾ cup of the liquid. Melt butter in saucepan. Gradually stir in whole wheat flour and salt. Add milk and cook, stirring constantly, until smooth and slightly thickened. Stir in peanut butter, then the reserved hot onion liquid. Place onions in a greased 1½-qt. baking dish and pour sauce over onions. Sprinkle with crumbs or wheat germ. Bake uncovered at 350° *20 minutes* or until bubbly.

BROCCOLI IN CHEESE CUSTARD
(6 servings)

1 lb. broccoli	3 T melted butter or
¾ cup instant nonfat dry	margarine
milk	2 T lemon juice
1¼ cups hot water	1 t salt
2 eggs, slightly beaten	⅛ t pepper
½ cup shredded Cheddar	
cheese	

Wash broccoli and slit the very thick stems. Cook in a small amount of boiling salted water until barely tender. Drain well and chop. Combine dry milk and hot water in a large bowl and beat until smooth. Stir in eggs, cheese, butter, lemon juice, salt and pepper. Place broccoli in a greased 5-cup casserole. Pour custard over broccoli. Set casserole in a shallow pan of hot water on oven rack. Bake at 350° *35 to 40 minutes* or until a knife inserted near center comes out clean. Serve hot.

STUFFED MUSHROOMS
(6 servings)

12 large or 24 small
  mushrooms
1 T butter or margarine
2 T oil
1 t minced shallot or 1
  clove garlic, minced,
  and 1 t minced onion
1 T minced parsley
¼ cup wheat germ or fine
  dry bread crumbs

½ t salt
⅛ t pepper
2 T vegetable broth, dry
  white wine or hot
  water
2 T grated Romano or
  Parmesan cheese

Snap off mushroom stems and mince fine. Heat butter and 1 tablespoon of the oil in a skillet. Add minced mushroom, shallot and parsley. Cook until lightly browned. Stir in wheat germ or crumbs, salt, pepper and enough broth to make a mixture which clings together. Arrange mushroom caps, cup side up, in a greased shallow baking dish. Fill with crumb mixture. Brush with oil and sprinkle with cheese. Bake at 400° *10 to 15 minutes.* Serve large mushrooms as a main course or vegetable, small mushrooms as appetizers.

CHEESE CREAMED MUSHROOMS
(4 servings)

24 large mushrooms
1 T lemon juice
1 cup sour cream
½ t salt

⅛ t pepper
3 or 4 T grated Parmesan
  cheese

Wash mushrooms quickly and drain. Snap off stems and reserve for another use. Place mushrooms, cup side up, in a well greased baking dish in which they will fit rather snugly. Sprinkle lightly with lemon juice, then drop sour cream from a spoon in blobs over the top. Sprinkle with salt, pepper and cheese. Cover and bake at 300° *30 minutes.* Uncover just before serving and serve hot.

LEEKS OR ONIONS AU GRATIN
(4 to 6 servings)

3 cups thickly sliced leeks
  or onions
  Boiling salted water

2 T butter or margarine
½ cup shredded Swiss
  cheese

In preparing leeks, wash very thoroughly as they hold dirt tenaciously. It is preferable to use white parts only. Cook leeks or onions in a small amount of boiling salted water until tender. Drain well, reserving liquid for soups or sauces. Spread leeks or onion in a shallow greased baking dish. Dot with butter. Sprinkle with cheese and bake at 400° until melted. Other cheeses may be used, including Cheddar, mozzarella mixed into the leeks or onions with Parmesan or Romano on top, Edam, Gouda, or crumbled goat cheese.

POTATOES SUZETTE
(6 servings)

6 medium to large baking
  potatoes
½ cup hot milk
2 T butter or margarine,
  melted
  Salt, pepper

6 eggs
6 T buttered whole wheat
  bread crumbs
2 T grated Parmesan or
  Romano cheese

Scrub potatoes, place in a shallow pan and bake at 400° *1 hour* or until pierced easily with a fork. Cut a thick slice from one side of each potato and scoop out potato pulp, leaving a sturdy shell. Mash potato very smooth, working in hot milk, butter and 1 teaspoon salt and a dash of pepper. Pile mixture back into potato shells, filling about half full. Break an egg into each potato and sprinkle with salt and pepper, bread crumbs and cheese. Bake at 350° until egg is set but not hard, about *12 minutes*.

SWISS CHEESE POTATOES
(4 to 6 servings)

4 large russet potatoes	2 cups milk
1 t salt	1½ cups shredded Swiss
¼ t pepper	cheese
⅛ t nutmeg	1 T butter, margarine or
1 egg	oil

Peel potatoes and grate coarsely. Combine with salt, pepper, nutmeg, egg, milk and 1 cup of the cheese. Mix well and turn into a greased 1½-qt. baking dish. Dot with butter or brush with oil. Sprinkle with remaining cheese. Cover and bake at 350° *45 minutes*. Uncover and bake *20 to 30 minutes* longer, until potatoes are tender and mixture set.

SPINACH CHEESE PUDDING
(6 servings)

2 lb. spinach	⅓ cup grated Parmesan
2 cups cottage cheese	cheese
1 t salt	2 eggs
¼ t nutmeg	Additional Parmesan
2 T minced onion	cheese

Wash spinach thoroughly and cook in the water which clings to leaves until barely tender. Drain well and chop fine. Mix spinach with cottage cheese, salt, nutmeg, onion, Parmesan cheese and eggs until well blended. Pour into a greased 1-qt. baking dish. Bake at 350° *30 minutes*. Serve with additional Parmesan cheese.

ZUCCHINI LOAF
(8 servings)

4 zucchini (about 1 lb.)	1 clove garlic, minced
1 onion, diced	½ t thyme
1 green pepper, diced	3 eggs, slightly beaten
2 cups cooked brown rice	¼ cup oil
1 t salt	½ to ¾ cup shredded
⅛ t pepper	Cheddar cheese

Wash zucchini and grate coarsely. Combine with onion, green pepper, cooked rice, salt, pepper, garlic, thyme, eggs, oil and cheese. Mix well and pack lightly into a greased 9 x 5-in. loaf pan. Bake at 350° *1 hour* or until set. Let stand in pan *10 minutes*, then carefully turn out onto small platter. Or slice and serve from pan. Serve with Tomato or Mushroom Sauce (page 239, 237), if wanted.

SPAGHETTI WITH BROCCOLI
(8 servings)

½ lb. broccoli
1 T oil
2 or 3 cloves garlic, crushed
1½ lb. tomatoes, peeled, seeded and chopped
1 t salt
¼ t pepper
¼ cup shelled pine nuts
1 lb. thin whole grain spaghetti
1 cup grated Parmesan cheese

Wash broccoli and cook in a small amount of boiling salted water until barely tender, about *10 minutes*. Drain broccoli, cut off flower heads and chop stems. Combine broccoli heads and stems in a bowl, cover and keep warm while preparing sauce and spaghetti. Heat oil in a large skillet, add garlic and cook until brown. And tomatoes, salt and pepper. Simmer uncovered until slightly thickened and well blended, about *20 minutes*. Stir in pine nuts. Meanwhile, cook spaghetti until barely tender in a large quantity of boiling salted water. Drain well and place in a large shallow bowl or deep platter. Add a few spoonfuls of the sauce and toss lightly. Top with remaining sauce and the broccoli. Sprinkle with Parmesan cheese.

Eggs and Cheese

EGGS and cheese provide valuable high quality protein, minerals and vitamins, and are especially important in the diet of nonmeat eaters. They are tremendously versatile in cookery. Here you'll find them in casseroles, omelets, pasta dishes, quick and easy, simple and semi-elaborate dishes. But a good egg needs only the simplest cooking and a little salt and pepper to make it gourmet fare. A good piece of cheese needs only to be removed from the refrigerator an hour or so before serving and brought forth with good bread for keen enjoyment.

EGGS IN CREAM
(6 servings)

½ cup cream, yogurt or milk   6 eggs
1 small whole dried chile, optional   ½ t salt
Minced parsley or paprika

Pour cream into a small bowl and, if used, add chile. Let stand at room temperature 30 minutes to 1 hour. Remove chile from cream. Break an egg into each of six greased individual baking dishes. Pour cream over egg and sprinkle with salt. Bake at 350° *15 minutes* or until egg is firm as desired. Dust with parsley or paprika and serve.

This simple way of preparing eggs offers unlimited possibilities in flavoring. If chile seasoning is not your choice, try a bay leaf or two, a slice or two of onion or garlic, fresh coriander (cilantro) or mix mustard or chili powder into the cream before pouring over the eggs.

ORIENTAL STEAMED EGGS
(4 servings)

6 eggs   1 t salt
1 cup hot stock or water   1 green onion, minced

Beat eggs gently with hot stock, salt and onion. It is important not to overbeat. Pour into a greased small bowl or custard cups. Place on a rack in a pan, pour in boiling water to a depth of about 1 in., cover pan and steam for *10 minutes* or until a wooden pick inserted in the center of each custard comes out clean. Sautéed mushrooms, chopped seafood or chicken may be added to steamed eggs. Or put an asparagus tip in the bottom of each custard cup.

CALIFORNIA CRAB FLAKE EGGS
(4 to 6 servings)

1 cup sliced mushrooms
¼ cup butter or margarine
¼ cup chopped green
    onion

8 eggs
½ t salt
1 cup flaked crab meat
Minced parsley

Cook mushrooms in butter until lightly browned. Add onion and cook over low heat until onion is tender but not browned. Beat eggs slightly with salt. Pour over mushroom mixture and cook over low heat, lifting with spatula at edges to allow uncooked portions to run underneath. When eggs are beginning to set add crab flakes and cook until set but still moist. Turn onto a warm platter and sprinkle with parsley.

TORTILLA ESPAÑOLA
(6 servings)

3 T olive oil
3 T butter or margarine
3 cups diced cooked
    potato

1 medium onion, diced
8 eggs
½ t salt
⅛ t pepper

Heat 2 T each oil and butter in a 10-in. omelet pan or skillet over medium heat. Add potatoes and onion and cook until potatoes are lightly browned. Remove potatoes and onion from skillet. Wipe skillet clean with a paper towel or cloth, then reheat with remaining oil and butter. Beat eggs just until well mixed and stir in salt and pepper. Return potatoes and onion to skillet and pour eggs over vegetables. Cook over low heat, running a spatula around edges occasionally to allow uncooked portions to run underneath. When omelet is almost firm, loosen edges and invert plate over skillet. Turn out omelet onto plate. Wipe out any bits which stick to pan and add a little additional oil. Heat oil and slide omelet back into skillet. Cook over low heat until lightly browned. Invert onto serving plate. Cut into wedges to serve.

EGGS FOO YUNG
(4 to 8 servings)

8 eggs
2 large green onions with
   tops, thinly sliced
2 stalks celery, diced

½ cup fresh bean sprouts
   (about 2 oz.)
Oil for frying
Brown Sauce (below)

Beat eggs just until well blended and ropy. Stir in green onions, celery and bean sprouts. Heat about ⅛ in. oil in a heavy skillet. Drop egg batter in by the quarter cupful and cook until lightly browned on one side, turn and brown on the other. Serve hot with Brown Sauce.

BROWN SAUCE
(1 cup)

2 t cornstarch
2 T soy sauce
2 t sugar

2 t vinegar
1 cup beef broth
Salt, if needed

Blend cornstarch with soy sauce, sugar and vinegar. Slowly pour in beef broth. Stir over low heat until thickened and transparent. Serve hot.

PINK PICKLED EGGS
(6 servings)

6 hard-cooked eggs,
   shelled
1½ cups beet juice (drained
   from cooked beets)
¾ cup vinegar
1 bay leaf

½ t whole allspice
1 t salt
2 or three whole black
   peppercorns
2 cloves garlic, peeled

Place eggs in a quart jar. Combine beet juice, vinegar, bay leaf, allspice, salt, peppercorns and garlic in a saucepan. Heat but do not allow to boil. Pour hot liquid over eggs, cool, then cover and refrigerate overnight or longer.

SCALLOPED EGGS
(4 to 6 servings)

Whole wheat bread
  crumbs
Butter or margarine
6 hard-cooked eggs, sliced
2 green onions with tops,
  sliced

Salt, pepper
Milk, cream, plain yogurt
  or sour cream

Grease a shallow baking dish such as a pie pan and
sprinkle in a thin layer of crumbs. Dot with about a half
teaspoonful of butter, then cover with a layer of sliced
eggs, green onions and salt and pepper. Repeat layers, then
finish with a layer of crumbs on top and dot lightly with
butter. Pour in milk, or cream until it can be seen just
below the top layer of eggs. If yogurt or sour cream is
used, spoon it in between layers of eggs and crumbs
and fill in with milk or cream after casserole is assembled.
Bake at 350° until bubbly, about *20 minutes.*

BASQUE POTATOES AND EGGS
(4 servings)

4 T oil, butter or margarine
3 cups sliced cooked
  potatoes
¼ cup minced onion

½ t salt
⅛ t coarsely ground pepper
4 eggs, beaten

Melt butter in a large heavy skillet, add potatoes and onion
and press down with the back of a spatula to make a
compact cake. Brown on one side, turn and brown the
other. Sprinkle with salt and pepper. Pour eggs over
potatoes, turn heat very low, cover and cook *7 to 10
minutes,* until eggs are set. Serve from skillet in which
eggs and potatoes are cooked.

COTTAGE EGG SCRAMBLE ON TOAST
(4 servings)

6 eggs
¼ cup mayonnaise, sour
    cream or water
⅛ t pepper
½ t salt
2 T butter, margarine or
    oil

¼ cup finely chopped green
    onions or parsley
½ cup creamy-style cottage
    cheese
6 slices whole wheat toast

Beat eggs with mayonnaise, pepper and salt just until well blended. Do not beat until foamy. Melt butter in a 9- or 10-in. skillet and tilt so bottom and sides are well coated. Add eggs and cook over moderate heat, stirring now and then, until eggs are set but still moist. Add onions and cottage cheese. Stir gently to mix well. Pile onto hot toast and garnish with more green onions or parsley, if wished.

PUFFY COTTAGE CHEESE OMELET
(4 to 6 servings)

4 eggs, separated
2 T whole wheat flour
½ t salt
2 cups creamy cottage
    cheese

2 T butter, margarine or
    oil
1 T honey
Honey or fruit preserves

Beat egg whites until soft peaks form when beater is lifted. Beat egg yolks until thick and lemon colored. Add flour and salt and continue beating until well blended. Stir in 1 cup cottage cheese. Fold egg whites gently into egg yolk mixture.

Heat butter in 10-in. skillet and tilt to coat sides and bottom. Pour egg mixture into hot skillet and cook over low heat until omelet begins to puff and is lightly browned on bottom, about *5 minutes*. (Carefully lift edge to check for browning.) Place in a 350° oven until top of omelet is dry, about *15 minutes*. Mix honey into remaining 1 cup cottage cheese. Spoon over half the omelet, crease omelet in center and fold over cheese filling. Carefully remove to warm platter. Serve at once with honey or fruit preserves.

EGG PUFF
(2 to 4 servings)

3 eggs, separated ½ t salt
½ cup milk
½ cup shredded Cheddar
    cheese

Beat egg yolks until thick and light colored. Beat in milk, cheese and salt. Wash beaters thoroughly and dry them, then beat egg whites until stiff peaks form when beaters are raised. Fold egg yolk mixture into egg whites and mix well. Pour mixture into a well-greased 1-qt. top of double boiler. Place over boiling water, cover and cook *20 minutes* without lifting top. Tilt double boiler top to see if any uncooked liquid runs free. If so, cover and cook *5 minutes* longer. Turn out onto warm plate and serve at once.

NOTE: This recipe should not be doubled as it is difficult to cook a larger quantity uniformly.

COUNTRY OMELET
(2 to 3 servings)

1 cupful finely shredded or ¼ cup slivered uncooked
    leaves of tender young   bacon or cooked ham,
    greens (mustard,   optional
    turnip, chard, spinach) 4 to 5 eggs
2 T oil, butter or margarine Salt, pepper

To prepare greens, wash thoroughly and drain. Keep leaves whole. Larger leaves should be shredded. Heat oil or other fat in a skillet. Add bacon or ham, if used, and greens. Cook just until bacon is crisp and greens wilted. Mix eggs with salt and pepper to taste. Pour over greens and stir and cook until eggs are set but still moist. Serve at once.

NOTE: This omelet was the invention of a southern black woman who made what she called a "green scramble" when she thinned the greens growing in her yard, so the greens were small and immature. The tiny leaves, if you grow greens, are ideal, but larger greens can be used if you shred them.

HUEVOS REVUELTOS
(Mexican Scrambled Eggs)
(4 to 6 servings)

3 T oil, butter or margarine
1 small onion, minced
1 clove garlic, minced
1 small hot chile, peeled
   and minced

1 medium tomato, peeled
   and chopped
6 eggs
½ t salt

Heat oil in a skillet. Add onion, garlic and chile and cook until onion is tender but not browned. Add tomato and cook and stir until most of the moisture is evaporated. Beat eggs just enough to blend and add salt. Add eggs to tomato mixture and cook over low heat, pushing cooked portions to center and letting uncooked portions run to edge from time to time until set but still moist. Turn onto a platter and, if wished, garnish with finely chopped cilantro (fresh coriander) or parsley.

NOODLES DELUXE
(4 to 6 servings)

4 oz. whole wheat noodles
1 egg
½ cup cottage cheese
2 green onions with tops,
   sliced

1 t salt
¼ t freshly ground pepper
Milk or cream, optional
1 cup shredded Cheddar
   cheese

Cook noodles in boiling salted water until tender but not mushy. Drain. Meanwhile, beat egg in a well-greased 1½-qt. baking dish. Stir in noodles, cottage cheese, green onions, salt, pepper and, if needed, milk or cream to make moist but not soupy. Add half the Cheddar cheese and fold gently but thoroughly to mix. Sprinkle top with remaining Cheddar cheese. Bake at 350° *20 minutes* or until top is golden and sauce is bubbly.

Variations on Noodles Deluxe. This dish can be varied endlessly. Fold in cooked green peas, soy beans or bean sprouts with Cheddar cheese. Add some chopped walnuts or almonds. Stir in bits of pimiento or green pepper. For a meat main dish, slivers of ham, chicken, turkey or tuna fish may be mixed with noodles and sauce.

BAKED RICE AND CHEESE
(6 servings)

1 cup sliced mushrooms
4 T butter or margarine
3 cups cooked brown rice
2¼ cups shredded sharp
    Cheddar cheese

½ t salt
Cayenne
1 cup milk, about
¼ cup wheat germ

Cook mushrooms in 2 tablespoons butter until lightly browned. Arrange layers of rice, cooked mushrooms, then cheese in a greased 1½-qt. baking dish. Season with salt and cayenne. Repeat layers until dish is almost full, reserving ¼ cup cheese for the topping. Pour in milk, using enough so it comes about half way to the top of the layered rice and cheese. Mix remaining cheese and wheat germ and sprinkle over casserole. Dot with remaining butter. Bake at 350° *30 minutes* or until bubbly.

CLASSIC MACARONI AND CHEESE
(6 servings)

8 oz. whole wheat elbow
    macaroni
2 T butter or margarine
2 T flour (whole wheat,
    rye or unbleached
    white)
1 t dry mustard
1 t salt

Dash cayenne
2 cups milk
2 cups shredded sharp
    Cheddar cheese
¼ cup fine dry whole wheat
    bread crumbs
1 T oil

Cook macaroni until barely tender and drain. Meanwhile, melt butter in saucepan over moderate heat and blend in flour, dry mustard, salt and cayenne. Add milk and cook and stir until smooth and thickened. Add 1½ cups cheese and stir until melted. Mix drained macaroni lightly into sauce. Turn mixture into a greased 1½-qt. baking dish.

Stir crumbs in oil over low heat until moistened throughout. Sprinkle crumbs, then remaining cheese over macaroni. Bake at 350° *40 minutes* or until bubbly.

SPRING GARDEN MACARONI AND CHEESE
(6 to 8 servings)

8 oz. whole wheat elbow macaroni
1 t dry mustard
1½ t salt
⅛ t cayenne
1½ cups sour cream
1 cup cottage cheese
1 egg, slightly beaten

¼ cup diced celery
¼ cup diced green pepper
¼ cup thinly sliced green onion tops
2 T minced parsley
1 cup shredded sharp Cheddar cheese

Cook macaroni until barely tender and drain. Blend mustard with salt and cayenne, then blend in a tablespoonful or two of sour cream. Stir in remaining sour cream, cottage cheese, egg, celery, green pepper, green onion and parsley and ½ cup of the Cheddar cheese. Add to macaroni and toss to mix well. Turn into a well-greased 2-qt. baking dish. Sprinkle remaining Cheddar cheese over top and bake at 350° *40 to 45 minutes,* until bubbly and cheese is lightly browned.

CHEESE-ONION PIE
(4 to 6 entree servings)

4 cups coarsely chopped onions
3 T butter or margarine
3 eggs
1½ cups milk or cream

¼ t cayenne
½ t salt
1 unbaked 9-in. pie shell
1 cup shredded Swiss or Cheddar cheese

Cook onions in butter or margarine until tender but not browned. Set aside. Beat eggs lightly, then beat in milk, cayenne and salt. Spread onions in pie shell. Sprinkle with cheese, then carefully pour in custard mixture. Bake at

450° *10 minutes*. Reduce heat to 325° and bake *25 to 30 minutes* longer or until a knife inserted in center comes out clean. Cool a few minutes, cut into wedges and serve as a main dish or serve slender wedges as an appetizer.

ALMOND CHEESE SOUFFLÉ
(4 to 8 servings)

3 T butter or margarine
4 T rye flour
1 cup milk
1 t salt
½ t paprika
½ cup sliced mushrooms, sautéed in a little oil

½ cup shredded Cheddar cheese
4 eggs, separated
¼ t cream of tartar
¼ cup toasted diced almonds

Melt butter in a saucepan and blend in flour. Stir in milk and cook, stirring constantly, until smooth and thickened. Add salt, paprika, mushrooms and cheese. Cook over low heat until cheese is melted, stirring now and then. Beat egg whites until foamy, add cream of tartar and beat until stiff but not dry. Without washing beater, beat yolks slightly and stir into the hot sauce. Stir in almonds. Fold half the egg whites thoroughly into cheese mixture, then fold remaining egg whites in lightly. Some flecks of egg white may remain unblended. Turn into an ungreased 1-qt. soufflé dish. Set in a pan of hot water and bake at 375° *30 minutes* or until puffed, brown and as firm as desired. Serve immediately.

BROCCOLI SOUFFLÉ
(4 to 6 servings)

3 T butter or margarine
3 T whole wheat flour
1 cup milk, scalded
1 t salt
1 t grated onion

4 eggs, separated
1 cup drained chopped cooked broccoli
1 egg white

Melt the butter and blend in flour. Gradually stir in milk, blending well. Return to heat and cook and stir until sauce is thickened and smooth. Add salt and onion, then cool slightly. Beat egg yolks until light and lemon colored. Add to cooled sauce, blending well. Add broccoli. Beat the five egg whites until stiff but not dry. Fold half the whites into the cooled sauce, mixing lightly but thoroughly. Fold in remaining egg whites lightly. Turn into a 1-qt. soufflé dish. Set in a pan of hot water and bake at 375° *35 to 40 minutes,* until puffed. Serve at once.

COTTAGE CHEESE SOUFFLÉ
(4 servings)

4 eggs	2 T minced parsley
½ cup milk	1 t salt
¾ cup creamy cottage	⅛ t pepper
cheese	1 T butter or margarine

Separate eggs and beat egg yolks with milk, cottage cheese, parsley, salt and pepper until smooth. Beat egg whites until stiff but not dry. Fold into the cottage cheese mixture. Melt butter in a 9- or 10-in. skillet. Pour in the omelet mixture and cook over low heat until set and the edges are beginning to turn golden. Finish cooking in an oven heated to 375°. Bake *15 to 20 minutes,* until top is puffed and golden brown. Serve at once.

MAKING COTTAGE CHEESE

Cottage cheese is easy to make, and well worth the trouble if you get the knack of producing just the flavor you prefer. Flavor depends on freshness of the milk used, flavor imparted by the buttermilk you use as a starter but, most of all, on eating the cottage cheese fresh.

A gallon of milk yields only about a pint of cottage cheese, so making less than two quarts is hardly worth the trouble. You need two large kettles, one which fits inside the other. Use stainless steel, good quality enamelware, heavy tinplate or other acid-resistant material—no aluminum or galvanized metal.

Pour milk into small kettle and place in larger container. Pour water around kettle of milk. Heat slowly until milk is about 72° (room temperature) throughout. Add ¼ cup fresh cultured buttermilk. Cover the container with cheese cloth and let stand 16 to 24 hours. Milk is sufficiently curdled when it appears custardlike throughout with a thin layer of watery whey on top. If milk cools too much during the curdling period, reheat water jacket, but be careful not to overheat.

When milk has curdled, cut the curd by slashing through the curd first in one direction, then in the other. Cut to the bottom of the pan. The curd should be cut into pieces about the size of a large green pea. Let stand 10 minutes to allow the whey to separate. Now heat water slowly in the jacket to raise the temperature of curds and whey to about 100° and maintain at this temperature for *30 minutes* or until pieces of curd are firm to the finger. Stir the curds and whey while heating.

Dip off some of the whey, then pour the mixture onto a fine cheese cloth in a colander over the sink. Let the curd drain two or three minutes, then pull corners of cloth in to form a bag around cheese and dip up and down in cold water to rinse out excess whey and to cool the cheese. Then rinse the cheese in ice water to chill. Set cheese cloth with cheese in colander again and let drain until whey no longer drips out.

Turn the cheese out into a bowl, add 1 teaspoon salt for each pint of cottage cheese and, if wished, stir in sweet or sour cream to moisten or cream slightly. Mix well, cover and chill until ready to use.

HOMEMADE YOGURT

1 qt. milk
1 T yogurt

Bring milk slowly to a boil. Remove from heat and at once cool to about 115°, until it feels barely warm when a drop is flicked onto the inside of the wrist. Blend a small amount of the warm milk into the yogurt in a 1-qt. jar. Gradually stir in the remaining milk. Cover, then wrap with a heavy wool blanket, insulated bag or several thicknesses of newspaper or toweling. The idea is to keep the yogurt comfortably warm while it is processing. Some people set the jar of yogurt in a pan of warm water and add warm water to the pan occasionally. Let the yogurt stand 6 to 8 hours, until it is set and solid, like a firm custard. Chill yogurt. Serve within a day or two for sweetest flavor as yogurt becomes more sour as it ages.

Berry Yogurt. Sweeten ¼ cup crushed strawberries, blueberries or blackberries with 1 to 2 teaspoons honey. Carefully stir in 1 cup yogurt, being careful not to agitate yogurt too much or it will separate.

Honey Yogurt. Slowly stir 2 teaspoons honey into 1 cup yogurt. Serve cold on fruit or cereals.

Fish and
Seafood

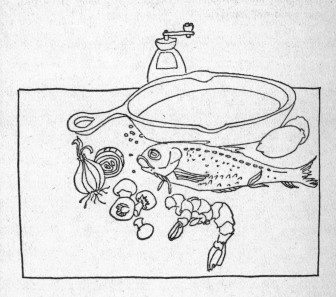

FINE fresh fish needs no fancy embellishments, and many of the recipes here are flawlessly simple. Fish is an excellent source of high quality protein and is usually lower in fats and calories than meats or poultry. Some recipes here can be adapted to pan fish you might catch anywhere. Others require fish from a fish dealer, and it is worth the trouble to find a dealer who sells high quality fresh fish, clean and well handled.

OVEN-PLANKED FISH
(6 servings)

1 3- or 4-lb. fish, dressed
1½ t salt
⅛ t pepper
2 to 3 T oil

Paprika
Seasoned mashed potatoes, optional
Lemon slices, parsley

A hardwood plank, ovenproof glass, ceramic or metal platter can be used for planking fish. If plank is used, oil thoroughly and place in a cold oven to heat while oven is preheating. Wipe the fish with a damp towel and sprinkle inside and out with salt and pepper. Place on hot oiled plank or greased platter and brush with oil. Bake at 400° *35 to 45 minutes* or until fish flakes easily with a fork. Remove fish from oven and spoon a border of potatoes around fish or press the potatoes through a pastry tube. Work quickly so the fish does not cool. Sprinkle fish with paprika and, if wished, brush potatoes with oil. Broil until potatoes are tinged with brown, about *5 minutes.* Garnish with lemon slices and parsley sprigs.

HERBED FISH
(4 servings)

1½ lb. fish fillets or steaks
1 T crushed fennel seeds,
dill weed or thyme
2 T butter or margarine,
melted

Juice of 1 lemon
Salt, cayenne, paprika

Rub fish on both sides with fennel seeds, dill or thyme. Place in a well-greased shallow pan. Brush with butter and sprinkle lemon juice over top. Season lightly with salt and cayenne. Bake at 375° *30 minutes* or until fish flakes easily with a fork. Baste several times with pan juices while baking. Sprinkle with paprika and place under broiler for *3 or 4 minutes* to brown lightly. Serve with lemon wedges, if wished.

SESAME HALIBUT
(4 servings)

4 halibut steaks or other fish fillets or steaks	2 T lemon juice
1 large clove garlic, split	½ t salt
2 T oil	⅛ t pepper
	2 T sesame seeds

Rub fish steaks well with garlic. Brush with oil and sprinkle with lemon juice, salt, pepper and sesame seeds. Place on a well-greased shallow baking pan or in a hinged wire grill. Broil or grill over glowing coals *4 to 5 minutes* or until browned. Turn and grill or broil *4 to 5 minutes* longer or until fish flakes easily with a fork.

FISH FILLETS JARDINIÈRE
(3 to 4 servings)

1 lb. broccoli	¼ cup diced leek, white part only
2 T butter, margarine or oil	1 t salt
1½ cups diced peeled carrot	1 t honey
½ cup minced onion	1 lb. fish fillets
½ cup diced celery	

Cook broccoli until barely tender, drain and chop fine. Melt butter in large skillet. Add carrot, onion, celery and leek. Sprinkle with ½ teaspoon salt and the honey. Simmer over low heat until vegetables are lightly browned. Cover with hot water and add broccoli. Bring to a boil.

Place fish in another large skillet and sprinkle with remaining ½ teaspoon salt. Pour vegetables with liquid over fish, cover and simmer until fish flakes easily with a fork, *8 to 10 minutes*. Drain off excess liquid and arrange fish and vegetables on a large platter.

POACHED SALMON WITH EGG SAUCE
(8 to 10 servings)

4 lb. salmon in one piece
4 or 5 whole black pepper-
    corns
1 bay leaf

2 slices lemon
2 qt. water
Egg Sauce (page 237).

Wrap salmon securely in cheesecloth, leaving ends free to facilitate removing salmon from poaching liquid after it is cooked. Add black peppercorns, bay leaf and lemon slices to water in a large kettle and bring to a boil. Carefully lower fish into the water and simmer, being careful not to boil, until fish flakes easily with a fork. This will take *6 to 8 minutes a pound*. Remove fish from broth, carefully remove cheesecloth and place fish on a serving platter. Carefully pick off skin, if wished. Garnish with lemon and parsley and serve with Egg Sauce.

POACHED FISH FILLETS
(4 to 6 servings)

1½ lb. fish fillets
¾ cup water, fish stock or
    chicken broth
¼ cup dry vermouth or
    dry white wine
½ t salt (less if using
    broth)

Dash cayenne
1 bay leaf
1 slice onion
1 small carrot, thinly
    sliced

If fish fillets are thick, split with a sharp knife. Roll fillets jelly roll fashion and fasten with wooden picks or skewers. Arrange fish rolls side by side in a deep skillet or large shallow saucepan. Pour water and wine over fish and add salt, cayenne, bay leaf, onion and carrot. Bring to a boil. Cover, reduce heat and simmer *10 minutes* or until fish flakes easily with a fork. Carefully lift fish from broth with a slotted spoon, letting excess broth drain into pan. Place fish on a platter and serve warm or cover, chill well and serve cold. Remaining broth may be thickened with arrowroot (a tablespoonful of arrowroot to each cupful) and served as a sauce with the fish. Or broth may be refrigerated or frozen and used as a base for soup.

Oven-Poached Fish. Arrange rolled fish fillets in a baking dish. Combine other ingredients, bring to a boil and pour over fish. Cover tightly and bake at 350° *15 minutes* or until fish flakes easily with a fork. Serve as above.

STEAMED FISH PORTUGUESE
(6 servings)

2 cloves garlic, split
2 T oil
1 onion, chopped
½ lb. mushrooms, sliced
4 T minced parsley
3 tomatoes, peeled and chopped

½ cup water, fish stock or dry white wine
½ t oregano
½ t salt
2 lb. fish fillets (rockfish, cod, haddock or others)

Cook garlic in oil in a large skillet until golden. Discard garlic, add onion and mushrooms and cook until tender but not browned. Add parsley, tomatoes, water, oregano and ½ teaspoon salt. Simmer uncovered until some of the liquid has evaporated, about *10 minutes,* stirring now and then. Cut fish into serving pieces and arrange over vegetables. (Thin fillets can be rolled and the rolls set on end over the vegetables.) Cover and simmer *15 minutes* or until fish flakes easily with a fork. Serve hot with boiled small potatoes or cooked brown rice.

BAHAMIAN FISH STEAM
(6 to 8 servings)

1 lb. fish trimmings (bones, head, tail)
2 cups water
1 bay leaf
1 t salt
½ t whole black peppercorns

1 rib celery, sliced
1 small carrot, sliced
2 lb. firm-fleshed fish fillets (rock cod, grouper, sea bass)
2 onions, sliced
2 limes or lemons

Place fish trimmings in a saucepan with water, bay leaf, salt, whole peppercorns, celery and carrot. Bring to a boil and simmer *15 minutes.* Strain fish stock, discarding bones and trimmings, whole spices and vegetables. (This can be done the night before and the stock refrigerated overnight.)

About a half hour before serving, bring fish stock to a boil in a large skillet. Arrange fish fillet in stock and top with sliced onions. Squeeze lime juice over the fish, cover tightly and simmer *10 to 15 minutes,* until fish looks opaque. Serve with grits and butter, spooning some of the fish stock over grits and passing lime wedges to squeeze over fish and grits.

BARBECUED SALMON
(10 to 20 servings)

1 whole salmon	3 or 4 sprigs parsley
Salt, pepper	Lemon Butter or Horse-
1 lemon, sliced	radish Mayonnaise
1 medium onion, sliced	(pages 238, 240)

A large cut of salmon may be prepared this way, but the whole fish looks more impressive. Wrap the head and tail with waxed paper, then foil, to protect from charring. If the fish is larger than 6 pounds, wrap damp towels between the waxed paper and foil.

Sprinkle cavity of fish with salt and pepper. Fill with lemon and onion slices and parsley. Close opening with skewers or wooden picks. Wrap fish loosely in foil. Place over glowing coal on a charcoal grill. Brush fish with oil. Cover the grill with its hood or a large tent of aluminum foil. Cook over hot coals until fish flakes easily with a fork, about *1 hour.* If possible, add hickory chips or hardwood to fire for extra smoke about 10 minutes before fish is done. Remove to a hot platter and serve hot with lemon butter or horseradish mayonnaise. Salmon prepared this way also can be baked in a 350° oven, but should be basted occasionally with a mixture of hot water and melted butter. Allow ¾ lb. of fish to a serving.

BARBECUED FISH
(6 to 8 servings)

1 3- to 5-lb. whole fish	¼ t rosemary
1 t salt	1 lemon, thinly sliced
¼ t pepper	1 large onion, thinly sliced
1 t marjoram	1 cup Tomato Sauce (page
¼ t oregano	239)
¼ t basil	¼ cup dry red wine

Skin and fillet fish, cutting out any dark portions of meat.
Place on a large piece of heavy-duty aluminum foil or in a
greased shallow baking dish. Blend salt, pepper, marjoram,
oregano, basil and rosemary and sprinkle over fish. Overlap lemon and onion slices over fish fillets to cover them.
Combine tomato sauce and wine and pour over fish. Wrap
foil loosely around fish, but seal top and sides securely.
Grill over glowing coals *45 minutes* to *1 hour*. Or bake
uncovered in oven heated to 400° *45 minutes* or until fish
flakes easily with a fork.

CHARCOAL GRILLED HALIBUT
(4 to 6 servings)

4 to 6 halibut steaks	¼ cup minced parsley
3 T lemon juice	1 T grated onion
½ cup oil	½ t dry mustard
Salt, pepper	

Arrange fish in a shallow dish. Combine lemon juice, oil,
salt and pepper to taste, parsley, grated onion and mustard.
Pour over fish, cover and let marinate about 4 hours in the
refrigerator. Place fish in a hinged wire grill which has
been well greased or in a greased shallow baking pan.
Grill over glowing coals *10 minutes* on each side or until
fish flakes easily with a fork. Baste with remaining
marinade several times while grilling. Or fish marinated
this way may be broiled.

CAMPFIRE FISH
(1 serving)

Freshly caught pan fish
Thinly sliced onion, optional
Oil, butter, margarine or
    bacon fat

Salt, pepper
Lemon juice
Minced parsley
Lemon wedges

Clean fish but leave whole. For easier eating, the main backbone may be removed, but be careful not to split fish in halves. Carefully push onion into cavity of fish and place fish in center of a large sheet of aluminum foil. Brush generously with fat, sprinkle with salt and pepper and squeeze lemon juice over fish. Sprinkle lightly with parsley. Fold foil carefully up around fish and seal with double folds of foil at edges of packet. Press the foil firmly to fish and turn edges up to hold in juices. Place packet at the edge of campfire, over glowing fire in a grill or on a baking sheet in the oven heated at 450°. Bake *15 minutes* or until fish flakes easily with a fork. Serve the fish with lemon wedges.

STUFFED WHOLE FISH
(6 servings)

1 3- to 4-lb. fish (whitefish,
    sea bass, red snapper)
Salt, pepper
2 cups cooked brown rice
1 t basil
¼ cup minced parsley
¼ t thyme

1 t crushed chiles
1 small onion, minced
2 T butter or margarine
2 cups Tomato Sauce
    (page 239)
⅓ cup oil

Carefully cut backbone from fish, leaving fish whole with head intact. Sprinkle fish inside and out with salt and pepper. Combine rice, ¼ teaspoon basil, parsley, thyme and crushed chile. Cook onion in butter until tender but not browned and add to rice mixture. Fill fish cavity with rice stuffing. Secure open edges with wooden picks or skewers and lace firmly with string.

    Place fish in a well-greased or foil-lined baking dish. Combine tomato sauce, oil, and remaining ¾ teaspoon basil. Pour over fish. Bake at 325° *45 minutes* or until fish flakes easily with a fork. Baste from time to time with pan juices while baking. Cut fish crosswise and spoon some of the pan juices over each serving.

GRILLED FISH STEAKS
(6 servings)

2 lb. salmon or other fish steaks
¼ cup vinegar
2 T lemon juice
1 clove garlic, minced
½ t salt
¼ t pepper
1 cup oil
Paprika

Place fish steaks in a shallow dish. Mix vinegar and lemon juice with garlic, salt and pepper. Add oil and beat to blend. Pour over fish and marinate *30 minutes,* turning fish once. Remove fish and reserve marinade to use for basting. Grill fish over charcoal fire, placing it in a wire rack to facilitate turning, or broil 3 to 4 in. from source of heat. Allow *8 minutes* for the first side and *6 minutes* for the second. Sprinkle generously with paprika before removing from fire. Fish is done when it flakes easily with a fork.

MARINATED ROAST FISH
(6 servings)

6 1-lb. fish (butterfish, sole, small mackerel or red snapper), cleaned
1 cup oil
¼ cup lemon juice
1 t salt
¼ t freshly ground pepper
Lemon wedges

Place fish in a shallow dish. Beat together oil, lemon juice, salt and pepper and pour over fish. Cover and marinate 1 hour, turning fish occasionally. Place fish side by side in a shallow baking dish. Beat together the marinade well and pour over fish. Roast at 400° *15 minutes* or until fish flakes easily with a fork. Baste with pan juices once or twice while baking. Arrange on a hot platter and garnish with lemon wedges.

PAN-FRIED FISH FILLETS
(4 to 6 servings)

1½ lb. fish fillets   Oil, butter or margarine
  Salt, pepper, paprika
  Cornmeal or unbleached
    flour, optional

Sprinkle fish with salt, pepper and paprika. If wished, roll in cornmeal or flour (whole wheat or rye may be used as well as white flour). Use enough fat so it reaches about half way up sides of fish pieces. Heat fat in a large skillet. Add fish a few pieces at a time, being careful not to overcrowd skillet and cook until browned on both sides, turning once. This will take about *4 minutes* on each side for medium-thick fillets. Drain on paper towels or brown paper bags and serve with lemon or lime wedges. Hushpuppies (page 264) may be fried in drippings after fish is cooked.

SAUTÉED PAN FISH AMANDINE
(4 servings)

4 pan fish, ½ to ¾ lb.   Additional butter or
  each   margarine
2 T butter or margarine   ½ cup blanched slivered
2 T oil   almonds
  Salt, pepper   1 t lemon juice

Sand dabs, small butterfish, trout or almost any small fish is suitable for this recipe. Have fish dressed and scaled or skinned, as the skin of the fish demands, but leave them whole. Heat 2 tablespoons butter and the oil in a large skillet. Add fish and cook over low heat *5 minutes* on one side. Turn and cook until fish is lightly browned and flakes easily when tested with a fork. Add more butter as needed. Remove fish to a warm platter and sprinkle with salt and pepper. Heat 2 tablespoons butter in another skillet. Add almonds and cook until lightly browned. Add lemon juice and pour over fish.

FISH IN SOY SAUCE
(4 servings)

4 small whole fish (floun-
    der, trout, butterfish)
3 to 4 T oil
½ t salt
¼ t pepper

¼ cup soy sauce
2 green onions, chopped
3 T water
1 slice ginger root, optional

Have fish cleaned, but the head and tail may be left on. The head helps keep fish moist while cooking. Heat oil in a large skillet. Salt and pepper the fish, then cook until lightly browned on each side. Pour off most of the oil and pour the soy sauce over the fish. Sprinkle with the green onion and add the water and ginger. Cover and simmer *5 minutes*. Turn the fish, cover and cook *5 minutes* longer. If fish flakes easily with a fork it is done. Serve hot with brown rice.

RED SNAPPER IN ORANGE SAUCE
(4 servings)

1 small onion, minced
¼ cup orange juice
1 t grated orange peel
1 t salt
4 large red snapper, rock-
    fish or sea bass fillets

Freshly grated nutmeg
Cayenne
1 T butter or margarine

Mix onion, orange juice, peel and salt in a shallow baking dish. Add fish and turn to coat with the marinade, then place skin side up in dish and let marinate at room temperature about half an hour. Turn the fish flesh side up, sprinkle lightly with nutmeg and cayenne, and dot with butter. Bake at 400° *10 to 12 minutes,* basting once or twice with marinade. Fish should flake easily with a fork when done. Serve hot with pilaf or brown rice.

SOUR CREAM BAKED SALMON
(6 servings)

1 lb. salmon steaks
Lemon juice
1 t salt
¼ t pepper

¼ t dill weed
1 cup sour cream
Minced parsley
6 lemon slices

Brush lemon juice over both sides of salmon steaks, cover and refrigerate 1 hour. Place salmon steaks in a greased shallow baking dish and sprinkle with salt, pepper and dill weed. Spread sour cream over fish and sprinkle lightly with parsley. Bake at 350° *30 to 35 minutes* or until fish flakes easily with a fork. Garnish each steak with lemon slices.

BREADED FISH
(6 servings)

2 lb. fish steaks or fillets
Lemon juice
1 t salt
1 t thyme

Mayonnaise, about ¼ cup
Buttered whole wheat
bread crumbs
Lemon wedges

Brush fish generously with lemon juice on both sides. Cover and refrigerate 1 hour. Arrange fish in a shallow baking dish. Sprinkle with salt and thyme. Spread a thin layer of mayonnaise over each fish steak or fillet, then sprinkle with buttered crumbs. Bake at 350° *30 to 40 minutes,* depending on thickness of fish. Fish is done when it flakes easily with a fork. Garnish with lemon wedges.

GREEK BAKED FISH
(6 servings)

1 2 to 2½-lb. whole fish,
dressed
Salt, pepper
Juice of 1 lemon
½ cup olive oil
2 onions, sliced
3 tomatoes, sliced

2 T minced parsley
1 cup Greek style black
olives
½ cup dry white wine
1 lemon, sliced
Parsley sprigs

Sprinkle fish with salt, pepper and lemon juice. Grease a shallow baking dish with some of the oil. Place half the onions and tomatoes in dish, sprinkle lightly with salt and place fish over vegetables. Cover fish with remaining onions and tomatoes, parsley and olives. Pour remaining oil and wine over fish and vegetables. Bake at 350°, basting now and then with liquid in pan, until fish flakes easily with a fork, *40 to 60 minutes*. Garnish with lemon slices and parsley sprigs.

OVEN-FRIED FISH
(4 servings)

2 t salt
Dash pepper
1 cup milk
½ cup wheat germ, corn-
. meal or fine dry bread
crumbs

4 fish fillets or steaks
¼ cup melted butter or
margarine or oil

Add salt and pepper to milk in a shallow dish. Spread wheat germ, cornmeal or crumbs on waxed paper. Dip fish first in milk mixture, then in crumbs. Place in a greased shallow pan. Drizzle fat over fish. Bake at 500° *10 to 12 minutes,* until fish flakes easily with a fork.

BROILED FLORIDA MACKEREL
(6 servings)

6 fillets mackerel
½ t salt
Dash pepper
Juice of 1 lime

½ cup butter or margarine
Paprika
Lime wedges

Sprinkle fish with salt, pepper and lime juice. Let stand about 20 minutes. Melt butter in a shallow pan about 6 in. from broiler heat. (Use reduced heat if broiler pan cannot be lowered.) Heat butter until bubbling. Place fish skin side up in butter, turn flesh side up and broil *3 to 5 minutes* or until fish flakes easily with a fork. Sprinkle generously with paprika, slip back in broiler for about half a minute and serve. Remove to a warm platter and garnish with lime wedges.

FISH FILLETS WITH RAISINS
(4 servings)

4 fillets sole, red snapper
  or sea bass
¼ t basil
1 small bay leaf, crumbled
Salt
Freshly ground pepper
½ cup chopped onion

1 carrot, peeled and diced
½ cucumber, sliced
3 or 4 clams, shucked and
  chopped fine
½ cup raisins
½ cup dry white wine or
  grapefruit juice

Arrange fish in a greased baking dish and sprinkle with basil, bay leaf, salt and pepper. Top with onion, carrot and cucumber. Sprinkle chopped clams and raisins around fish. Pour wine over all. Cover and bake at 350° *25 minutes* or until fish flakes easily with a fork. Serve with boiled new potatoes or brown rice.

SAN PEDRO FISH BAKE
(4 to 6 servings)

1 3-lb. whole fish (red
  snapper, sea bass, rock
  cod, whitefish)
2 large onions, sliced
3 ribs celery, sliced
3 tomatoes, peeled and cut
  in wedges
¼ cup minced parsley
½ cup water, fish or chicken
  broth

½ cup dry white wine or 2
  T lemon juice
1 bay leaf
1 clove garlic, minced
  (optional)
½ t salt
¼ t pepper
Paprika

Have fish cleaned and, if wished, the backbone removed. But do not have fish split and it will be juicier if the head is left on. Spread onions, celery and tomatoes in a greased shallow baking dish. Place fish over bed of vegetables and sprinkle with parsley. Pour broth and wine around fish and add bay leaf. Sprinkle fish with garlic, salt, pepper and paprika. Cover and bake at 350° *30 to 45 minutes*, until fish flakes easily with a fork and vegetables are tender. Remove bay leaf and serve fish and vegtables hot from baking dish. Garnish with lemon, if wished.

BROILED FISH FILLETS
(4 to 6 servings)

¼ cup butter, margarine
    or oil
½ t salt
¼ t pepper
½ t paprika
1 T lemon juice
1½ lb. fish fillets
Minced parsley

Heat butter in a small skillet and stir in salt, pepper, paprika and lemon juice. Arrange fish on a greased rack in a broiler pan (or thin fillets may be placed in pan without rack). Brush with the seasoned butter. Broil 4 to 5 in. from source of heat until fish flakes with a fork, about *10 minutes*. Thick fillets should be turned about halfway through the cooking period. Sprinkle with parsley. Serve with lemon or lime wedges or a sauce.

MAHI-MAHI POLYNESIA
(6 servings)

2 lb. mahi-mahi fillets (or
    snapper, whitefish or
    sole)
1 cup buttermilk
1 cup cornmeal
    Salt, pepper
¼ cup oil
½ cup butter or margarine
½ cup finely chopped fresh
    pineapple
¼ cup slivered almonds
    Juice of 1 lime
¼ cup toasted shredded
    coconut
    Lime slices

Dip fish in buttermilk, then in cornmeal. Season with salt and pepper. Heat oil with ¼ cup of the butter in a large skillet until butter melts. Add fish a few pieces at a time, being careful not to overcrowd, and cook until browned on both sides, turning once, and until fish flakes when tested with a fork. Remove to heated platter and keep warm.

In a small skillet, melt remaining butter until foamy. Add pineapple, almonds and lime juice and cook until heated through. Pour pineapple sauce over fish and sprinkle with coconut. Garnish with lime slices.

COLD HALIBUT WITH CUCUMBER
(4 servings)

1½ lb. halibut steaks
  1 stalk celery with leaves, sliced
  1 onion, sliced
  ½ lemon, sliced
  1 T honey
  1 t salt
  4 whole black peppercorns

2 whole cloves
1 bay leaf
Boiling water
Cucumber Cream) page 240)
Sliced cucumber, tomato wedges

Arrange halibut in a single layer in a large skillet. Add celery, onion, lemon, honey, salt, whole peppercorns, cloves and bay leaf. Add enough boiling water to barely cover fish. Cover and simmer over low heat *20 minutes.* Allow fish to cool in stock. Carefully lift fish from pan into a shallow dish, pour stock over fish, cover and refrigerate 24 hours. To serve, drain fish and place on a platter. Spoon cucumber sauce over fish and garnish with thinly sliced cucumber and tomato wedges.

CHRYSANTHEMUM BOWL
(4 servings)

1 lb. shrimp, shelled
1 lb. scallops or 1 dozen shelled oysters or clams
1 lb. thin fish fillets
1 bunch watercress
½ bunch spinach or Swiss chard
½ bunch Chinese cabbage

Green onion
2 oz. bean thread or 4 oz. vermicelli
4 eggs
4 T soy sauce
Sesame oil, optional
Hot cooked brown rice
1½ to 2 qt. chicken broth

This style of cookery calls for a Chinese firepot, a brass bowl with a funnel in the center which holds hot charcoal, but an electric skillet or wok or a fondue pot may be used. Each diner (this is for four) needs a dinner plate, a soup bowl and spoon, a pair of chopsticks for cooking, though fondue fork may be used by the less adept, a fork or separate chopsticks for eating.

Prepare shrimp, scallops and fish, cutting fish into 2-in. squares. Arrange on a platter. Wash and dry greens, separate into leaves which can be managed with chopsticks and arrange on the platter with the fish. Cut green onion, including tops, into 2-in. lengths and frill one end of each section by slivering finely. Pile onion pieces in center of platter. Soak bean threads in cold water 10 to 15 minutes to soften and cut into 6-in. lengths with kitchen shears. Place bean thread or vermicelli, which needs no preparation, in a separate dish.

Wash eggs and break one into each diner's soup bowl. Stir in 1 tablespoon soy sauce and a drop or two of sesame oil. Just before cooking, place a mound of hot rice on each plate.

Meanwhile, bring broth to a boil in the firepot or in another pan and pour into the firepot bowl. The broth should boil slowly during cooking. Each guest spears a morsel of fish, seafood or green and quickly cooks it in the boiling broth. This takes only a minute or two for seafood, just long enough to wilt the greens. The hot food then is dipped into the egg sauce and eaten, with a green onion. When the cooking is completed the bean thread or vermicelli is added to the boiling broth. When the noodles are tender, the soup is ladled into each diner's remaining egg sauce and is drunk as the finale to the meal.

NOTE: Chrysanthemum pot cookery is applicable to meats or chicken, all cut into small thin pieces so cooking is rapid. Other vegetables might be whole mushroom caps, thin cuts of sweet potato, zucchini or fresh asparagus.

SHRIMP SAUTÉ
(4 servings)

1 lb. jumbo shrimp
¼ cup olive oil
2 cloves garlic, minced
½ t salt
⅛ t pepper
¼ t dried basil
1 T butter or margarine
Minced parsley

Shell shrimp, leaving tails intact, and split almost through down center. Flatten slightly. Heat oil in a large skillet, add garlic and shrimp. Sprinkle with salt, pepper and basil. Sauté until shrimp turns pink and opaque, *3 to 5 minutes.* Add butter in small pieces. Sprinkle with parsley.

SCALLOPED OYSTERS
(6 to 8 servings)

2 cups fine whole wheat
    bread crumbs
½ cup butter or margarine,
    melted
½ t nutmeg
1 qt. oysters
1 t salt
Few grains cayenne
1 cup rich milk

Mix bread crumbs, butter and nutmeg. Spread a layer of crumbs in a greased 1½-qt. baking dish. Top with a layer of oysters and sprinkle lightly with salt and cayenne. Repeat layers until all oysters and crumbs are used, ending with crumbs. Carefully pour milk over casserole. Bake uncovered at 400° *20 to 25 minutes,* until bubbly. Serve hot.

SHRIMP AND COCONUT IN GREENS
(4 servings)

1 onion, minced
2 cloves garlic, crushed
1½ t crushed red chiles
1 cup shredded coconut
2 or 3 T water, can use
    water drained from
    coconut
1 lb. small shrimp, shelled
Juice of ½ lemon
½ t salt
⅛ t turmeric
1 firm tomato, cut in 4
    slices
Ti, banana or Swiss
    chard leaves or
    aluminum foil

Mix onion, garlic, chiles, coconut, water, shrimp, lemon juice, salt and turmeric. Wash leaves and spread a large leaf or two overlapping leaves flat on a board for each serving. Place a slice of tomato on each leaf then top with some of the shrimp mixture. Wrap neatly, turning in ends to seal well. Place in a shallow baking dish and bake at 350° *35 minutes* or cook over charcoal, turning now and then. Remove wrapping and serve.

Meats and Poultry

MEATS and birds have been the foundation of the American diet since before the white man came. This doesn't mean you are obliged to eat them, but it is easier to plan an adequate diet around meat and poultry, at least occasionally.

CALIFORNIA BEEF JERKY

1 well-trimmed flank steak	Salt, freshly ground
½ cup soy sauce	pepper
1 clove garlic, minced	

Cut steak lengthwise with the grain into strips no more than ½ in. thick. Toss with soy sauce and garlic. Spread beef strips in a single layer on a wire rack placed on a baking sheet. Sprinkle with salt and pepper. Place a second rack over meat and flip over. Remove the top rack and sprinkle meat again with salt and pepper. Bake at 150° to 175° overnight or *10 to 12 hours*. Store in a tightly covered jar or tin.

NOTE: Jerky is a favorite snack of campers and hikers in California, a heritage from pioneer outdoorsmen and, before them, Indians. To prepare it this way, an oven which maintains a relatively even low temperature is essential. If your oven fluctuates at very low temperatures, jerky may be air dried. Cover the rack of meat with cheesecloth to prevent insect infestation and set outdoors in clear dry weather, bringing in each night. Air drying generally takes three or four days. Taste the jerky after three days and if it is dried and leathery throughout, it is sufficiently processed.

10-WAY MEAT LOAF
(8 servings)

1 egg	½ t basil
⅔ cup milk	¼ t thyme
2 cups soft whole wheat or rye bread crumbs	1 onion, minced
1 t dry mustard	½ cup minced celery with leaves
1½ t salt	¼ cup minced parsley
¼ t pepper	2 lb. ground beef

Beat egg, add milk and bread crumbs and let stand until crumbs have absorbed milk. Blend in mustard, salt, pepper, basil, thyme, onion, celery and parsley. Add meat and mix well. Pack lightly into a 9 x 5-in. loaf pan or shape into a loaf and place in a shallow baking pan. Bake at 375° *1 hour and 15 minutes*. Let stand 5 minutes and turn out of pan onto platter. Slice to serve.

Meat Loaf Ring: Pack mixture into a 6-cup ring mold and bake at 375° *1 hour*.

Individual Loaves: Shape mixture into eight oval loaves and place in a shallow baking pan. Bake at 400° *45 minutes*.

Meat Loaf Cups: Pack mixture lightly into eight 6-oz. custard cups. Bake at 400° *45 minutes*.

Cottage Cheese Meat Loaf. Add 1 cup cottage cheese to meat mixture and increase salt to 2 teaspoons.

Cheddar Cheese Meat Loaf. Add ½ to 1 cup shredded or chopped Cheddar cheese to meat mixture.

Oatmeal Meat Loaf. Substitute 1½ cups uncooked oatmeal for the 2 cups bread crumbs in meat mixture.

Wheat Germ Meat Loaf. Substitute wheat germ for half or all the bread crumbs in meat mixture.

Mushroom Meat Loaf. Sauté ½ cup thinly sliced mushrooms in 1 tablespoon butter or oil until lightly browned and add to meat mixture. Serve with mushroom sauce, if wished.

Green Pepper Meat Loaf. Chop 1 large green pepper and add to meat mixture.

Tomato Meat Loaf. Chop 1 or 2 large tomatoes which have been peeled and add to meat mixture. Slice an additional peeled tomato over top of the loaf and sprinkle with basil 15 minutes before it is done.

Meat Loaf with Eggs. Hard cook three eggs and shell. Pack half the meat mixture into a loaf pan. Carefully arrange eggs lengthwise in center of loaf and cover with remaining meat mixture. Bake and slice as usual. Each serving will be centered with a slice of egg.

Stuffed Meat Loaf. Pack half the meat mixture into a loaf pan. Then carefully pack in a layer of mashed cooked carrots, mashed green peas, bread stuffing or Brown Rice Stuffing (page 150). Cover with remaining meat mixture. Bake and slice as usual.

BEEF PATTIES WITH CREAM
(4 servings)

1½ lb. ground lean beef
1 t salt
¼ t pepper
¼ t nutmeg
2 T oil
    Whole wheat or rye
    flour

¼ cup butter or margarine
½ cup heavy cream
1 T lemon juice
    Additional salt, pepper

Combine beef, salt, pepper, nutmeg and oil. Mix lightly with a fork to prevent packing meat. Shape into four patties about 1 in. thick. Coat with the flour. Heat butter in a heavy skillet. Add meat and brown lightly on each side. Lower heat and cook *2 minutes* longer for medium rare. Remove patties to a warm platter. Add cream and lemon juice to pan juices. Bring to a boil and cook rapidly until thickened. Sauce will curdle somewhat. Pour over meat, dust with parsley and serve with hot brown rice or mashed potatoes.

SUKIYAKI
(4 servings)

1 lb. tender beef, pork or chicken, cut in paper-thin slices 3 in. long and 1 in. wide

2 onions

½ bunch celery, sliced, optional

½ lb. spinach, Chinese cabbage or chard

1 bunch green onions, cut in 2-in. lengths

½ cup sliced large mushrooms

4 1-in. cubes soy bean curd

1 bamboo shoot, sliced

⅓ cup soy sauce

2 T honey

¼ cup chicken broth, beef broth or sherry

½ cup shirataki (rice noodles), optional

¼ cup oil or beef suet

Slice onions in halves lengthwise, then thinly crosswise. Prepare other vegetables and meat. Arrange in strips or piles on a platter. One attraction of sukiyaki is the display of foods before cooking. Mix soy sauce, honey and broth and pour into a small pitcher. Place noodles in a bowl. A sukiyaki pot set over a hibachi is the traditional utensil for Sukiyaki, though an electric skillet or automatic wok may be used. Heat oil in the pot. Add beef and brown quickly. Push to one side with chopsticks or tongs and add the sauce. Cook *2 or 3 minutes,* then add vegetables. Turn and cook vegetables with meat for *3 or 4 minutes.* Add noodles, mix well and serve over hot brown rice.

GAUCHO STEW IN A PUMPKIN SHELL
(8 servings)

2 lb. beef chuck or round
1 large onion, chopped
2 cloves garlic, minced
3 T oil
2 large tomatoes, peeled and chopped
1 large green pepper, chopped
Salt, pepper
1 t honey
1 cup dried apricots

3 white potatoes, peeled and diced
3 sweet potatoes, peeled and diced
2 cups beef or vegetable broth
1 medium pumpkin
Melted butter or margarine
1½ cups corn, cut off the cob

Trim visible fat off meat and cut the meat into 1½-in. cubes. Brown meat, onion and garlic in hot oil in large pot. Add tomatoes, green pepper, 1 tablespoon salt, ½ teaspoon pepper, honey, apricots, white and sweet potatoes and broth. Cover and simmer *1 hour*.

Meanwhile, cut top of pumpkin and discard. Scoop out seeds and stringy portions. Brush inside of pumpkin with butter and sprinkle lightly with salt and pepper. Stir corn into stew and carefully ladle into pumpkin shell. Place pumpkin in a shallow baking dish and bake at 325° *1 hour* or until pumpkin and meat are tender. Carefully transfer pumpkin to a large bowl and ladle out stew, scooping out pumpkin along with each serving.

OVEN BEEF STEW
(8 servings)

2 lb. beef chuck or round
2 T soy sauce
4 carrots, sliced
2 large onions, sliced
1 cup thinly sliced celery
1 cup thinly sliced mushrooms

1 clove garlic, minced
2 t salt
¼ t pepper
Juice of 1 lemon
1 cup meat or vegetable broth or water
1 small potato, peeled

Trim visible fat from meat and cut the meat into 1½-in. cubes. Place in a 2½-qt. baking dish, add soy sauce and toss to coat meat well. Add carrots, onions, celery, mushrooms and garlic. Toss again to mix meat and vegetables. Combine salt, pepper, lemon juice and broth. Coarsely grate potato into the broth mixture and pour over stew. Cover tightly and bake at 325° *2½ hours* or until meat and vegetables are tender. Stir three or four times while baking. Potato will thicken liquid somewhat to make a smooth gravy. Serve stew with mashed or boiled potatoes or brown rice.

STEAK IN LEMON BARBECUE SAUCE
(4 to 6 servings)

1 T oil
1 small onion, chopped
1 cup sliced peeled
    tomatoes (3 or 4)
¼ cup honey
1 t dry mustard

¼ t ground cloves
¼ t allspice
¼ cup lemon juice
1 thick chuck steak, about
    2½ lb.

Heat oil in a large ovenproof skillet. Add onion and cook until tender but not brown. Add tomatoes and stir and cook until most of the liquid of tomatoes is evaporated. Stir in honey, mustard, cloves, allspice and lemon juice. Bring to a boil. Place chuck steak in sauce and turn so both sides are coated with sauce. Cover and bake at 325° to 350° until fork tender, about *1½ hours*. Serve with mashed or boiled potatoes, brown rice, whole wheat spaghetti or noodles.

STUFATINO
(Italian Beef Stew)
(4 servings)

4 thick slices beef shin
    Flour
3 T olive oil
2 or 3 cloves garlic,
    minced
1 onion, chopped
1 t salt

½ t marjoram leaves
¼ t pepper
3 tomatoes, peeled and
    chopped
½ cup dry red wine, beef
    stock or water

Dredge beef in flour. Heat oil in a Dutch oven or other large pot. Add meat and brown on both sides. Brown in two batches if kettle will not accommodate meat easily. Add garlic and onion and cook until lightly browned. Sprinkle salt, marjoram, pepper and tomatoes over meat. Mix tomatoes into oil around meat, then add wine. Cover and simmer over low heat *1½ hours* or until meat is fork tender. Serve with brown rice or hot cooked spaghetti.

GREEN PEPPER STEAK
(4 servings)

1 lb. boneless beef chuck
    or round
2 T oil
1 small onion, diced
1 clove garlic, minced
½ cup diced celery
2 large green peppers, cut
    in strips

1 small sweet red pepper,
    chopped (optional)
½ cup beef stock
1 t salt
⅛ t pepper
2 t cornstarch
2 T water
1 t soy sauce

Cut beef in thin strips and brown slowly in hot fat. Add onion, garlic, celery, green and red pepper. Cook until onion is tender but not browned. Add beef broth, salt and pepper. Cover and simmer *30 minutes* or until beef is tender. Mix cornstarch, water and soy sauce to form a smooth paste. Add to meat, stirring until blended, and simmer *5 minutes*. Serve hot with brown rice.

FLANK STEAK WITH BROWN RICE STUFFING
(6 servings)

1 flank steak, about 1½ lb.
1 T chopped onion
1 small clove garlic,
    minced
1 T vinegar
4 T oil
1 t salt

½ t pepper
Brown Rice Stuffing
    (page 150)
Whole wheat flour
½ cup beef broth or water
6 small potatoes, peeled

Score meat in shallow diamond markings on one side. Combine onion, garlic, vinegar and 2 tablespoons oil. Mix well and brush over meat. Marinate meat *1 hour*. Spread meat flat on waxed paper. Sprinkle with salt and pepper and spread with stuffing. Roll meat as for jellyroll and tie. Dust lightly with flour. Heat remaining 2 tablespoons oil in Dutch oven or other heavy pot, add meat and brown on all sides. Add beef broth and any remaining marinade. Cover tightly and bake at 350° until meat is tender, about *2 hours*. Place potatoes around meat about a half hour before it is done. If needed, add hot broth or water while cooking.

BROWN RICE STUFFING
(1½ cups)

1 cup cooked brown rice	½ t dry mustard
2 T minced onion	1 t honey
3 T chopped green pepper	½ t salt
½ cup diced celery	⅛ t pepper
1 small bay leaf, crumbled	

Combine all ingredients well and use as stuffing for flank steak.

MAPLE POT ROAST
(6 servings)

1 3-lb. boneless chuck roast	¼ t allspice
3 T oil	1 t salt
¼ cup maple syrup	¼ t pepper
¼ cup cider vinegar	3 cups beef stock or water
2 bay leaves	Parsley
2 medium onions, cut in wedges	

Brown beef on all sides in hot oil in a heavy pot. Add maple syrup, vinegar, bay leaves, onions, allspice, salt, pepper and beef stock. Cover and simmer *2 hours* or until meat is tender. Slice beef and keep warm. Skim fat from sauce and press sauce through a sieve or puree in blender until smooth. Garnish meat with parsley sprigs and serve with sauce on the side.

NOTTINGHAM HOTPOT
(4 to 5 servings)

4 medium potatoes,
   peeled and sliced
1½ lb. beef chuck, cut in
   1½-in. cubes
1 medium onion, sliced

3 tomatoes, peeled and
   sliced
1 pt. small oysters
1 t salt
⅛ t pepper

A deep bean pot with cover is ideal for cooking this traditional British dish, but any heavy casserole with cover will do. Layer the potatoes, beef cubes, onion, tomatoes and oysters in the pot. Sprinkle with salt and pepper. If tomatoes are normally juicy no water or other liquid is needed in a hotpot. Cover and bake in a very slow oven (250°) for *6 to 12 hours*. Serve in warm bowls.

KOREAN BEEF BARBECUE
(4 servings)

8 thin tournedos (beef
   fillet steaks)
1 T honey
4 large cloves garlic,
   minced

2 t crushed toasted
   sesame seeds
2 T minced green onion
1½ t sesame or other oil
3 T soy sauce

Place meat in a shallow dish and brush with honey on both sides. Let stand *5 minutes*. Mix garlic, sesame seeds, green onion, oil and soy sauce. Pour over meat and turn to coat well. Let stand about half an hour. Broil or grill meat over charcoal until done as desired. Serve at once with brown rice and vegetables.

BAY LEAF KEBABS
(6 servings)

2 to 2½ lb. boneless beef
   chuck or sirloin tip
2 T water
⅓ cup oil
½ cup cider vinegar

1 small onion, minced
2 cloves garlic, minced
1½ t salt
½ t pepper
Bay leaves

Cut meat into 1½-in. cubes. Combine water, oil, vinegar, onion, garlic, salt and pepper. Crumble 2 bay leaves into the marinade. Heat marinade and pour over meat. Cover and marinate *4 or 5 hours* at room temperature or overnight in the refrigerator. Thread meat on skewers, placing a whole bay leaf between each piece of meat. Broil or grill over charcoal about *20 minutes* for medium rare, basting often with marinade. Serve with pilaf and sautéed green pepper.

WHITE BEANS AND LAMB NORMANDY
(8 to 10 servings)

2 cups dried navy beans
2 T minced parsley
½ cup chopped celery
¾ cup diced onion
2 t dry mustard
½ t thyme
2 t salt

¼ cup brown sugar, packed
1 cup dry white wine or
   apple juice
1 lb. lamb stew meat, cut
   in 1-in. cubes
3 T oil
1 clove garlic, quartered

Soak beans overnight in water to cover generously. Add parsley, celery, onion, mustard, thyme, salt, brown sugar, wine or apple juice and more water to cover, if needed. Cover and simmer until just tender, about *1½ hours*. Brown lamb in oil with garlic. Add to beans, mix well and turn into a greased baking dish. Add about 2 tablespoons water to drippings in which lamb was browned, heat until bubbling and pour over beans and lamb. Cover and bake at 325° *30 minutes*, moistening occasionally with additional wine or hot water. Uncover and bake *30 minutes* longer.

SINI KUFTA
(Armenian Baked Lamb Strata)
(6 servings)

2 lb. ground lean lamb	¼ t pepper
2 small onions, chopped	¾ cup fine bulgur
½ cup minced parsley	1 T grated onion
⅛ t allspice	1 T butter or margarine
2 T pine nuts	1 to 2 T meat broth or
1½ t salt	water

Cook 1 lb. of the lamb with chopped onions until lightly browned, stirring to keep meat crumbly. Add parsley, allspice, pine nuts and half the salt and pepper to cooked lamb. Set aside. Mix remaining lamb, bulgur, grated onion and salt and pepper. Knead thoroughly until smooth, adding a little water if needed to make a pasty consistency. Press half the lamb-bulgur mixture into a greased 8- or 9-in. baking dish, flattening with dampened hands. Spread cooked lamb mixture over lamb in baking dish, then spread remaining uncooked lamb over top. Cut into diamond shapes, dot with butter and sprinkle with broth or water. Bake uncovered at 350° *1 hour*. Cut diamond shapes apart, remove kufta to a platter and serve warm, at room temperature or chilled. Pilaf is the appropriate accompaniment. This kufta also may be cut in small diamonds and served as an hors d'oeuvre.

LEEK AND LAMB STEW
(6 to 8 servings)

3 lb. boneless lamb stew meat	1 cup water or broth
3 T oil	1½ t salt
1 large onion, chopped	¼ t pepper
2 tomatoes	4 or 5 leeks

Cut lamb into 1-in. cubes. Heat oil in a Dutch oven or other large heavy pot, add lamb a few pieces at a time and brown on all sides. Add onion and cook until tender but not browned. Peel tomatoes, cut off stem ends and squeeze to remove as much of the seeds and thin juice as possible.

Dice tomato into pot and cook and stir a minute or two. Add water, salt and pepper. Cover and simmer *30 minutes*. Cut leeks into 1-in. slices, discarding green tops. Add to stew, cover and simmer *1 hour* longer or until meat is tender. Serve with pilaf.

LAMB COCONUT CURRY
(6 to 8 servings)

2 t curry powder
2 t salt
1 lb. boneless lamb, cut in
½-in. cubes
1 small onion, minced
1 clove garlic, minced,
(optional)

1 T oil
1 cup Thin Coconut Cream
(page 297)
1 T lime or lemon juice

Blend curry powder with salt and lamb and let stand for 10 or 15 minutes. Cook onion and garlic in oil until golden brown. Add lamb and cook slowly until lightly browned, stirring to brown evenly. Add Coconut Cream, cover and simmer *20 to 30 minutes*, until lamb is tender. Add lime or lemon juice. Serve at once with hot cooked brown rice, dahl and curry condiments such as diced green onion, hard-cooked egg and chutney.

LAMB SHANKS WITH FRUIT
(4 servings)

4 small lamb shanks
Whole wheat flour, salt,
pepper
1 cup water
1 cup pitted cooked prunes
1 cup cooked dried
apricots

¼ cup honey
½ t cinnamon
½ t allspice
¼ t cloves
2 T lemon juice
½ t grated lemon peel
¼ t salt

Roll lamb shanks in flour seasoned with salt and pepper. Place in a baking dish large enough so they are not piled on top of each other. Cover tightly and bake at 350° until meat is tender, *1½ to 2 hours*. Drain off fat.

Meanwhile, combine water, prunes, apricots, honey, cinnamon, allspice, cloves, lemon juice and peel and salt. Bring to a boil and simmer about *5 minutes*. Pour fruit mixture over and around lamb shanks. Cover and bake at 400° *30 minutes*. Serve with brown rice or noodles.

CLASSIC GOULASH
(6 to 8 servings)

2 lb. boneless pork, veal or beef	3 green peppers
1 T oil	1½ t salt
2 medium onions, sliced	¼ t pepper
4 tomatoes	1 t paprika, preferably imported rose

Trim visible fat off meat and cut the meat into 1½-in. cubes. Brown on all sides in hot oil. Add onions and cook until tender but not browned. Peel tomatoes and cut into chunks over pot so juices are not lost. Remove seeds and ribs from green pepper and cut the peppers into strips and add to meat. Cook over moderate heat until juices begin to run from tomatoes. Add salt, pepper and paprika. Cook uncovered *10 minutes*, stirring two or three times. Taste and correct seasoning, if necessary. Cover and simmer *45 minutes* or until meat is tender, stirring occasionally. Serve over cooked noodles or brown rice.

VIENNESE PORK STEW
(6 servings)

2 lb. boneless pork shoulder	1 cup shredded cabbage
2 onions	1½ t salt
2 T butter, maragine or oil	¼ t pepper
3 large potatoes	1 t caraway seeds
3 carrots	1 cup beef broth or bouillon

Cut pork into 1½-in. cubes. Slice onions and cook in butter until tender but not browned. Skim out onions with a slotted spoon and reserve pan drippings. Peel and slice potatoes and carrots. Spread half the potatoes in a greased 2-qt. casserole, then add a layer of pork, carrots, cabbage and onions. Sprinkle each layer with salt, pepper and caraway seeds. Top with remaining potatoes. Pour pan drippings over potatoes, sprinkle with more salt, pepper and caraway seeds. Pour broth over casserole. Cover and bake at 325° *2 hours* or until pork is tender. Remove cover last 10 minutes of baking to brown top lightly.

LEMON PORK CHOPS
(4 servings)

4 thick pork chops	1 unpeeled lemon, sliced
1 t salt	1 green pepper, sliced
¼ t pepper	2 cups tomato juice
1 large onion, sliced	

Trim fat off chops and fry out in a large heavy skillet. Add chops and brown well on one side. Sprinkle with salt and pepper, turn and brown the other side. Pour off excess fat. Add onion, lemon, green pepper and tomato juice. Turn heat low, cover and simmer *1 hour* or until meat is tender.

NATURAL JELLIED VEAL
(5 to 6 servings)

1 veal knuckle	1 T salt
1 lb. veal shank meat, diced	2 T lemon juice
1 onion, sliced	2 eggs, hard-cooked
6 whole black peppercorns	Thinly sliced cooked
1 bay leaf	carrot or green pepper
Water	strips

Have the veal knuckle sawed into three or four pieces. Place in a kettle with diced meat, onion, whole black peppercorns and bay leaf. Add enough water to barely cover the meat and bones. Add salt and lemon juice. Cover, bring to a boil, turn heat low and simmer *2 hours*. Remove meat and bones from stock. Shred the meat fine and discard the bones. Strain the broth, return to kettle and boil rapidly uncovered until reduced to 1 cupful. This should form broth which will jell naturally. Pour a thin layer of the broth into a greased 8 x 4-in. loaf pan. Slice eggs and arrange in broth with carrots or green pepper to form a design. Spread the chopped meat over the vegetables carefully. Pour in the broth. Chill several hours, until firm. Slice and serve on lettuce or as one of the meats on a cold plate.

YUGOSLAV VEAL
(6 to 8 servings)

1 cup yogurt
1 T grated lemon peel
1 T chopped mint leaves
1 3- to 4-lb. boned and
    rolled veal roast

2 large onions, sliced
3 T oil

Mix yogurt, lemon peel and mint lightly. Place meat in a shallow dish and brush yogurt mixture over meat. Let marinate at room temperature *45 minutes* to *1 hour*. Cook onions in oil until tender but not browned. Spread onions in a deep casserole or Dutch oven. Place meat on onions and pour any marinade remaining in the dish over meat. Roast uncovered at 325° *2 to 2½ hours,* basting meat with pan juices often. Let roast stand *20 or 30 minutes* after removing from oven before carving. Serve with boiled potatoes or pilaf.

VEAL WITH SOUR CREAM
(6 to 8 servings)

2 lb. veal cutlet, ¼ in.
    thick
Whole wheat flour, salt,
    pepper
¼ cup oil
2 t minced shallot or 1
    green onion

3 tomatoes, peeled and
    quartered
1 cup sliced mushrooms
2 cups sour cream

Pound veal cutlets thin, coat with flour and season lightly with salt and pepper. Brown lightly on both sides in oil in large skillet. Add shallot when veal is turned. Drain off excess oil and add tomatoes and mushrooms. Cook and stir until saucy in consistency. Add sour cream, cover and simmer *20 to 30 minutes,* being careful not to boil. Serve with whole wheat noodles, spaghetti or brown rice.

LIVER AND ONIONS
(4 servings)

2 onions, sliced
3 to 4 T oil
1 lb. liver, cut in cubes

Wheat germ
Salt, pepper

Cook onions in oil in large skillet until golden. Coat liver well with wheat germ. Push onions to one side of skillet, add liver and cook until lightly browned. Be careful not to overcook liver. Remove liver and onions from skillet, sprinkle lightly with salt and pepper and serve at once with brown rice.

LIVER VENETIAN
(4 to 5 servings)

1 lb. calf's, beef or lamb
    liver, sliced ¼ in. thick
Salt, pepper
Whole wheat flour
½ cup oil

3 or 4 onions, sliced
Juice of 2 lemons
Minced parsley
Lemon wedges

Cut liver in serving pieces and sprinkle lightly with salt and pepper. Coat thoroughly in whole wheat flour. Heat oil in a large skillet and add liver, making sure pieces do not overlap. Brown on both sides, about *2 minutes* per side. Place liver on a warm platter. Add onions to pan drippings and cook until tender but not browned. Skim onions from pan with a slotted spoon and spread over liver. Add lemon juice to pan drippings, heat until bubbly and pour over liver. Sprinkle generously with parsley and garnish with lemon wedges.

LIVER LOAF
(8 servings)

1½ lb. beef or pork liver
   Boiling water
½ lb. ground fresh lean
   pork or beef
1 large onion, minced
¼ cup minced parsley
½ cup wheat germ

1 cup uncooked oatmeal
2 eggs
1½ t salt
¼ t pepper
½ t rubbed sage
½ to 1 t crushed red chiles

Cover liver with boiling water and let stand *10 minutes*. Drain well. Grind liver, using fine blade of food grinder or slice into blender and grind a few pieces at a time. Mix well with pork or beef, onion, parsley, wheat germ, oatmeal, eggs, salt, pepper, sage and crushed chiles. Pack lightly into a 9 x 5-in. loaf pan. Bake at 350° *1½ hours* or until done through. Make a small cut near center with a sharp knife to check. If juices run red bake a few minutes longer. Let stand in pan about *10 minutes,* turn out onto platter and serve hot, or chill and serve sliced as part of a cold meat platter or as sandwich filling.

BRAISED HEART WITH VEGETABLES
(6 servings)

1 beef heart or 2 veal
   hearts
   Boiling water
   Salt, pepper
2 T oil
1 cup broth or water

1 rib celery, sliced
½ small onion, minced
1 carrot, sliced
1 small white turnip, diced
1 bay leaf
Juice of ½ lemon

Wash hearts carefully and remove veins, arteries and clotted blood. Cover with boiling water and simmer *1 hour* or until almost tender. Cool, remove all fat, cords and artery cases. Cut meat into 1-in. cubes. Sprinkle lightly with salt and pepper and brown in oil in heavy pan. Add broth, celery, onion, carrot, turnip and bay leaf. Cover and simmer *1 hour* or until tender. Add lemon juice and simmer *10 minutes* longer. Serve with brown rice, mashed or boiled potatoes.

LEMON AND LIME CHICKEN
(4 servings)

1 2½- to 3-lb. broiler-fryer,
cut up
¼ cup lime juice
¼ cup lemon juice
⅓ cup dry white wine or
orange juice

1 clove garlic, minced
1 t salt
⅛ t pepper
¼ t thyme
¼ cup butter or margarine

Place chicken in a bowl. Combine lime and lemon juices, wine, garlic, salt, pepper and thyme. Pour over chicken, turn to coat well and let stand *30 minutes*. Arrange chicken in a single layer in a well-greased 13 x 9-in. baking pan. Dot with butter. Bake uncovered at 425° *40 to 50 minutes* or until chicken is fork tender. Turn as needed to cook evenly.

HONEY-GLAZED CHICKEN
(4 servings)

1 2½- to 3-lb. broiler-fryer,
cup up, or 3 lb. parts
1 t salt
¼ cup butter or margarine

6 T honey
3 T prepared mustard
2 t curry powder or more
to taste

Season chicken with salt. Heat butter in a 13 x 9-in. baking pan in a 375° oven. Remove from oven and stir in honey, mustard and curry powder. Turn chicken in sauce to coat evenly. Arrange chicken in a single layer in the pan and return to oven. Bake uncovered *45 minutes* or until tender. Baste and turn chicken several times while baking. Serve on a hot platter, lined with shredded lettuce, if wished.

BREAST OF CHICKEN WITH VEGETABLES
(4 servings)

2 broiler-fryer breasts
Paprika
1½ t salt
1 t tarragon
2 green peppers, cut in
  strips

2 tomatoes, peeled and
  quartered
1 medium onion, sliced
½ cup chicken broth

Remove skin from chicken and split breasts. Place in a shallow pan and sprinkle with paprika, ½ teaspoon salt and ½ teaspoon tarragon. Broil at moderate heat until browned. Turn chicken and sprinkle with paprika, ½ teaspoon salt and remaining tarragon. Broil until the second side is browned. Transfer chicken to a baking dish and add green pepper, tomatoes and onions. Pour chicken broth over chicken and vegetables and sprinkle with remaining ½ teaspoon salt. Bake at 375° *20 minutes* or until chicken is tender. Be careful not to overcook, as chicken breasts tend to dry out.

CHICKEN TANDOORI
(4 or 8 servings)

2 cups yogurt
Juice of 1 lemon
1½ t coriander
¼ t cayenne

Salt, pepper
4 chicken breasts, split
Oil

Combine yogurt, lemon juice, coriander, cayenne and salt and pepper to taste. Mix well but do not stir vigorously or custardy texture of yogurt will break down. Arrange chicken in a single layer in a shallow baking dish and paint with yogurt mixture. Cover and marinate in refrigerator several hours or overnight. Turn chicken two or three times while marinating.

When ready to bake, turn chicken skin side up and brush lightly with oil. Bake at 375° *40 to 45 minutes*, basting often with marinade in baking dish. Test with fork for doneness. Spoon fresh yogurt over chicken just before serving, if wished, and serve with hot brown rice or a rice, barley or wheat pilaf.

CHICKEN WITH PAPAYA
(4 to 6 servings)

2 cloves garlic, split
3 T oil
1 3-lb. broiler-fryer, cut up
1 cup boiling chicken broth
    or water

1 t salt
1 T grated ginger root
1 firm, half-ripe papaya,
    peeled and cubed

Cook garlic in oil in a large skillet until golden, and discard. Add chicken to oil and cook until lightly browned, turning to brown evenly. Add broth, salt and ginger. Cover and simmer *15 minutes* or until chicken is almost tender. Add papaya and cook *15 minutes* longer, or until chicken and papaya are tender. Serve with hot brown rice.

Cubes of winter squash such as Hubbard or banana may be substituted for papaya, but allow *25 to 30 minutes* cooking time for squash.

CHICKEN TARRAGON
(4 to 5 servings)

1 3-lb. broiler-fryer, cut up
  Salt, pepper, paprika
¼ cup butter or margarine
1 large onion, thinly sliced

½ lb. mushrooms, sliced
1 T dried tarragon leaves
    or 2 T fresh

Sprinkle chicken lightly with salt, pepper and paprika. Cook in butter until browned. Remove chicken and keep hot. Add onion and mushrooms to pan drippings and cook until tender but not browned. Return chicken to pan and sprinkle with tarragon. Cover tightly and cook *20 minutes* or until thickest pieces of chicken are fork tender. Serve with brown rice or Green Rice.

AFRICAN CURRY
(8 servings)

4 large tomatoes, chopped
2 large onions, chopped
4 chicken breasts, split, or
    2 broiler-fryers, cut
    up
1½ cups water
1 t turmeric
½ t cayenne
½ t coriander

½ t ginger
¼ t cinnamon
½ t cardamom
1 cup raisins
2 bananas, sliced
2 firm tart apples, cut in
    chunks
Curry condiments

Combine tomatoes, onions and chicken in large pot. Add water, turmeric, cayenne, coriander, ginger, cinnamon and cardamom. Bring to a boil, reduce heat, cover and simmer *30 minutes* or until chicken is tender, stirring occasionally. Add raisins, bananas and apples and simmer *5 minutes* longer. Serve with hot brown rice or a pilaf, chopped egg, shredded coconut, sliced almonds or walnuts and chutney.

CHICKEN CACCIATORE
(4 servings)

12 small artichokes,
    optional
Water, lemon juice
¼ cup oil or more as
    needed
1 2½- to 3-lb. broiler-
    fryer, cut up
Whole wheat flour
2 cups chopped peeled
    tomatoes

2 cloves garlic, minced
1½ t salt
½ t oregano
½ t basil
½ t pepper
½ lb. mushrooms, sliced
½ cup dry sherry, optional
Minced parsley

Pull tough outer leaves off artichokes, trim stems to short stubs, invert each artichoke on a board, whack sharply with heel of the hand or cleaver to spread leaves and scoop out fuzzy portions with a teaspoon. Immediately drop each artichoke into water to cover with 2 or 3 tablespoons lemon juice.

Heat oil until almost sizzling in skillet. Coat chicken

with whole wheat flour, add to hot oil and brown on all sides. As chicken browns, transfer to a large casserole. Pour off excess oil and add tomatoes, garlic, salt, oregano, basil, pepper and mushrooms to drippings. Bring to a boil, pour over chicken, cover and bake at 350° *30 minutes*. Add artichokes, cover and bake *30 minutes* longer or until chicken and artichokes are tender. Add sherry and bake *10 minutes* longer. Garnish with parsley. Serve with brown rice, noodles or spaghetti.

CHICKEN STEW WITH WALNUTS
(6 to 8 servings)

1 3- to 3½-lb. stewing chicken	¼ t pepper
3 T butter or margarine	¼ t marjoram
½ cup walnut halves	⅛ t paprika
1 T grated orange peel	1 clove garlic, minced
3 cups water	2 T arrowroot
1 t salt	1 cup sliced celery

Cut chicken into serving pieces. Melt 1 T butter in a large heavy pan. Add walnuts and orange peel and cook and stir until nuts are lightly toasted. Skim out nuts with a slotted spoon. Add remaining butter and melt in drippings. Add chicken and brown on all sides. Add water, salt, pepper, marjoram, paprika and garlic. Bring to a boil, cover tightly and simmer *1½ hours* or until chicken is tender but not falling off the bones. Blend arrowroot to a paste with a small amount of water and stir into stew. Add celery and cook *10 minutes* longer. Add walnuts and cook *5 minutes* longer. Sprinkle with more grated orange peel just before serving, if wished. Serve hot with brown rice.

CHICKEN IN A POT
(4 servings)

1 3-lb. broiler-fryer
Salt, pepper, paprika
1 lb. green beans, cut in 2-in. lengths
4 carrots, sliced
2 large potatoes, cut in quarters
2 T butter or margarine
Minced parsley

Sprinkle chicken cavity with salt, pepper and paprika. Hook wing behind back to hold neck skin and tie legs together. Place chicken in a deep casserole or Dutch oven. Sprinkle with paprika. Arrange vegetables around chicken. Sprinkle chicken and vegetables lightly with salt and pepper and dot with butter. Cover tightly and bake at 400° *1 hour* or until chicken and vegetables are tender. Remove cover, brush chicken and vegetables with pan drippings and roast *15 minutes* longer. Sprinkle with parsley and serve from casserole or remove to a platter.

JAPANESE CHICKEN NOODLE
(4 servings)

6 Japanese dried mushrooms
Hot water
1 carrot
2 green onions
4 cups chicken broth
1 to 1½ cups chopped cooked chicken
1 t soy sauce
Salt
3 oz. Japanese buckwheat or yam noodles
Crushed dried red chiles, optional

Put mushrooms in a bowl and add hot water to cover. Soak *15 minutes* or longer. Peel and slice carrot into a kettle. Slice green onions into kettle. Add broth, chicken and soy sauce. Slice mushrooms into broth, discarding stems which are hard. Add salt to taste. Bring to a boil, add noodles and boil *3 minutes*. Serve in soup bowls and pass chiles to sprinkle over noodles at table.

NOTE: Buckwheat and yam noodles are to be found in Japanese markets. If not available, very thin vermicelli may be substituted.

ROAST CHICKEN OR TURKEY

1. Make sure bird is thoroughly thawed, if frozen. Remove neck and giblets and put in saucepan with water to cover, holding liver in refrigerator; add to saucepan an onion, peeled and quartered, 2 or 3 ribs of celery, sliced, and salt and pepper to taste. Simmer until giblets are tender, *30 minutes* for a broiler-fryer chicken, about *40 minutes* for a roasting chicken, *1 hour to 1½ hours* for a turkey. Add liver and simmer *10 minutes*.

2. Wipe bird with a clean towel and if necessary, wad up towel and stuff into cavity to soak up liquid.

3. Prepare stuffing, if it is to be used. If bird is to be stuffed, no further seasoning is needed. If it is not to be stuffed, rub neck and body cavities lightly with salt and pepper. To stuff, spoon stuffing lightly into neck cavity and fasten flap of skin to back with a skewer. Turn bird on its back and fold wings under the back. Lightly spoon stuffing into body cavity and skewer vent opening closed, sew or tuck legs under flap of skin to hold stuffing in place. Poultry should be stuffed just before roasting to avoid danger of spoilage.

4. Place chicken or turkey back side down or, if you have a V-rack, breast side down in a shallow pan. (Roasting breast down produces juicier breast meat.) Brush bird with oil or melted butter or margarine.

5. For turkey, roast at 325° Roast chicken at 375° to 400°. Legs should be cut loose to allow heat to penetrate thigh joints after about half the estimated roasting time has elapsed. When legs are cut loose, turkey generally needs a loose covering to prevent overbrowning. Some cooks use a loose cap (not tightly pressed to bird) of aluminum foil. I prefer a clean cloth soaked in oil.

6. Roast chicken or turkey until meat thermometer inserted in thickest portion of thigh muscle registers 180°. This produces juicy meat, but done at the joints. The leg should twist easily when done. If you prefer drier meat, roast a half hour longer or until thermometer registers 190°.

Chickens roasted at 375° take from about *45 minutes* for a small broiler-fryer to *1½ hours* for a roasting chicken.

Turkeys take about *3 to 4 hours* for a 6- to 8-lb. bird,

4 to 4½ hours for 8 to 12 lb., *4½ to 5 hours* for 12 to 16 lb., *5 to 6½ hours* for 16 to 20 lb. or *7 to 8 hours* for a turkey weighing 20 to 24 lb.

Let a turkey stand *20 to 30 minutes* before carving, a chicken, *15 to 20 minutes,* to absorb the juices and make it easier to carve.

A-PLUS POULTRY STUFFING
(Enough for 10- to 12-lb. turkey)

6 cups dry whole wheat bread cubes
1 large onion, chopped
½ cup chopped parsley
3 ribs celery with leaves, chopped
½ cup oil
1½ t salt

¼ t freshly ground pepper
1 T rubbed sage (or to taste)
4 carrots, shredded
Hot broth or water to moisten, about 1½ cups

To prepare bread, cut into ½-inch slices and cube by stacking several slices on a board and cutting in checkerboard design through the bread. Bake at 325° until dry and crisp. Put bread cubes in a large bowl. Cook onion, parsley and celery in hot oil in a large skillet until tender but not browned. Sprinkle bread cubes with salt, pepper and sage. Add carrots and pour onion mixture over bread. Mix lightly. Add hot broth or water to moisten as wished. If you prefer a dry stuffing, add liquid just until stuffing looks moist but falls apart when pressed into a large ball on spoon. If you prefer a moist stuffing, a large ball of the mixture should hold its shape on the spoon.

Cornbread Stuffing. Omit carrots in A-Plus Stuffing and use 6 cups cornbread and 2 cups dry whole wheat bread cubes. Add chopped pecans, if wanted.

Garden Stuffing. Add ½ cup finely shredded spinach, 1 tomato, peeled and chopped, and 1 zucchini, thinly sliced, to A-Plus Stuffing.

Raisin or Date Stuffing. Add ½ cup seedless raisins or snipped pitted dates to A-Plus Stuffing.

Mushroom Stuffing. Add 1 cup sliced mushrooms to onion mixture while sautéing in oil.

BROWN RICE STUFFING FOR POULTRY
(Enough for 6- to 8-lb. turkey)

1 cup uncooked brown rice	1 large onion, chopped
2½ cups chicken or vegetable broth	¼ cup oil
	½ cup shelled pine nuts or slivered almonds
1 t salt	1 t rubbed sage
3 cups chopped celery	½ t rosemary or marjoram
½ lb. mushrooms, sliced	¼ t pepper

Combine rice, broth and salt in a saucepan. Bring to a boil, stir lightly, cover and simmer over very low heat *50 minutes* or until tender and liquid is absorbed. Meanwhile, cook celery, mushrooms and onion in oil until tender but not browned Stir in nuts, sage, rosemary or marjoram and pepper. Cook and stir *2 or 3 minutes.* Combine with rice, mixing well. Stuff lightly into ready-to-cook turkey, chicken or Cornish game hens. Or bake and serve as an accompaniment to unstuffed poultry.

Wild Rice Stuffing. Reduce brown rice in recipe above to ½ cup and broth to 1¼ cups. Cook ½ cup wild rice separately. Combine with rice and vegetables.

KASHA STUFFING
(Enough to stuff a 6-lb. roasting hen)

1 cup kasha (buckwheat groats)	1 small onion, chopped
2 cups chicken stock	½ cup chopped celery
Salt to taste	¼ cup minced parsley
¼ cup butter or oil	1 t sage
	1 cup pine nuts, optional

Combine kasha, chicken stock and salt to taste in a saucepan. Bring to a boil and boil uncovered *1 minute.* Cover tightly, turn heat low and simmer *12 to 15 minutes* until kasha is tender and liquid absorbed. Cool kasha.

Melt butter in a large skillet. Add onion, celery and parsley. Cook until onion is tender but not browned. Combine cooked kasha, sautéed onion mixture, sage and pine nuts. Mix well. Stuff lightly into neck and body cavities of a roasting hen. Double or triple recipe to use for turkey.

SKILLET BARBECUED TURKEY DRUMSTICKS
(4 large servings)

¼ cup oil
4 turkey drumsticks
1 cup Laurie's Tomato
    Sauce (page 241)
2 T brown sugar
2 T lemon juice

½ t salt
¼ t pepper
½ t cayenne (or less to
    taste)
1 small onion, sliced
Water

Heat oil in large skillet or shallow saucepan. Add drumsticks and brown on all sides. Combine tomato sauce, brown sugar, lemon juice, salt, pepper, cayenne and onion. Mix well and pour over turkey. Cover and simmer *1 to 1½ hours,* until turkey is fork tender. Add a small amount of water while cooking if needed to thin sauce. Serve hot with brown rice, mashed potatoes or a pilaf.

TURKEY ALMOND
(4 servings)

2 to 4 T oil
2 cups diced cooked
    turkey
½ cup sliced fresh water
    chestnuts or jicama
½ cup sliced bamboo shoots
½ cup sliced celery
½ cup sliced mushrooms

2 T sherry (optional)
½ cup turkey broth
½ t brown sugar
Salt, pepper
½ cup snow peas
2 t cornstarch
Toasted almond halves

Heat oil in skillet or wok. Add turkey and brown lightly. Remove turkey and set aside. Add water chestnuts, bamboo shoots, celery and the mushrooms to oil and cook until tender-crisp. Add sherry and broth, cover and steam about *30 seconds*. Add sugar, salt and pepper to taste, then add the peas, which have been strung like string beans. Add turkey. Blend cornstarch with a little water to make a smooth paste and gradually stir into turkey mixture. Cook and stir until slightly thickened. Sprinkle generously with almonds and serve with brown rice.

NOTE: Diced raw chicken or turkey may be used instead of the cooked turkey, in which case the chicken or turkey meat should be cooked until it is done, about *10 minutes*.

Vegetables

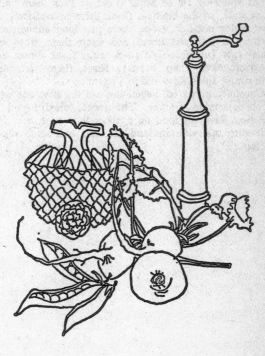

VEGETABLES benefit more than any other food from natural cooking. The three point program to the best vegetables you ever ate or hope to eat is: Pick them and run, don't walk, to the kitchen. Cook them immediately in the least water possible. Cook them just long enough to tenderize the toughest fibers and keep them from tasting grassy-raw (undercooked snap beans taste almost as bad as overcooked snap beans). Serve them immediately, with simple seasonings and in a warm bowl.

Carefully prepared, vegetables are the keystone of your most delectable dinners. The most colorful and often the most flavorful food on a plate, they contribute important nutrients, vitamins and minerals and some vegetable protein.

ARTICHOKES AURORA
(4 servings)

4 medium artichokes   1 t salt
   Boiling salted water   ¼ t pepper
1 small onion, minced   ½ t basil
3 T oil   1½ cups corn cut from cob
2 cups chopped peeled
   tomatoes

Trim artichoke stems to 1-in. stubs. Cut off leaf tips with scissors or a sharp knife. Place artichokes upright in 1½ in. boiling salted water. Cover pan and cook until a fork pierces artichoke easily, *20 to 45 minutes*. Turn upside down on board to drain.

Meanwhile, cook onion in 2 T oil in large skillet until tender but not browned. Add tomatoes, salt, pepper and basil and simmer uncovered until slightly thickened, about *15 minutes*, stirring often. Add corn and cook *3 or 4 minutes*.

Separate center leaves of artichokes and scoop out chokes with a sturdy teaspoon or grapefruit knife. Fill artichoke centers with corn mixture. Brush with remaining oil and serve at once. Or place in shallow pan, cover and reheat in a moderate oven (350°) when ready to serve.

ARTICHOKE WITH LEMON SAUCE
(6 servings)

24 tiny artichokes   ½ t salt
¼ cup butter, margarine or   ⅛ t pepper
   oil   1 bay leaf
1 clove garlic, minced   2 egg yolks
1 cup chicken broth   Juice of 1 lemon

Pull off tough outer leaves of artichokes and snip off tips of remaining leaves.

Heat fat in a large skillet and add garlic and artichokes.

Toss artichokes to coat with butter and cook until artichokes turn a bright green, *3 to 4 minutes*. Add chicken broth, salt, pepper and bay leaf. Bring to a boil, cover, reduce heat and simmer *10 to 15 minutes* or until artichokes are tender. Remove artichokes from broth with a slotted spoon and keep warm. Remove chokes with a teaspoon, scooping out from between leaves at top. Discard bay leaf. Beat egg yolks with lemon juice until frothy. Gradually stir hot broth into egg mixture, then return sauce to skillet and cook, stirring constantly, until sauce is slightly thickened. Pour over artichokes and serve at once.

ASPARAGUS SAUTÉ
(6 servings)

1½ lb. asparagus	1 t honey
¼ cup butter or margarine	1 t lemon juice
1 t salt	

Snap off base ends of asparagus and wash spears thoroughly. Cut off tips, then cut stems into thin diagonal slices. Heat butter in a large skillet or wok. Add asparagus and cook, tossing with chopsticks or tongs until asparagus is tender-crisp and has a glazed appearance. Season with salt, honey and lemon juice. Serve at once.

ORIENTAL ASPARAGUS
(4 to 6 servings)

1 chicken breast	2 T soy sauce
1 lb. asparagus	2 t cornstarch
2 T oil	2 t cold water
2 cloves garlic, minced	½ t honey
½ cup chicken broth	½ t salt
1 T sherry wine or lemon juice	⅛ t pepper
	2 T toasted sesame seeds

Skin and bone chicken and cut meat into thin strips. Snap off bases of asparagus and wash spears thoroughly. Slice spears diagonally, leaving tips whole. Heat skillet, wok, or Dutch oven, add 1 T oil and garlic. Add asparagus and sauté *30 seconds*. Remove asparagus from fat with slotted spoon and keep warm. Add remaining oil to pan drippings and reheat. Add chicken and stir fry until tinged with brown. Add chicken broth, sherry and soy sauce and cook *2 to 3 minutes* or until chicken becomes snowy white and opaque. Add asparagus and stir with chicken *1 minute*. Blend cornstarch and water. Stir into asparagus mixture and cook and stir until sauce is thickened. Sprinkle with honey, salt, pepper, and sesame seeds.

STIR-FRY BEAN SPROUTS
(6 servings)

2 T oil	1 t grated fresh ginger
1 green onion, chopped	½ cup sliced mushrooms
1 clove garlic, minced	½ cup chopped walnuts
4 cups bean sprouts or half alfalfa and half bean sprouts	1 T soy sauce

Heat oil in large skillet or wok. Add green onion and garlic and cook until onion is crisp-tender. Add sprouts, ginger and mushrooms, and cook and stir until sprouts are heated through and coated with oil mixture. Add walnuts and soy sauce. Cook and stir a few seconds. Serve as a side dish or over brown rice.

BEET ROOTS AND TOPS
(3 to 4 servings)

1 large bunch beets with crisp-looking tops	Salt, pepper
Water	Butter or margarine

Wash beet roots thoroughly and cut off of greens, leaving about 1-in. stem on each beet. Place in saucepan with water to almost cover, cover the pan and boil beets *20 to 30 minutes* or until easily pierced with a fork. Meanwhile, cut stems off beet tops and wash leaves thoroughly. Shake off as much excess moisture as possible. Remove beets from pan and pour off beet liquid. Place greens in the pan and sprinkle lightly with salt. Cook until wilted, about *5 minutes*. Peel beets, slice into a warm bowl and sprinkle with salt and pepper. Place a pat of butter on beetroot. Cut beet greens coarsely, if wished, or leave uncut. Place greens over beetroot, sprinkle lightly with salt and pepper and top with another pat of butter.

NOTE: Beetroots with tops sufficiently fresh and crisp for cooking are difficult to find in most supermarkets. If your green grocer does not provide them, it is worth the effort of growing beets in your garden, even if it's only a window box or a flower bed in a condominium patio.

ORANGE LEMON BEETS
(6 servings)

1 bunch beets (about 6 medium)	2 T honey
¼ cup lemon juice	1½ t cornstarch
½ cup orange juice	Salt, pepper
2 T vinegar	¼ cup butter or margarine

Cut off beet tops, leaving a 1-in. stem on each beet. Cook beets in boiling water until tender, *20 to 40 minutes*, depending on size. Rinse in cold water, drain and slip off skins. Slice beets thin. Combine lemon and orange juices, vinegar, honey, cornstarch and salt and pepper to taste in saucepan. Bring to a boil, stirring constantly. Cook until sauce is thick and clear. Add beets and butter. Heat to serving temperature.

STIR-FRY BROCCOLI
(4 to 6 servings)

1 bunch broccoli, about 1 lb.	¼ t Chinese five spice or ground anise
¼ lb. mushrooms	¼ cup vegetable or chicken broth
2 T oil	Salt, pepper
½ onion	
1 T soy sauce	

Wash broccoli and drain, cut stems into ¼-in. slices and separate tops into flowerets. Wash mushrooms quickly, drain thoroughly and slice. Heat oil in a skillet or wok. Add broccoli and mushrooms and cook, stirring now and then, about *2 minutes*. Cut onion in thin slices and toss with broccoli. Sprinkle with soy sauce, spice and chicken broth. Cover tightly and simmer *3 or 4 minutes*, until broccoli is crisp-tender but still bright green. Sprinkle with salt and pepper to taste and boil rapidly to evaporate most of the liquid. Serve at once.

BRUSSELS SPROUTS WITH ALMONDS
(4 to 6 servings)

1½ lb. Brussels sprouts	½ t salt
Boiling salted water	Dash pepper
¼ cup butter or margarine	½ cup slivered almonds
½ t nutmeg	

Trim blemished leaves off sprouts and wash well. Cook in a small amount of boiling salted water until barely tender. Melt butter in a saucepan, being careful not to burn it. Add nutmeg, salt, pepper and almonds. Cook over low heat, shaking pan now and then, until almonds are lightly browned. Add Brussels sprouts, toss to coat well with sauce and serve at once.

DANISH CABBAGE
(6 servings)

1 medium head cabbage	¼ t salt
2 T honey	2 to 3 T water
1 T oil, butter or margarine	Poppy seed, optional

Chop cabbage fine. Combine honey and oil in a large skillet and cook and stir until well blended and turning golden. Add cabbage and stir until lightly browned. Sprinkle with salt and water. Cover and simmer *10 to 15 minutes*, until cabbage is tender. Turn out onto warm platter and sprinkle with poppy seed, if wanted.

RED CABBAGE WITH CRANBERRIES
(4 to 5 servings)

2 T butter or margarine
1 small onion, minced
1 small head red cabbage, shredded
1 t salt
½ cup water

2 cups fresh cranberries
½ cup honey
3 T red wine vinegar
½ t ground cardamom or cloves

Melt butter in a large saucepan, add onion and sauté until tender but not browned. Add cabbage, salt, and ¼ cup water. Cover and simmer *10 minutes*. Stir in cranberries and remaining ¼ cup water. Simmer until cranberries pop, about *5 minutes*. Add honey, vinegar and cardamom. Heat through and serve at once.

SHREDDED CARROTS
(6 servings)

3 T butter or margarine
4 cups coarsely shredded carrots
1 small onion, minced

½ t salt
Dash pepper
½ cup sauterne wine, chicken broth or water

Melt butter in saucepan or baking dish. Add carrots, onion, salt, pepper and wine or broth. Cover and cook over moderate heat *10 to 15 minutes*, until carrots are tender, or bake at 350° *25 to 30 minutes*.

BUTTER-STEAMED CARROTS AND POTATOES
(4 servings)

4 carrots
4 small potatoes
½ cup water or chicken broth
1 t salt

2 T butter, margarine or oil
1 T minced onion, optional
2 T minced parsley

Peel and slice carrots thin. Peel and dice potatoes. Put in saucepan with water or broth, salt, fat and onion. Cover tightly and bring to a boil. Turn heat low and simmer *15 minutes* or until vegetables are tender. Shake pan several times while cooking vegetables so they do not scorch. If heat is kept low no more liquid is needed, but check once or twice and add a little more if necessary. Sprinkle with parsley.

NOTE: Other fresh vegetables can be cooked this way, making the flavor of fresh vegetables possible for even hurried cooks. Try snap beans, green peas, zucchini or other summer squash and some of the greens.

CARROT POTATO COMBO
(6 servings)

½ cup boiling water
1 t salt
2 cups coarsely grated
   uncooked carrots
1 cup coarsely grated
   uncooked potatoes

1 T butter or margarine
⅛ t white pepper
¼ t nutmeg

Combine water, salt, carrots and potatoes in a saucepan. Cover and cook *4 to 5 minutes,* until vegetables are tender. Add butter, white pepper and nutmeg and toss gently. Serve at once.

CARROTS VICHY
(4 servings)

6 medium carrots
3 T butter or margarine
1 T honey

¼ cup water
¼ t salt
Minced parsley

Peel carrots and cut diagonally into thin slices. Place in heavy saucepan with butter, honey, water and salt. Cover and cook over medium heat, shaking pan occasionally, until carrots are tender and water absorbed. Uncover and sauté until carrots are tinged with brown, stirring often. Sprinkle with parsley and serve.

CARROT BAKE
(4 to 6 servings)

1 lb. small young carrots   2 T butter, margarine or oil
  Boiling salted water   Wheat germ or whole
1 t honey   wheat bread crumbs

Peel carrots thinly and cut crosswise in halves or leave whole. Place in a large shallow saucepan or skillet with boiling salted water to about half cover and the honey. Cover and boil until barely tender, *15 to 20 minutes*. Drain, reserving liquid for soups or sauces, and add butter to carrots. Season with more salt and pepper, if needed. Shake carrots in pan as butter melts. Spear carrots one by one with a fork, roll in wheat germ to coat well and arrange one layer deep in a greased shallow baking dish. Bake at 350° *15 minutes* or until lightly browned.

SPANISH CHAYOTE
(6 servings)

2 chayote squash, about   4 tomatoes, peeled and
  1½ lb.   diced
1 small onion, minced   1 t salt
½ green pepper, diced   ½ t honey
¼ cup oil   Grated Parmesan cheese

Peel chayote and cut into ½-in. cubes. If chayote seed is soft it may be cubed and cooked with the squash. As chayote matures, seed becomes more fibrous. If very tough, discard seed. Sauté chayote with onion and green pepper in oil *10 minutes* or until lightly browned. Add tomatoes, salt and honey. Cover and simmer until chayote is tender, about *5 minutes* longer. Sprinkle with cheese and serve hot.

NOTE: Chayote is a mild-flavored pale green squash used in the Caribbean, Mexico, South Florida and California. If not available, eggplant or zucchini may be used in this recipe.

BAKED CORN AND TOMATOES
(6 servings)

2 cups cooked corn, cut
  from the cob
2 cups chopped peeled
  tomatoes
1 t salt
¼ t pepper

1 t honey
½ t basil or ¼ t oregano
½ cup wheat germ or whole
  wheat bread crumbs
2 T butter or margarine

Mix corn, tomatoes, salt, pepper, honey and basil. Turn
into a greased baking dish. Top with wheat germ or crumbs
and dot with butter. Bake at 350° *30 minutes* or until
bubbly. If wished, shredded cheese or cottage cheese may
be added to the corn mixture for a heartier dish.

CORN AND OKRA
(6 servings)

¼ cup oil, butter or
  margarine
2 cups diced green pepper
½ cup diced onion
1½ cups corn, cut from
  the cob

1½ cups sliced okra
⅔ cup chicken broth or
  water
Salt, pepper

Heat fat in saucepan. Add green pepper and onion and
cook until tender but not browned. Add corn, okra, chicken
broth and salt and pepper to taste. Cover and simmer *5
minutes* or until okra is tender, stirring now and then.

GREEN CORN TAMALE
(6 servings)

8 or 9 ears corn
2 t salt
3 T melted butter or
  margarine
1 to 1½ cups cornmeal

½ lb. sharp Cheddar cheese,
  cut into strips
6 to 8 long green chiles,
  blanched and cut into
  strips

Shuck corn, reserving shucks, and cut kernels off cobs. Grind corn, using food grinder with fine blade, or process in blender until mushy. There should be about 3 cups ground corn. Add salt, butter and enough cornmeal to make a dough with thick spreading consistency. Rinse and drain corn shucks and spread flat.

Line bottoms and sides of a greased 1½-qt. baking dish with shucks. Spread a thin layer of corn dough over shucks, pressing down to hold shucks in place. Top with a layer of cheese and chiles, then remaining corn dough, spreading to edges. Fold corn shucks over top of tamale, cover with foil and bake at 350° *1 hour* or until firm but still moist.

To make individual tamales, spread a spoonful of mixture on each corn shuck, fill with a strip of cheese and chile and wrap up, encasing cheese and chiles. Fold under ends and place seam side down on rack in kettle. When all tamales are shaped and arranged in pan, pour in about 1 in. of boiling water, cover and steam *1 hour* or until tamales are firm.

CUCUMBER MUSHROOM CUPS
(6 servings)

2 cucumbers	1 green onion with top, sliced
Boiling water	
½ t salt	2 T butter or margarine
1 cup sliced mushrooms	Tiny parsley sprigs

Cut unpeeled cucumbers into 2-in. sections. Scoop out, leaving cups ½ in. thick. Cook in boiling water until barely tender, about *10 minutes*. Salt just before cooking is finished. Turn upside down on towels and drain. Cook mushrooms and green onion in butter until tender but not browned. Pile into cucumber cups. Top with a sprig of parsley. Serve hot.

TOMATO-STUFFED CUCUMBERS
(8 servings)

4 large cucumbers	1 cup drained chopped
2 T minced onion	peeled tomatoes
2 T minced parsley	1 t salt
4 T oil	¼ t oregano
1 cup whole wheat or rye bread crumbs	Dash pepper

Wash cucumbers and cut in halves lengthwise. Scoop out seeds carefully and boil shells in lightly salted water about *10 minutes*, until barely tender, not soft. Drain. Cook onion and parsley in oil until onion is tender but not browned. Mix in bread crumbs, tomatoes, salt, oregano and pepper. Cook slowly about *5 minutes*. Fill cucumbers with stuffing and place in a shallow baking dish. Pour water to a depth of ¼ in. around cucumbers. Bake at 350° *15 minutes*. Serve hot with meat or as one of the vegetables on a vegetable plate.

GRILLED EGGPLANT
(4 servings)

½ cup oil	1 large eggplant
2 cloves garlic, split	Salt, pepper, marjoram

Combine oil and garlic and let stand *3 or 4 hours* to flavor oil. Wash eggplant and cut into thick wedges or slices. Add to garlic oil and let marinate *1 hour*. Grill over charcoal fire, broil, or brown lightly in a hot skillet, turning as needed to achieve desired color and brushing with the garlic oil now and then. Sprinkle with salt, pepper and marjoram just before eggplant is done.

SWEET-SOUR EGGPLANT
(4 to 6 servings)

1 large eggplant	1 T honey
Olive or other oil	1 t chopped fresh mint
Salt, pepper	1 t oregano
¼ cup vinegar	1 clove garlic, minced

Wash and dry eggplant, but do not peel. Cut off stem and blossom ends, then cut eggplant lengthwise into ½-in. slices. Brush each slice with oil and broil until soft and lightly browned on both sides, about *5 minutes*. Sprinkle with salt and pepper. Combine vinegar, 3 T oil, honey, mint, oregano and garlic. Layer eggplant into a dish, sprinkling some of the sweet-sour sauce over each layer. Serve cold.

EGGPLANT PATTIES
(4 servings)

1 medium eggplant	⅛ t pepper
¾ cup fresh whole wheat bread crumbs	2 T minced parsley
	2 T grated onion
¼ cup grated Parmesan cheese	1 clove garlic, minced
	2 medium green peppers
2 eggs, beaten	1 cup oil
1 t salt	¼ cup yogurt
½ t basil	Minced parsley or chives
¼ t oregano	

Wash eggplant, wrap in foil and bake at 350° *45 minutes* or until tender when pierced with a fork. Cool, peel and finely chop the flesh. Combine eggplant, bread crumbs, Parmesan cheese, eggs, salt, basil, oregano, pepper, parsley, onion and garlic. Mix well but lightly. Trim ends from green peppers and slice each pepper into four rings. Press eggplant mixture into a flat cake in each green pepper ring. Heat oil, carefully add eggplant rings, and brown on each side. Top each patty with a little yogurt and sprinkle with parsley or chives.

DANDELION GREENS
(6 servings)

2 lb. (large bunches) dandelion greens	1 small onion, sliced, optional
Salt, pepper, butter or margarine	Vinegar or Old Sour (page 242)

Dandelion greens should be served in the spring, before the dandelions begin to blossom. After plants begin to blossom, the greens become excessively bitter. Cut off the roots and pick over the greens to remove any yellowed or tough leaves. Place in a large sink or pan and run in water vigorously to wash off as much dirt as possible, then lift greens up and down in water to wash thoroughly. If very gritty, greens may need to be washed through several changes of water.

Place greens in large kettle and add boiling water to a depth of ½ in. Cover and cook until tender, about *15 minutes*. Salt lightly just before greens are done. Drain in a colander, reserve pot liquor for soups or sauces. Turn green onto a platter and chop by cutting with two sharp knives. Sprinkle with salt and pepper and top with a pat of butter. Slice onion over greens, if wished. Serve with vinegar or Old Sour on the side for sprinkling on greens.

BRAISED SWEET ANISE (FINOCHIO)
(6 servings)

2 lb. sweet anise	½ cup beef broth, chicken
¼ cup butter, margarine or	broth or water
oil	⅛ t pepper
1 t salt	

Wash and peel anise bulb and stalks. Cut bulb and stalks into 1-in. slices. Feathery tops also can be washed and cut into pieces. Cook anise in butter until lightly browned. Sprinkle with salt and add broth and pepper. Cover and simmer until tender, about *10 minutes*.

GREENS AND POTATOES
(6 servings)

1 bunch turnip or
    mustard greens
1 bunch kale
½ lb. spinach
2 T oil
2 potatoes, peeled and
    cubed
¼ cup boiling water

1½ t salt
½ t honey or brown sugar
½ t cayenne
Cooked brown rice,
    optional
Salted roasted peanuts,
    optional

Wash greens thoroughly, lifting in and out of a large panful of water to remove sand and grit. Pinch leaves off stems of turnip or mustard and spinach. Shred kale coarsely, if very large. Heat oil in a large pot and add turnip or mustard greens, kale, potatoes, boiling water, salt and honey. Cover and simmer *15 minutes*. Add spinach and cook just until wilted, about *5 minutes*. Season with cayenne and more salt, if needed. Toss lightly, being careful not to mash potatoes. Serve with brown rice, if wanted, and sprinkle with chopped peanuts.

SOUL FOOD GREENS
(4 to 6 servings)

2 bunches mustard, turnip
    or collard greens or,
    a combination
Water

¼ lb. salt pork or ¼ cup oil
Salt, pepper
Pepper or plain vinegar

Wash greens thoroughly, lifting in and out of a large panful of water to remove all sand and grit. Pinch leaves off stems. Place leaves in large pot and add water to a depth of about 1 in. (More water may be used if large quantities of pot liquor are wanted.) Slice salt pork almost to rind and place on top of greens. Season lightly with salt and pepper. Cover, bring to a boil, turn heat low and cook until greens are tender, *30 to 45 minutes*. Remove greens from pot liquor with a slotted spoon and place on a warm platter. Chop by slashing with two sharp knives. Place salt pork on top if it is to be served. Pass pepper or plain vinegar to serve on greens. The pot liquor may be served separately in teacups or small soup cups. Hot corn bread is traditionally crumbled into the pot liquor.

GREENS CHINESE STYLE
(2 to 4 servings)

½ lb. or 1 small bunch greens—mustard, kale, turnip, chard, beet, Pokchoi or Chinese cabbage
2 T oil
1 clove garlic, minced
4 or 5 mushrooms, sliced
1 green onion, sliced
1 t salt
1 t honey

Wash greens thoroughly, shake off excess moisture and pinch off stems. Shred leaves coarsely with a sharp knife. Heat oil in a wok or large skillet. Add garlic, mushrooms and green onion. Cook until green onion is slightly wilted, then add greens. Cook over medium heat, stirring occasionally, until wilted. Sprinkle with salt and honey, cover and cook over low heat until greens are tender, about *10 minutes* for mustard or turnip greens, about *5 minutes* for chard, kale, beet and Chinese greens. Serve at once.

BUTTERED KALE
(6 servings)

2 large bunches kale (2 lb.)
Salt, pepper, butter or margarine

Wash kale in a large quantity of cold water, lifting and agitating in water to remove all sand and grit. Shake off as much water as possible and shred kale coarsely, discarding tough stems. Place in large kettle with whatever water still clings to leaves. Add salt and pepper. Cover and cook until tender, *20 to 25 minutes*. Drain, reserving pot liquor for soups or other uses. Top with butter.

SCALLOPED KALE
(6 servings)

3 cups drained cooked
kale
3 hard-cooked eggs,
chopped
½ cup sour cream or plain
yogurt

1 cup shredded Cheddar or
Swiss cheese
Salt, pepper

Combine kale, eggs and sour cream or yogurt. Layer into greased 1½-qt. baking dish with cheese, ending with cheese. Bake at 400° *15 minutes* or until bubbly.

CREAMED KOHLRABI
(6 servings)

6 kohlrabi
2 qt. cold water
2 T vinegar
Boiling salted water

½ cup milk
½ cup cottage cheese
½ t paprika
½ t salt

Peel kohlrabi and cut into 1-in. cubes or slices. As pieces are cut, drop into water acidulated with vinegar to prevent darkening. Just before cooking, drain well. Place in saucepan with boiling salted water to about half cover, cover pan and simmer *20 to 25 minutes* or until tender. Drain well, reserving liquid for soups or sauces. Beat together milk and cottage cheese until smooth. Add paprika and salt. Pour over kohlrabi and toss well.

ARMENIAN LEEKS AND RICE
(6 servings)

3 or 4 large leeks
½ cup water
2 cups chopped peeled
tomatoes
1 T salt

½ t coarsely ground pepper
½ cup olive oil
½ cup brown rice
Juice of 1 lemon

Wash leeks thoroughly, discarding gritty portions. Slice leeks (tops and bottoms) thin and place in large saucepan with water, tomatoes, salt, pepper, olive oil and rice. Cover tightly and simmer *1 hour to 1 hour and 10 minutes,* until rice is tender. Add lemon juice. Taste and add more salt, if needed. Serve hot or cold as a meat accompaniment.

NOTE: The amount of olive oil in this dish may be cut in half, but the rich oily consistency makes this dish typical—and more filling.

STIR-FRY LETTUCE
(4 servings)

2 T safflower, soy, corn or cottonseed oil
1 t sesame oil, optional
¼ cup sesame seeds
2 or 3 green onions, thinly sliced
¼ lb. mushrooms, thinly sliced
1 medium head lettuce, coarsely shredded
¼ t salt

Heat the oils in a large skillet, Dutch oven or wok, add sesame seeds and stir until golden. Add green onions, mushrooms, lettuce and salt. Cook and stir until lettuce is barely wilted. Toss well and turn onto hot platter.

VEGETARIAN WILTED LETTUCE
(6 servings)

1 large head lettuce
½ small red onion
½ t salt
¼ t pepper
3 T oil
1 T honey
3 T cider vinegar

Wash lettuce thoroughly and drain well. Pat dry to remove all water. Shred lettuce coarsely into a bowl. Slice onion thin, separate into rings and distribute over letttuce. Sprinkle with salt and pepper. Heat oil in a skillet. Mix honey and vinegar and add to oil. When bubbling, pour over lettuce and toss well. Serve at once.

MUSHROOMS IN THEIR NATURAL JUICES
(6 servings)

36 medium mushrooms   6 slices toast
  Salt, pepper
 2 T butter or margarine,
   about

Select mushrooms with a pronounced cup shape. Break off stems and reserve for other uses. Rinse cups quickly and drain on towels. Arrange cupped side up in a greased shallow baking dish. Sprinkle with salt and pepper and place a bit of butter in each mushroom cup. Bake at 400° *15 minutes* or until cups are filled with their own liquor. Serve hot on toast.

NOTE: For variation, garlic butter may be used for filling mushroom cups or use snail butter (soft butter blended with shallots, garlic and minced parsley).

MUSHROOM BAKE
(6 servings)

¼ cup butter, margarine or   ¼ cup dry white wine
   oil   (optional)
 4 small green onions,   1 t salt
   chopped   ¼ t pepper
 1 T minced parsley   1 lb. mushrooms
½ cup chicken broth or
   water

Heat butter, margarine or oil in a skillet. Add green onions and parsley and cook until green onions are tender. Add chicken broth, wine, salt and pepper. Trim stems of mushrooms and place mushrooms in a 1-qt. baking dish. Pour green onion mixture over mushrooms, cover and bake at 350° *20 minutes*. Serve with meat, poultry or a pilaf.

MUSHROOMS PAPRIKASH
(6 servings)

1 lb. mushrooms, sliced
1 onion, diced
¼ cup oil, butter or
   margarine
1 T whole wheat flour
1 t salt

1 T paprika, preferably
   sweet
Dash cayenne, optional
¼ t pepper
1 cup sour cream

Cook mushrooms and onion in fat until mushrooms are tender. Stir in whole wheat flour, salt, paprika, cayenne and pepper. Cook slowly about *2 minutes*. Stir in sour cream. Heat, but do not boil. Serve at once.

BAKED OKRA
(4 servings)

1 lb. okra
2 T oil
2 onions, chopped
4 tomatoes, peeled and
   chopped

1 t salt
1 T lemon juice

Wash okra and cut off tip ends. Wash and drain well again. Heat oil in saucepan, add okra, onions, tomatoes and salt. Cover and simmer until okra is tender, about *15 minutes*. Turn into a greased shallow baking dish and bake uncovered at 400° until lightly browned, about *30 minutes*. Sprinkle with lemon juice just before serving.

SAVORY GREEN ONIONS
(6 servings)

3 bunches green onions
1 cup chicken or beef broth

1 hard-cooked egg
1 T butter or margarine

Trim green onions, leaving on most of the green tops. Place onions on a sheet of foil in a wide skillet, add broth, cover and cook until onions are barely tender, *7 to 10 min-*

utes. Arrange onions in six bundles on a warm platter. Mash egg and sprinkle over onions. Top each bundle with half a pat of butter. Serve hot as a vegetable.

ALMOND ONION CUPS
(6 servings)

6 large onions	¼ t salt
Boiling salted water	¼ t pepper
Oil	¼ cup raisins
¼ cup cream or 3 T milk	¼ cup toasted slivered
2 T butter or margarine	almonds
¼ t prepared mustard	

Peel onions and cut a thick slice off top of each. Scoop out centers of onions, leaving sturdy shells. Cook the onion shells in boiling salted water until tender but not limp, *20 to 25 minutes.* Drain onions upside down. Place in a greased shallow baking dish. Brush onion shells with oil. Chop onion trimmings and combine with cream or milk, 1 T of the butter, mustard, salt, pepper, raisins and half the almonds. Spoon mixture into onion shells, packing lightly. Top with remaining almonds and dot with remaining butter. Bake at 400° *15 to 20 minutes* to heat through.

FRENCH FRIED ONION RINGS
(4 to 6 servings)

4 onions	1 t salt
Milk	Pepper
1 cup whole wheat flour	Fat for frying

Slice onions ¼ in. thick, remove skin and separate slices into rings. (Centers can be saved for another use or if you don't mind small onion rings, use them, too.) Soak onions in milk to cover for *30 minutes.* (This is an ideal use for nonfat dry milk liquefied as directed on the package. The milk can be reserved for use in white sauces or Sauce Soubise.) Mix flour, salt and pepper. Drain onion rings and dip in flour to coat thoroughly. If time allows, spread on a tray and refrigerate for *45 minutes* to *1 hour*. This makes coating stick better when onion rings are fried. Heat deep fat to 375°. Put a few onion rings at a time in deep fry basket, lower into hot fat and fry until browned. Drain on absorbent paper. Serve at once.

STEAMED PARSNIPS OR SALSIFY
(4 to 6 servings)

Allow 1½ lb. parsnips or salsify for 4 to 6 servings. Peel and immediately plunge into water mixed with a little lemon juice to prevent darkening. Slice or cube the vegetable. Place in a saucepan with 1 in. boiling salted water, cover and boil gently *10 to 15 minutes,* until tender. Serve hot with butter or margarine.

GLAZED BAKED PARSNIPS OR SALSIFY
(4 to 6 servings)

1½ lb. parsnips or salsify	Dash nutmeg
¼ cup water	Salt, pepper
2 T brown sugar	1 T butter or margarine
1 T lemon juice	

Peel parsnips or salsify, immediately plunging into water mixed with a little lemon juice to prevent darkening. Cut vegetable into thin strips and place in a baking dish with ¼ cup water. Sprinkle with brown sugar, lemon juice, nutmeg and salt and pepper to taste. Dot with butter. Cover and bake at 350° *1 hour* or until vegetable is tender. Stir once or twice while baking and add a little more hot water, if needed.

PIQUANT SAUTÉED PARSNIPS OR SALSIFY
(4 to 6 servings)

1½ lb. parsnips or salsify	Salt, pepper
2 T oil	1 clove garlic, minced
2 T butter or margarine	2 T minced parsley

Peel parsnips or salsify immediately plunging into cold water mixed with a little lemon juice to prevent darkening. Cut vegetables into ½-in. cubes. Heat oil and butter in a large skillet. Add parsnips or salsify and cook slowly until tender and tinged with brown. Add salt and pepper to taste, garlic and parsley. Cook, stirring now and then, for *2 or 3 minutes* longer.

HERBED GREEN PEAS AND MUSHROOOMS
(4 servings)

1 cup sliced mushrooms	⅛ t pepper
1 small onion, minced	⅛ t nutmeg
2 T oil, butter or margarine	2 cups drained cooked
¼ t salt	green peas
¼ t marjoram	

Cook mushrooms and onion in butter until onion is tender but not browned. Add salt, marjoram, pepper, nutmeg and peas. Mix lightly, cover and heat through.

FRENCH PEAS
(4 to 6 servings)

1 cup shredded lettuce	1 t honey
4 green onions, chopped	1 t salt
3 cups shelled green peas	¼ t chervil or ½ t chopped
2 T butter or margarine	mint
¼ cup boiling water or	
chicken broth	

Line a saucepan with lettuce, then add green onions, peas, butter, boiling water, honey, salt and chervil. Cover, bring to a boil, turn heat low and cook *15 to 25 minutes* or until peas are tender. Drain off any remaining liquid, taste and add salt to peas if needed.

PEPPERS

Chiles must be skinned before using in cooked or uncooked dishes and sweet peppers should be skinned for use in salads and relishes. To do this, spear each pepper on a long-handled fork or skewer. Hold over a high gas flame or under a preheated broiler and heat until skin blisters, turning peppers to blister evenly. Peel off skin, which should be burned to filaments. Peppers or chiles then can be sliced and served raw or cooked as needed.

The same method may be used for skinning a tomato. Turn it slowly over the flame until the skin pops in several places, being careful not to burn it.

BAKED POTATO CAKE
(3 servings)

1 egg	Dash pepper
½ cup milk	⅛ t nutmeg
½ t salt	2 or 3 potatoes

Grease a 9- or 10-in. pie pan liberally with butter, margarine or oil. Beat egg lightly and stir in milk, salt, pepper and nutmeg. Grate potatoes coarsely, using coarse shredder or chop coarsely in a blended. Add to egg mixture and mix well. Spread in prepared pie pan. Bake at 375° *30 to 35 minutes*, until golden brown. Cut into wedges and serve hot.

NOTE: This recipe can be multiplied ad infinitum, but use a separate pie pan for each two to three potatoes, and one egg and half cup of milk to preserve the character of this dish.

APRICOT SWEET POTATOES
(8 servings)

2 lb. sweet potatoes	¼ cup butter or margarine
½ lb. dried apricots	1 t grated orange peel
Water	¼ cup chopped walnuts
1 cup brown sugar, packed	

Cook sweet potatoes in boiling water until tender, cool, peel and cut into thick slices. Barely cover apricots with water and simmer until tender. Drain well, reserving ¼ cup of the liquid. Layer sweet potatoes and apricots into a 10 x 6 x 2-in. baking dish, sprinkling each layer of apricots with brown sugar. Mix the reserved apricot liquid, butter and orange peel and pour over potatoes. Bake at 375° *45 minutes*, basting two or three times with liquid in baking dish. Sprinkle with nuts and bake *5 minutes* longer.

Orange Sweet Potatoes. Substitute sliced unpeeled oranges and orange juice for apricots and apricot liquid in recipe above.

THANKSGIVING SWEET POTATOES
(4 servings)

3 medium sweet potatoes	2 T melted butter or
½ cup cream	margarine
⅓ cup brown sugar, packed	2 eggs, lightly beaten
½ t salt	½ cup chopped pecans
½ t nutmeg	

Put sweet potatoes in a saucepan with enough water to about half cover. Cover pan and boil sweet potatoes until tender, about *30 minutes*. Drain, cool and remove peels. Mash potatoes with a fork, then with an electric mixer or large spoon, beat in cream, brown sugar, salt, nutmeg, butter and eggs. Fold in pecans. Turn into a greased 1-qt. baking dish. Bake at 350° *30 minutes* or until heated through.

SWEET POTATO PUFF
(4 servings)

1½ lb. sweet potatoes	⅛ t pepper
Boiling water	¼ cup milk or cream
2 T butter or margarine	1 egg, separated
1 t salt	

Cover sweet potatoes with water, bring to a boil and cook covered until tender, about *25 minutes*. Drain and peel as soon as cool enough to handle. Place potatoes in a bowl and mash with a potato masher, spoon or electric mixer. Work in butter, salt, pepper and cream while mashing. Beat in egg yolk. Beat egg white until it stands in stiff peaks and fold into sweet potato mixture. Turn into a 1-qt. baking dish and bake at 375° until puffy and lightly browned, about *35 minutes*.

SWEET POTATO TZIMMES
(4 to 6 servings)

3 sweet potatoes
4 carrots
½ onion, minced
3 T oil

½ cup brown sugar, packed, or honey
1 t salt
Water

Cook sweet potatoes in skins until tender. Peel and slice. Peel carrots. Cook onion in oil in a large skillet or saucepan. Stir in brown sugar, salt and carrots, which have been sliced. Add sweet potatoes and water to barely cover. Cover pan tightly and simmer vegetables *2 hours* or until soft and blended almost to a thick paste. Taste and add more salt, if needed. Serve hot with meats.

SWEET POTATOES WITH PECANS
(6 to 8 servings)

6 to 8 small sweet potatoes
½ cup chopped pecans
¼ cup butter or margarine

½ cup brown sugar, packed
¼ cup orange juice

Boil sweet potatoes in jackets in a small amount of boiling water until tender. Drain and peel. Roll one side of each potato in pecans, pressing lightly so pecans adhere. Arrange pecan side up in a single layer in a well-greased shallow baking dish. Melt butter and stir in sugar and orange juice. Cook and stir about *5 minutes,* until syrupy. Pour over sweet potatoes. Bake uncovered at 350° *30 minutes* or until glazed. Spoon syrup over sweet potatoes when served.

PUMPKIN

Cut a small pumpkin in half, scoop out the seeds and stringy portions, then turn face down on a baking pan and bake at 325° *1 hour* or until easily pierced with a fork through the skin. Remove the pumpkin from the oven, cool enough to handle, then scoop out the pulp and mash it. Season to taste with salt, pepper and butter and serve as a vegetable or use in pumpkin pie, other recipes or this casserole.

PUMPKIN MAPLE CASSEROLE
(6 servings)

3 cups mashed cooked pumpkin	1 t cloves
½ cup maple syrup	½ t cinnamon
2 T butter or margarine, melted	½ t nutmeg
1 t salt	3 eggs
1 t ginger	1 cup chopped walnuts or pecans

Combine pumpkin, ¼ cup maple syrup, butter, salt, ginger, cloves, cinnamon and nutmeg. Beat in eggs. Turn into a well-greased 1-qt. baking dish. Bake at 375° *20 minutes.* Pour remaining maple syrup over top, sprinkle with nuts, and bake *20 minutes* longer or until heated through.

SUMMER SQUASH WITH DILL
(4 servings)

1 lb. yellow crookneck or   ¼ t salt
    pattypan squash   ½ t dill weed
¼ cup water   2 T butter or margarine
¼ cup chopped green onion   Dash pepper

Wash squash and cut off blossom and stem ends. (Pattypan squash should be cut shallowly so as to waste no more of the edible vegetable than necessary.) Cut squash into eighths or quarters, depending on size. Combine with water, green onion, salt and dill in a saucepan. Cover and simmer until squash is barely tender. Stir in butter and pepper and serve hot.

BAKED SQUASH PARMESAN
(8 servings)

2 acorn squash   ¼ cup grated Parmesan
    Salt, pepper, nutmeg   cheese
2 T melted butter or
    margarine

Cut acorn squash in halves lengthwise and remove fibers and seeds with a sharp-edged spoon. Sprinkle lightly with salt, pepper and nutmeg. Turn cut sides down on a baking sheet and bake at 400° *30 minutes*. Turn cut side up and cut each half into halves again, making quarters. Brush with melted butter and sprinkle with cheese. Bake *10 or 15 minutes* longer.

CIDER SQUASH CUPS
(4 servings)

2 acorn or butternut
   squash
½ cup water
2 cups toasted whole wheat
   or cornbread cubes
¼ t sage or marjoram
¼ t nutmeg
1 t salt

⅛ t pepper
2 T oil or melted butter or
   margarine
1 T lemon juice
¼ cup apple cider or juice
1 large red apple
2 T raisins
Apple slices (optional)

Cut squash in halves and scoop out seeds and stringy fibers. Place halves cut side down in a baking pan containing about ½ in. water. Bake at 400° *30 minutes* or until squash is almost tender. (Acorn squash usually takes longer than butternut squash.)

Combine bread cubes, sage or marjoram, nutmeg, salt, pepper, butter, lemon juice and cider. Toss lightly to mix. Core but do not peel the apple. Dice and add to the stuffing mixture along with raisins. Mix well.

Turn squash halves cut sides up and fill with stuffing. Garnish with apple slices and bake at 400° *20 minutes* longer or until squash is tender and stuffing lightly browned.

COUNTRY FRIED TOMATOES
(4 to 6 servings)

4 large firm tomatoes, ripe
   or green
2 T minced chives, optional
   Cornmeal, salt, pepper
¼ cup butter, margarine or
   oil

Brown sugar
1 cup cream or evaporated
   milk

Cut tomatoes in ½-in. slices. Sprinkle with chives and let stand *30 minutes*. Dredge heavily in cornmeal seasoned with salt and pepper. Heat fat in skillet. Add tomatoes a few at a time, being careful not to overcrowd. Brown slowly on both sides. Pour off excess fat. Return tomatoes to skillet, springle with brown sugar, add cream and simmer a few minutes to thicken sauce. Serve on toast, if wished.

HERBED TOMATO BAKE
(6 servings)

6 medium tomatoes
2 cloves garlic, minced
2 T minced fresh basil or
    parsley

Salt, pepper
2 T butter or margarine

Cut off stem ends and thin slice at blossom ends of tomatoes, then cut each into two thick slices. Arrange in a well-greased shallow baking dish. Sprinkle with garlic, basil or parsley, salt and pepper. Dot with butter. Bake at 350° *20 to 30 minutes* or until tomatoes are soft, but still hold their shape.

SCALLOPED FRESH TOMATOES
(6 servings)

6 large tomatoes
1 t salt
¼ t pepper
½ cup brown sugar, packed,
    or 6 T honey

2 cups fine whole wheat
    bread crumbs
2 T oil

Peel tomatoes and cut out cores. Arrange in a greased baking dish. Sprinkle with salt and pepper and spoon brown sugar or honey over each tomato. Pack half the crumbs around tomatoes. Combine remaining cup of crumbs with oil and pack on first layer of crumbs. Bake uncovered at 375° *1 hour* or until tomatoes are tender.

BAKED STUFFED TOMATOES
(6 servings)

6 large tomatoes
¼ cup chopped green
    pepper
2 T oil
½ t salt

¼ t basil
¼ t pepper
2 T minced parsley
2½ cups coarsely crumbled
    cornbread

Cut a thin slice from stem end of each tomato. Gently squeeze out seeds and most of the pulp, leaving firm shells. Chop ½ cup of the squeezed-out tomato pulp and set aside. Turn tomatoes upside down to drain. Cook green pepper in oil until tender but not browned. Add salt, basil, pepper, parsley, cornbread and chopped tomatoes. Mix lightly. Stuff lightly into tomato shells. Place in a greased shallow baking dish. Bake at 350° *15 to 20 minutes*.

ITALIAN STYLE ZUCCHINI
(6 servings)

¼ cup oil
1 onion, chopped
2 large tomatoes, peeled
   and chopped
6 zucchini

1 t salt
¼ t pepper
Parmesan cheese,
   optional

Heat oil in skillet, add onion and cook until tender but not browned. Add tomatoes and cook until blended into pan drippings, stirring once or twice. Wash and slice zucchini into tomato and onion mixture. Sprinkle with salt and pepper. Cover and cook *15 to 20 minutes* or until zucchini is tender. Sprinkle with cheese, if wished.

SWEET-SOUR ZUCCHINI
(6 servings)

6 medium zucchini
1 T oil
½ t salt
⅛ t pepper

3 T vinegar
1 T honey
1 T minced fresh basil

Cut off ends of zucchini and cut squash lengthwise into thin slices. Fry in hot oil in a large skillet until lightly browned and barely tender. Sprinkle with salt and pepper. Remove from oil with slotted spoon and place in a flat serving dish. Combine vinegar and honey and add to oil remaining in skillet. Boil *2 minutes*. Pour over zucchini and sprinkle with basil. Serve warm or cold.

ZUCCHINI PANCAKES
(4 servings)

1 lb. zucchini
2 eggs, slightly beaten
1 t honey
¼ t baking powder
2 to 4 T wheat germ
½ t salt
Oil for frying

Scrub zucchini well and trim ends. Shred on a coarse grater and drain. Mix squash pulp with eggs, honey, baking powder, enough wheat germ to form a batter and salt. Drop by spoonfuls into a small amount of hot oil in skillet. Cook until browned on one side, turn and brown other side. Serve as a vegetable.

ZUCCHINI CASSEROLE
(8 servings)

2 lb. small zucchini, sliced
¼ cup sliced green onion
¼ cup oil
6 tomatoes, peeled and sliced
Salt, pepper
2 cloves garlic, minced
1 green pepper, chopped
½ cup grated Parmesan cheese, optional
2 T minced parsley

Sauté zucchini and green onion in oil in an ovenproof skillet until lightly browned. Place tomatoes over zucchini and sprinkle with salt, pepper, garlic and green pepper. Cover and bake at 350° *20 minutes.* Sprinkle with cheese and bake *20 minutes* longer. Sprinkle with parsley just before serving.

MEXICAN ZUCCHINI SUCCOTASH
(5 to 6 servings)

1 lb. zucchini, sliced
Boiling water
1 onion, chopped
1 clove garlic, minced
2 T oil
½ t salt
1 cup corn cut off cob
1 or 2 peeled green chiles, diced
1 small tomato, peeled and chopped
1 cup shredded Jack or Cheddar cheese

Cook zucchini in small amount of boiling salted water until barely tender. Drain. Cook onion and garlic in oil in large skillet. Add zucchini, salt, corn, chiles and tomatoes. Sprinkle with cheese. Cover and simmer *10 minutes.*

ZUCCHINI PROVENCAL
(4 to 8 servings)

4 large zucchini, 8 to 10 in. long	1 large clove garlic
2 small onions	2 T minced parsley
2 small tomatoes, peeled	4 T oil
1 small green pepper, seeds and pithy ribs removed	1 t salt
	⅛ t pepper
	4 T grated Parmesan cheese

Cut zucchini in halves lengthwise and make shallow cuts in crisscross pattern on cut side. Cook the zucchini in a small amount of boiling water (as little as possible to prevent burning) for *3 minutes,* then drain. Carefully scoop out pulp, leaving sturdy shells. Finely chop the zucchini pulp, onions, tomatoes, green pepper and garlic. Heat oil in skillet, add the onion and cook until tender but not browned. Add tomatoes, green pepper, garlic and parsley. Cook and stir until liquid which cooks from vegetables is evaporated. Arrange zucchini shells side by side in a shallow baking dish. Spoon tomato mixture into shells. Sprinkle with cheese. Bake at 350° *15 minutes* or until heated through.

ZUCCHINI WITH YOGURT
(6 servings)

1 pt. yogurt	1 to 1½ lb. zucchini
1 clove garlic, minced	Oil for frying
½ t salt	Freshly ground pepper or minced parsley
1 T oil	
1 T vinegar, optional	

Combine yogurt, garlic, salt, 1 T oil and vinegar. Mix gently. Vigorous stirring will break down structure of yogurt. Cover and chill thoroughly. Meanwhile, wash zucchini and slice diagonally. Fry in 1 in. oil in a skillet until tinged with brown, about *4 minutes*. Drain on absorbent paper. Arrange in overlapping circles on a platter or chop plate. Spoon yogurt sauce over zucchini and sprinkle with pepper or parsley. Serve hot or cold with meat, or as an appetizer.

Salads
and
Salad Dressings

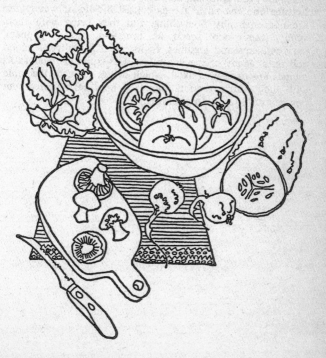

SALADS are all important in a natural foods diet. Nowhere does the natural crispness and goodness of fresh things show to better advantage. Salads function in various roles as part of a simplified menu scheme. There are salads here to start a meal, to go with a hearty main course dish, to follow the main course, or to work as a salad-dessert at the end of a meal. There are also salads that serve as the main course, the huge Greek salad, for example.

Salads are important, too, for the nutrients they provide. Lettuce and the paler greens consist mostly of water, and are not especially nourishing. But they bring with them such vitamin-rich foods as tomatoes, green peppers, various beans and legumes, fruits, meats, poultry, seafood and nuts. Many of the vegetables and fruits in these salad recipes are used uncooked, which brings them to the table with their nutrient quota intact, if kept refrigerated and covered until just before serving.

GREEN SALAD WITH JERUSALEM ARTICHOKES
(6 servings)

2 or 3 Jerusalem artichokes
½ cup slivered toasted
    almonds
½ t tarragon
¼ t grated lemon peel
¼ t nutmeg

½ cup oil
¼ cup lemon juice
½ t salt
    Spinach, Boston or Bibb
    lettuce

Cook artichokes in boiling water until barely tender, *10 to 15 minutes*. Peel and slice. Combine almonds, tarragon, lemon peel, nutmeg, oil and lemon juice and beat until well blended. Add salt. Tear greens into a salad bowl, using about 6 cups broken greens. Chill well. Add sliced artichokes to greens and enough of the almond dressing to moisten well. Toss and sprinkle with a little more nutmeg.

SALADE BEIGE
(6 servings)

¼ lb. mushrooms
    Lemon French Dressing
    (page 233)
1 bunch watercress

1 small head butter
    lettuce
12 cherry tomatoes
    Freshly ground pepper

Rinse mushrooms quickly under running water and drain well. Slice thinly from caps through stems. Place sliced mushrooms in a shallow bowl and cover with Lemon French Dressing. Let marinate *1 hour or longer*. Wash watercress and lettuce and drain well. Tear leaves off stems of watercress leaves and lettuce into bite-size pieces. Combine watercress leaves and lettuce in bowl with cherry tomatoes, which have been washed and drained. Drain mushrooms, reserving dressing, and add to salad. Add as much more dressing as is needed to moisten greens, and toss lightly. Sprinkle with freshly ground pepper. Any remaining dressing may be reserved for other salads.

VEGETARIAN WILTED SPINACH
(4 to 6 servings)

1 bunch spinach	¼ cup oil
½ small red onion	3 T wine vinegar
1 t salt	¼ cup salted soy beans
¼ t freshly ground pepper	pine nuts or almonds

Wash spinach thoroughly, pinch leaves off stems and dry leaves thoroughly. Put in earthenware or heat-resistant glass bowl, breaking up large leaves. Cut onion into thin slices and separate into rings. Scatter over spinach. Sprinkle with salt and pepper. Let stand at room temperature for *20 or 30 minutes.* Just before serving, heat oil until almost sizzling. Using a mitten to protect your hand, add vinegar. When mixture is bubbling, pour over spinach. Toss well, sprinkle with soy beans or nuts and toss again. Serve at once.

SPINACH SALAD WITH SEEDS
(4 servings)

1 bunch spinach	1 T wine vinegar
2 green onions	½ t salt
¼ cup salted sunflower or pumpkin seeds	⅛ t pepper
	3 T oil

Wash spinach thoroughly, pinch off stems and drain leaves thoroughly, blotting off any excess moisture with a towel. Tear leaves into bite-size pieces into a salad bowl. Slice green onions with tops and sprinkle over spinach. Refrigerate until just before serving. Sprinkle seeds over spinach. Combine vinegar, salt and pepper and stir until blended. Beat in oil. Pour over salad and toss until leaves are coated with dressing. If salad is still too dry, sprinkle on a little more oil and toss again.

CHICORY AND ONION SALAD
(6 servings)

1 large bunch chicory
¼ lb. fresh bean sprouts
1 small red onion
6 T oil
6 T lemon juice

½ t salt
⅛ t pepper
2 T minced fresh tarragon
   or 1 T dried
Freshly ground pepper

Wash chicory and drain thoroughly. Tear into bite-size pieces into large bowl. Pour boiling water over bean sprouts, let stand a minute and drain well. Add to chicory. Peel and thinly slice onion and separate into rings. Add to salad. Beat together oil, lemon juice, salt, pepper and tarragon. Add to salad and toss well. Grind a few sprinkles of pepper over each serving of salad at the table.

DANDELION SALAD
(6 servings)

6 cups very tender dandelion shoots
Lemon French Dressing (page 233)
1 hard-cooked egg, chopped

This is an early springtime salad only, and generally a pick-it-yourself proposition. Only the very tenderest dandelion greens, the first early shoots, are suitable and few markets stock such delicacies. Harvest the tiny greens, wash thoroughly and wrap in a towel to dry. Put in a bowl and toss with just enough dressing to moisten well. Sprinkle egg over the salad.

WATERCRESS AND WALNUT SALAD
(4 to 6 servings)

2 cups washed and drained
   watercress leaves
1 cup broken washed and
   drained Boston lettuce

⅔ cup coarsely chopped
   walnuts
Lemon French Dressing
   (page 233)

Combine watercress and Boston lettuce in a bowl. Add walnuts and enough dressing to moisten, but not enough to puddle in the bottom of the bowl. Toss lightly but thoroughly. Add a few more drops of dressing if not moist enough. Serve at once.

ROMAINE SPROUT SALAD
(4 servings)

1 small bunch romaine	2 green onions
½ cup bean sprouts	French Salad Sauce
Boiling water	(page 232)

Wash romaine and dry thoroughly. Put bean sprouts in a bowl, cover with boiling water and let stand about *1 minute*. Drain well, then pat dry with a towel. (Bean sprouts need not be blanched if you prefer the uncooked flavor.) Break romaine into bite-size pieces into a salad bowl. Add bean sprouts and slice in green onions with the green tops. Refrigerate until ready to serve. Toss with just enough dressing to coat leaves well. Serve at once.

GARBANZO GREEN SALAD
(8 servings)

1 clove garlic, split	1 cup drained cooked
1 head Boston lettuce	garbanzo beans
½ bunch chicory	½ t oregano
½ bunch leaf or red leaf	1 t salt
lettuce	¼ freshly ground pepper
2 or 3 stems dill	1 T wine vinegar
2 green onions, sliced	¼ cup olive oil
12 small artichokes, cooked,	
drained and chilled	

Rub large salad bowl with cut sides of garlic and discard garlic. Wash and drain greens thoroughly. Break into bite-size pieces into the bowl. Snip off feathery leaves of dill and discard the tough stems. Add dill, green onions, artichokes and garbanzos to greens. Cover and chill until ready to serve. Just before serving sprinkle with oregano, salt and pepper. Add vinegar and olive oil and toss thoroughly. If not moist enough, add a little more vinegar and oil, but be careful not to drown salad.

CUCUMBER CHEESE SALAD
(2 to 3 servings)

2 oz. blue cheese   1 cucumber
1 cup yogurt   Minced fresh dill

Crumble cheese and blend gently with yogurt. Wash cucumber and peel, if wished. Slice thinly. Arrange slices in overlapping concentric circles on a plate and top with dressing. Sprinkle with dill.

SPICED CUCUMBER SALAD
(6 to 8 servings)

4 cucumbers   ½ t crushed red chiles
  Salt   1 clove garlic, crushed
¼ cup oil
2 T vinegar
2 t honey
1 t ground coriander or 1
    T minced cilantro
    (fresh coriander
    leaves)

Peel cucumbers and shred coarsely or slice very thin. Place in bowl and sprinkle generously with salt. Cover and let stand *2 or 3 hours*. Drain well and rinse with cold water, then pat dry with paper toweling. Combine with oil, vinegar, honey, coriander, chiles and garlic. Mix well, cover and chill in refrigerator for several hours.

BOMBAY EGGPLANT SALAD
(6 to 8 servings)

1 large eggplant
3 large tomatoes
1 medium onion, minced
2 T minced cilantro or 2 t
   ground coriander
3 cloves garlic, minced
   (optional)

2 small green chiles, peeled
   and minced
1 t salt
1 T cider vinegar
3 to 4 T oil

Cut eggplant in quarters and steam until tender, about *20 minutes.* (If you do not have a steamer, quartered eggplant may be placed in a colander then the colander suspended over boiling water in a large pot, which then is covered.) Cool, and carefully peel off skin and chop eggplant flesh. Peel and chop tomatoes. Combine eggplant, tomatoes, onion, cilantro, garlic and chiles. Add salt, vinegar and oil and toss to mix well. Taste and add more salt, if needed. Cover and chill. This salad may be served as a side dish with curried meat, fish, poultry or vegetables or may be served on lettuce as a salad with salted yogurt or sour cream spooned over it.

COLD SOY CELERY
(5 to 6 servings)

4 to 6 ribs celery
4 T soy sauce ·
1 t salt
2 t honey

1 t freshly ground pepper
¼ cup oil
Watercress

Cut celery crosswise into 1-in. pieces, then slit lengthwise into three sections each. Scald in boiling water *2 minutes,* but do not boil. Drain and plunge into ice water for *1 minute.* Drain well. Put celery in a bowl and add soy sauce, salt, honey, pepper and oil. Toss gently to mix well, cover and put in refrigerator for several hours. Turn several times while chilling. Drain and serve on a platter or individual salad plates, garnished with watercress.

ZUCCHINI CHIFFONADE
(6 servings)

5 or 6 small zucchini
  Boiling salted water
3 T minced onion
3 T diced green pepper
2 T minced parsley
1 hard-cooked egg, finely
  chopped

¼ cup vinegar
1 T honey
1 t salt
¼ cup oil
Crisp greens

Wash zucchini and cut into ¼-in. slices, discarding ends. Cook in a small amount of boiling salted water about *3 minutes,* until barely tender. Drain and chill well. Combine the onion, green pepper, parsley and egg. Stir in the vinegar, honey, salt and oil. Mix well. Line a platter with greens and mound zucchini in the center. Pour dressing over zucchini and serve.

CARROT SALAD
(6 servings)

2 cups shredded raw carrot
1 cup shredded cabbage or
  diced celery
½ cup raisins, plumped
1 T lemon juice

½ t salt
½ cup mayonnaise or Sour
  Cream Dressing
  (page 229)
Crisp greens

Combine shredded carrot and cabbage, raisins, lemon juice and salt. Mix well and add dressing. Toss to mix well. Chill until ready to serve. Spoon onto crisp greens.

NOTE: To plump raisins, cover with hot water, let stand about *5 minutes,* then drain well.

DUTCH COLESLAW
(6 to 8 servings)

3 cups shredded cabbage
1 green or sweet red
  pepper, chopped fine
1 t salt

1 t honey
½ cup Sour Cream Dressing
  (page 229)

Mix cabbage, pepper, salt and honey. Pour dressing over salad and mix well. Serve at once.

THREE-DAY HONEY COLESLAW
(8 servings)

1 medium head white
    cabbage
½ cup honey
½ cup oil

½ cup vinegar
1 T salt
2 or 3 green onions,
    chopped (optional)

Shred cabbage fine and put in a bowl. Combine honey, oil, vinegar and salt in a saucepan and bring to a rolling boil. Pour over cabbage, mix well, cover and let marinate in the refrigerator for three days. Just before serving, add green onion, if wanted. Lift coleslaw from marinade with slotted spoon.

GRANNY'S COLESLAW
(6 servings)

¼ cup vinegar
¾ t salt
⅛ t pepper
3 T honey
1 T butter or margarine
3 eggs, well beaten
2 T cream or rich milk

5 cups coarsely grated
    cabbage
¾ cup thinly sliced radishes
¼ cup grated onion
½ cup diced celery
½ cup diced green pepper

For dressing, blend vinegar, salt, pepper, honey and butter in top of double boiler. Heat to simmering over direct heat. Remove from heat and gradually beat in eggs. Place over boiling water and cook, stirring often, until smooth and thickened. Stir in milk or cream. Chill until ready to serve.

Chill cabbage in ice water, then drain well. Combine radishes, onion, celery and green pepper in bowl. Add cabbage, cover and chill well. Add dressing, toss to mix well and chill until ready to serve.

ARMENIAN SALAD
(6 servings)

2 large tomatoes	Pinch basil
1 cucumber	Pinch dill weed
½ cup minced flat leaf parsley	Pinch mint flakes or 1 t minced fresh mint
½ small red onion, thinly sliced	1 t salt
	⅛ t pepper
3 ribs celery, diced	Dash cayenne
½ bunch watercress, chopped	Juice of 2 lemons
	2 T oil

Peel tomatoes, squeeze out juice and seeds if excessively juicy, and cut into wedges into salad bowl. Peel and slice cucumber over tomatoes. Add parsley, red onion, celery, watercress, basil, dill weed, mint, salt, pepper and cayenne. Toss lightly. Add lemon juice and oil and toss again. Serve at once.

FARMER'S CHOP SUEY
(6 servings)

1 large cucumber	Dash pepper
1 medium green pepper	1 cup cottage cheese
1 cup thinly sliced radishes	1½ cups dairy sour cream
6 green onions, sliced	1 t lemon juice
3 tomatoes	Tomato wedges, radish roses
¼ t salt	

Peel and cube cucumber. Remove seeds and membranes from green pepper and cut the flesh into squares. Combine cucumber, green pepper, radishes and onions, mix well, cover and chill. Just before serving, peel tomatoes, core and cut into large cubes. Add to the chilled vegetables and toss gently. Combine salt, pepper, cottage cheese and sour cream and lemon juice. Mix well and spoon over salad. Garnish with tomato wedges and radish roses.

BULGARIAN SALAD
(6 servings)

6 green peppers	1 t salt
8 tomatoes	1 t sweet paprika
2 large onions	1/8 t pepper
1 cup vinegar	1/2 cup oil

Blister skin of peppers by spearing on a fork and holding over a flame or by broiling for a few minutes. Cool peppers, rinse and peel off charred skin. Remove seeds and cut peppers into thin strips. Peel tomatoes and cut into wedges. Peel onions and chop fine. Combine peppers, tomatoes and onions in a large bowl. Beat together vinegar, salt, paprika and pepper, then beat in oil. Sprinkle dressing over vegetables, cover and chill *2 hours* or longer. Drain vegetables and serve with Feta cheese and ripe olives or cottage cheese for a summer lunch.

ITALIAN TOMATO SALAD
(8 servings)

6 medium tomatoes	1 t salt
1 medium red onion, thinly sliced	1/2 t coarsely ground pepper
	2 cloves garlic, minced
1 large green pepper, halved lengthwise and sliced	2 or 3 sprigs fresh basil, chopped, or 1/2 t dried
	4 to 6 T olive oil

Wash and peel tomatoes, cut out cores, then squeeze tomatoes to press out as much juice and seeds as possible. Cut tomatoes into wedges. Combine with onion slices and green pepper slices in large bowl. Sprinkle with salt, pepper and garlic, then basil. Sprinkle with oil, mixing well with a wooden spoon and crushing some of the tomatoes and blend juice with oil and herbs. Cover and chill or serve immediately.

SALAD ORIENTAL
(6 to 8 servings)

6 cups thinly sliced Chinese
    cabbage
1 cup thinly sliced radishes
2 T toasted sesame seeds

Lemon French Dressing
    (page 233)
Salt, pepper

Combine Chinese cabbage, radishes and sesame seeds in a bowl. Sprinkle 2 or 3 T dressing over salad and toss until all dressing is mixed through salad. If leaves are not coated with dressing, add a tablespoonful or two more and toss again. Season to taste with salt and pepper. Serve at once.

ROMAN POTATO SALAD
(6 servings)

6 medium potatoes, about
    1½ lb.
2 cloves garlic
1 t salt
1 t oregano

¼ t freshly ground pepper
2 large tomatoes, peeled
    and quartered
6 T oil

Wash potatoes and cook in boiling salted water until tender, about *30 minutes*. When cool enough to handle, peel and cut into ½-in. cubes. Mash garlic with salt in a bowl, add hot potatoes, oregano, pepper and tomatoes. Drizzle oil over salad and mix gently. Cover and chill several hours.

GADO GADO SALAD
(4 to 6 servings)

½ lb. green beans
2 or 3 carrots
¼ lb. bean sprouts
2 potatoes
1 cucumber
2 tomatoes

2 hard-cooked eggs
Leaf lettuce
Chili-Peanut Sauce
    (page 230)
Crisp Onion Flakes
    (page 247)

Cut green beans diagonally into 1½-in. pieces, discarding tip ends, and cook until barely tender in a small amount of salted water. Drain and chill. Peel carrots and cut into matchstick strips about 2 in. long. Cook in a small amount of boiling salted water, drain and chill. Blanch bean sprouts *2 minutes* in boiling water and drain well. Cook potatoes in skins, cool and peel and slice or dice. Peel and slice cucumber. Peel tomatoes and cut into wedges. Shell eggs and cut into quarters. When ready to serve, line a large platter with lettuce. Arrange vegetables on the lettuce in separate mounds, making an attractive arrangement. Garnish with egg wedges. Serve with warm or chilled Chili-Peanut Sauce to be spooned on by each diner as wished and pass onion flakes.

MINT SNAP BEAN SALAD
(6 servings)

1 lb. green or wax beans	2 t finely chopped mint
Boiling salted water	Juice of 1 lime or lemon
1 small clove garlic,	½ cup oil
minced	Dash salt

Snap beans and break into 1 to 2-in. pieces. Cook in boiling salted water until barely tender. Drain, saving liquid for soups or sauces, and add garlic and mint to hot beans. Mix lightly. Combine lime or lemon juice and oil and salt. Pour over beans and mix well. Serve warm.

SOY SALAD MIMOSA
(8 to 10 servings)

1 lb. dry soy beans	3 green onions with tops,
3 t salt	sliced
¼ cup wine vinegar	2 cloves garlic, minced
¼ cup freshly ground	2 hard-cooked eggs
pepper	Crisp greens
6 T olive or other oil	

Cover soy beans with water and soak by the preferred method. Cover and bring to a boil, turn heat low and simmer until almost tender, about *1½ hours*. Add 2 teaspoons salt and cook until tender but not mushy. Drain hot beans, saving liquid for soups or sauces. Mix wine vinegar, remaining 1 teaspoon salt, pepper, olive oil, green onions and garlic. Add to hot beans and toss to mix well. Cover and chill several hours. Shell eggs, cut in halves and remove yolks. Chop whites fine, add to bean salad and mix lightly. Taste and add more salt, pepper and vinegar, if needed. (Beans soak up seasonings.) Pile beans onto a platter, garnish with crisp greens and sieve egg yolk over top.

RED KIDNEY BEAN SALAD
(6 servings)

3 cups drained cooked red
   kidney beans
1 small yellow onion,
   thinly sliced
½ green pepper, chopped
3 green onions, sliced

¼ cup olive oil
3 T lemon juice
Salt, pepper
2 tomatoes, peeled and
   sliced into wedges
½ cup minced parsley

Place kidney beans in a large bowl with yellow onion, green pepper and green onion. Sprinkle with olive oil, lemon juice and salt and pepper to taste. Cover and chill until ready to serve. Arrange tomatoes around edges of bowl and mound parsley in center. Toss lightly at table and serve.

PEAS AND RICE SALAD
(8 servings)

1 t dry mustard
½ t salt
⅛ t cayenne
3 T vinegar
½ cup oil
1 T honey
4 cups hot cooked brown
   rice

1 to 2 cups drained cooked
   green peas, kidney
   beans or garbanzo
   beans
2 green onions, chopped
2 hard-cooked eggs, diced
   (optional)
Minced parsley

Blend mustard, salt, cayenne and vinegar until well mixed. Beat in oil and honey. Toss dressing with hot rice, cover and marinate at room temperature 1 to 2 hours. Add peas or beans, green onions and eggs. Toss lightly to mix, cover and chill 2 or 3 hours. Dust with minced parsley.

TABOOLI
(8 servings)

½ cup bulgur	1 t salt
3 bunches parsley, minced	¼ t pepper
1 bunch green onions, chopped	1 T lemon juice
	3 T olive oil
2 large tomatoes, peeled and chopped	Inside romaine leaves
2 T chopped fresh mint or 1 T mint flakes	

Soak bulgur in cold water 15 minutes, then drain. Combine parsley, green onions and tomatoes. Add bulgur, the mint, salt and pepper, lemon juice and oil. Mix thoroughly, cover and refrigerate or let stand at room temperature at least 1 hour. Pile into a bowl and surround with inside leaves of romaine. Some of the salad is lifted in cupped end of the romaine leaf and eaten as finger food.

HEALTH SALAD
(4 to 6 servings)

4 dried figs	¼ cup chopped salted peanuts
2 crisp red apples	
1 T lemon juice	Mayonnaise or sour cream
2 carrots	

Soak figs in boiling water for 2 or 3 minutes, drain and snip into small pieces with scissors. Wash and core apples but do not peel. Cut into small squares. Add to figs along with lemon juice and toss to coat apples with lemon. Peel carrots and shred. Add to apple mixture and toss again. Add peanuts and enough mayonnaise to moisten and toss well.

APRICOT BANANA SALAD
(6 servings)

2 cups broken lettuce or
　　other salad greens
2 bananas
½ lemon
6 cooked dried apricots
1 cup cottage cheese,
　　optional

¼ cup chopped walnuts
Honey Yogurt or Fluffy
　　Honey Dressing
　　(pages 230, 232)

Arrange a bed of lettuce on each salad plate. Peel and slice bananas into bowl, squeeze lemon juice over bananas and toss to coat well. Pile bananas onto lettuce nests and top each with an apricot. If wished, put a scoop of cottage cheese at the side of each fruit mound and sprinkle with nuts. Serve with Honey Yogurt or Fluffy Honey Dressing.

TROPICAL FRUIT PLATE
(6 to 8 servings)

¼ cup pineapple juice
1 T lemon juice
½ t salt
½ t curry powder
⅛ t ginger
1 T honey
½ cup oil

1 pineapple
1 mango
1 papaya
1 grapefruit
Crisp greens
Cottage cheese, optional

To make pineapple juice, puree chopped fresh pineapple in a blender at highest speed until liquefied. Combine pineapple juice, lemon juice, salt, curry powder and ginger. Beat together until blended, then beat in honey and oil. Beat again just before serving.

To assemble fruit plate. Peel pineapple and cut into fingers, discarding core, then cut each finger in halves crosswise. Peel mango and slice, discarding seed. Peel papaya, scoop out seeds, then cut into lengthwise slices. Peel and section grapefruit. Arrange fruit on greens in alternating rows or wedges. Sprinkle with just enough dressing to give a glossy appearance. Spoon cottage cheese into center, if wanted. Pass remaining dressing.

CARLTON SALAD
(6 servings)

1½ cups cubed pineapple
Water
1 envelope unflavored
   gelatin
2 eggs
¼ t salt

1 t dry mustard
1 t vinegar
1 cup plain yogurt
2 unpeeled apples,
   chopped
Crisp greens

Place pineapple in a small saucepan with water to barely cover and simmer for about *5 minutes*. (Uncooked pineapple contains an enzyme which prevents gelatin from setting, so pineapple must be cooked or blanched before using with gelatin.) Drain pineapple reserving liquid, and cool. Soften gelatin in ¼ cup cold water. Measure juice drained from pineapple and add water to make 1 cup in top of double boiler. Blend eggs with salt, mustard and vinegar. Add pineapple juice. Cook and stir over boiling water until thick enough to coat a metal spoon. Add softened gelatin and stir until dissolved. Chill until mixture mounds slightly when dropped from a spoon. Beat gelatin until smooth, then fold in yogurt, apples and pineapple chunks. Turn in a 9-in. ring mold which has been rinsed in cold water. Chill until firm. Unmold and garnish with crisp greens.

PINEAPPLE-CHICKEN SALAD
(4 servings)

2 cups cubed cooked
   chicken or turkey
1½ cups cubed pineapple,
   drained
1 cup diced celery
1 t powdered or freshly
   grated ginger

½ cup slivered almonds
½ cup Sour Cream Dress-
   ing (page 229) or
   mayonnaise
Crisp greens

Combine chicken, pineapple, celery, ginger and almonds. Toss lightly. Add dressing and toss again. Cover and chill until ready to serve. Serve on crisp greens, passing additional dressing, if wanted.

BOMBAY TURKEY SALAD
(6 servings)

½ cup mayonnaise
¾ t salt
1½ t curry powder
1 T lemon juice
2 or 3 peaches, peeled
and cubed
2 cups cubed cooked
turkey

1 cup sliced celery
¼ cup sliced green onion
with tops
Crisp greens
¼ cup salted roasted
peanuts, chopped

Mix mayonnaise with salt, curry powder and lemon juice. Add peaches as they are cut, turkey, celery and green onion. Toss gently and pile onto crisp greens on a platter. Sprinkle with peanuts.

GREEK SALAD SUPPER
(4 servings)

4 or 5 potatoes
Salt, pepper
6 green onions
¼ cup minced parsley
1 green pepper
¼ cup vinegar
¾ cup olive or safflower oil
¼ cup mayonnaise
4 or 5 cups coarsely shredded romaine, escarole
or roquette

1 cucumber
2 small tomatoes
1 small avocado
4 radishes
½ lb. Feta cheese
½ lb. large shrimp, cooked
and shelled
½ t dried leaf oregano

Cook potatoes in their jackets in boiling water until tender but not mushy. Run cold water over potatoes to cool slightly, peel and cube into a bowl. Slice two of the green onions thinly and add to potatoes. Add parsley. Cut four rings out of center of green pepper, remove seeds and ribs and dice remaining pepper. Add to potatoes. Sprinkle with salt and pepper to taste. Beat together vinegar and oil and pour about half of it over the potato salad. Cover and chill several hours or overnight. Add mayonnaise to potato salad and mix lightly.

Spread greens on a platter. Mound potato salad in center. Peel cucumbers and cut into eight lengthwise wedges. Peel tomatoes and cut into four or eight wedges each. Peel avocado, remove seed and cut flesh into eight wedges. Arrange cucumber, tomato wedges and avocado around potato salad, building into a mound. Arrange radishes around mound. Cut cheese into strips or squares and intersperse at base of salad. Trim remaining green onions and arrange around salad. Scatter shrimp over top. Sprinkle with oregano and remaining oil and vinegar dressing. Sprinkle with more salt and pepper, if wanted. Serve with crusty bread and a hearty red wine.

PEASANT CHEESE SALAD
(4 servings)

¾ lb. Swiss or Gruyère cheese
4 potatoes, boiled and peeled
1½ cups cut green beans, cooked and drained
1 onion, chopped

Lemon French Dressing or French Salad Sauce (pages 233, 232)
Crisp greens
Radish roses, optional

Cut cheese into small squares or strips. Slice potatoes. Combine cheese, potatoes, beans and onion and toss lightly. Add just enough dressing to moisten and toss again. Cover and refrigerate several hours. Arrange in a bowl lined with greens and garnish with radish roses.

EGG SALAD CUPS
(6 servings)

6 hard-cooked eggs, finely chopped
1½ cups shredded Swiss cheese
½ cup mayonnaise

2 T minced chives
1 t prepared mustard
6 tomatoes
Watercress or chicory

Combine eggs, cheese, mayonnaise, chives and mustard and mix lightly. Wash tomatoes and cut a thin slice off blossom end. Cut each tomato into 6 wedges almost to stem end. Open out slightly and spoon egg salad between wedges. Place on salad plates and garnish with greens.

TAHITIAN FISH
(4 salad servings)

1 lb. fish fillets (whitefish, rockfish, sole)
4 small limes
2 small tomatoes

1 onion
½ t salt
1 cup Thin Coconut Cream (page 297)

Firm-textured, mild-flavored fish should be used in this recipe. Dice the fish fillets fine. Place in a small bowl and squeeze lime juice over the fish. Mix well and let stand about 10 minutes at room temperature. The fish will get a rather opaque appearance as the acid in the lime "cooks" the protein in the fish. Drain fish well. Peel and dice tomatoes; peel and dice onions. Add tomatoes, onion and salt to fish. Mix lightly, cover and refrigerate until ready to serve. Mix with Coconut Cream. Serve on crisp greens as a salad or appetizer.

PAPAYA CRAB SALAD
(4 to 6 servings)

1 cup crab meat (½ lb.)
½ cup thinly sliced celery
¼ cup minced green onion
4 hard-cooked eggs, chopped
½ t salt

Dash cayenne
½ cup mayonnaise, or as needed
2 or 3 papayas
Crisp greens
Green pepper rings

Pick over crab, removing any bits of cartilage. Combine crab meat, celery, onion, eggs, salt and cayenne. Toss lightly, add mayonnaise to moisten and toss until well mixed. Cut papayas in halves lengthwise, scoop out seeds and, if wished, peel papaya halves. Fill with crab salad and garnish with crisp greens and green pepper rings. If papaya is unavailable, avocado halves may be substituted.

ESCABECHE IN AVOCADO
(8 servings)

2 cloves garlic, minced
½ cup oil
1½-lb. fillet of sole
1 large onion, sliced
¼ t oregano
¼ cup lime or lemon
 juice

1 small tomato, peeled
 and chopped
¼ cup diced green pepper
Salt, cayenne
4 avocados
Lime or lemon juice

Cook garlic in oil in a large skillet until golden. Cut fish into ½-in. crosswise slices. Add fish, onion, oregano and lime juice to garlic oil. Cover and simmer *5 minutes* or until fish turns white and opaque looking. Cool in broth. Add tomato, green pepper, salt and cayenne to taste. Chill well.

When ready to serve, cut avocados in halves lengthwise and twist to separate halves. Remove seeds and brush cut surfaces with lime or lemon juice. Do not peel halves. Place on salad plates or in small bowls and fill with escabeche. Garnish with lime wedges, if wanted.

ORANGE SALAD CREAM
(1¼ cups)

1 t grated orange peel
2 T orange juice
2 T lemon juice
1 T honey

½ t dry mustard
1 t salt
⅛ t cayenne
1 cup sour cream

Blend orange peel and juice, lemon juice, honey, mustard, salt and cayenne well. Stir in sour cream. Chill well and serve on fruit or ham salad.

HOMEMADE MAYONNAISE
(1¼ cups)

2 egg yolks or 1 whole egg
½ t salt
⅛ t cayenne

½ t dry mustard
1 T lemon juice
1 cup oil

Drop egg yolks or whole egg into a platter or a small bowl. Using a wire whisk, egg beater, automatic beater or silver fork, beat in salt, cayenne and mustard until well blended. Beat in the lemon juice. Beat in 3 or 4 teaspoons oil drop by drop. This is important as the mayonnaise will not amalgamate unless first portion of oil is added very slowly.

When mayonnaise begins to thicken, add remaining oil about a teaspoonful at a time. Make sure the mayonnaise is completely smooth each time before adding the next teaspoonful of oil. When all oil is beaten in mayonnaise should be stiff and completely smooth. If too thick, thin with a little more lemon juice. Mayonnaise beaten on a platter usually is thicker than mayonnaise beaten in a bowl.

If you have a blender, mayonnaise is virtually foolproof. Beat together egg, seasonings and lemon juice. Then add oil in a fine stream with motor running. As mayonnaise begins to thicken, stop motor occasionally and scrape sides of blender container with rubber scraper.

SOUR CREAM DRESSING
(1¼ cups)

1 t salt	1 T lemon juice
⅛ t cayenne	2 T vinegar
1 T honey	1 cup sour cream

Blend salt and cayenne, then stir in honey, lemon juice and vinegar. Beat until smooth. Stir in sour cream.

LOW-FAT SALAD DRESSING
(½ cup)

½ cup buttermilk	1 t honey
4 t freshly grated horse-radish	Dash salt
	Dash pepper

Combine buttermilk, horseradish, honey, salt and pepper. Mix well, chill and stir before serving.

CHILI-PEANUT SAUCE
(2¼ cups)

1 onion, chopped
2 T oil
½ to 1 t cayenne
2 cups water

¼ cup peanut butter
1 t salt
1 T vinegar or lemon juice
1 t honey

Cook onion in oil until tender but not brown. Stir in cayenne, then water, then peanut butter. Bring to a boil, stirring often, and continue stirring and cooking until mixture is smooth. Season with salt, vinegar and honey. Serve warm or cooled over vegetable salad.

HONEY YOGURT DRESSING
(1 cup)

1 cup yogurt
1 T honey

1 t grated lemon peel
1 T toasted sesame seeds

Gently blend yogurt, honey, lemon peel and sesame seeds. Do not stir vigorously or structure of yogurt will break down. Serve with fruit salads. Sprinkle with more toasted sesame seeds, if wanted.

BUTTERMILK DRESSING
(1 cup)

1 cup buttermilk
1 clove garlic, crushed
¼ t dry mustard

1½ t cider vinegar
1 t honey

Mix buttermilk, garlic, mustard and vinegar thoroughly. Stir in honey. Chill at least *30 minutes,* beat to mix again and serve on green salads.

CUCUMBER CHEESE DRESSING
(about 2 cups)

1 cup cottage cheese
½ cup sour cream
½ t salt
¼ t paprika

1 t dry mustard
½ cup finely chopped
    cucumber, drained

Press cottage cheese through a fine sieve or puree in a blender to make smooth. Stir or beat in sour cream, salt, paprika, mustard and cucumber. Serve over mixed vegetable, tomato or green salads or serve as a sauce for cold poached fish.

DILL DRESSING
(1¼ cups)

½ cup heavy cream
1½ t freshly grated horse-
    radish

1 t dill weed
¼ t salt
¼ cup dairy sour cream

Whip cream until stiff, then fold in horseradish, dill, salt and sour cream. Cover and chill to blend flavors. Serve over greens, cucumber salad or cold poached fish.

DAIRY DRESSING
(2½ cups)

1 cup cottage cheese
1 cup dairy sour cream
½ cup buttermilk
1 t salt

⅛ t cayenne
1 clove garlic, minced
½ small onion, minced

Press cottage cheese through a fine sieve or puree in a blender until smooth. Stir or beat in sour cream, buttermilk, salt, cayenne, garlic and onion. Cover and chill until ready to serve. Serve on green salad or tomato salad.

YOGURT GARLIC DRESSING
(1 cup)

1 cup yogurt
1 t lemon juice
½ t grated lemon peel
1 clove garlic, minced

1 T minced parsley
1 T minced chives or green
    onion top

Gently blend yogurt, lemon juice and peel, garlic, parsley and chives. Be careful not to beat vigorously or structure of yogurt will break down. Cover and refrigerate for several hours to blend flavors. Serve with green salads, tomato or seafood salads.

FLUFFY HONEY DRESSING
(2 cups)

2 eggs
½ cup honey
¼ cup lemon juice
2 T orange juice

Dash salt
½ cup heavy cream, whipped
2 t grated lemon peel

Beat eggs in a small saucepan and stir in honey, lemon juice, orange juice and salt. Cook and stir over low heat until thickened. Cool and fold in whipped cream and lemon peel. Serve with fruit salad.

FRENCH SALAD SAUCE
(½ cup)

2 T prepared mustard, preferably Dijon style
2 T wine vinegar
4 T oil

Spoon mustard into a small bowl and beat in about half the vinegar with a small wire whisk. Gradually beat in oil and remaining vinegar. Serve at once. This sauce may be tossed with greens, served as a sauce for artichokes or mixed with shredded carrots for salad.

MACADAMIA DRESSING
(1½ cups)

1 cup oil
¼ cup lemon juice
1 t grated lemon peel
½ t salt

½ t dry mustard
¼ t pepper
1 cup finely chopped Macadamia nuts

Combine oil, lemon juice and peel, salt, mustard and pepper in a bowl or jar with a tight-fitting cover. Shake or beat together until blended. Let stand *1 hour* or longer to blend flavors. Just before serving add nuts. Serve on tuna salad, fruit salads or tossed greens.

LEMON GARLIC DRESSING
(10 tablespoons)

1 t salt
¼ t pepper
½ t paprika
1 clove garlic, minced, optional

2 T lemon juice
½ cup oil (cottonseed, soy, safflower or olive or peanut)

Combine salt, pepper, paprika and garlic in a small bowl or jar with a tight-fitting lid. Add lemon juice and beat or cover and shake vigorously until well mixed. Add oil and beat or shake again. Shake or beat to mix each time before using. This dressing will keep several days in the refrigerator.

LEMON FRENCH DRESSING
(1¼ cups)

¼ cup lemon juice (about 2 lemons)
½ t grated lemon peel, optional
½ t salt

1 t honey
⅛ t white pepper
1 cup safflower, soy, corn, sesame or cottonseed oil

Combine lemon juice, peel, salt, honey and white pepper. Beat together until well blended. Add oil and blend well. Beat again just before serving. Use as dressing for tossed green or fruit salads.

Relishes and Sauces

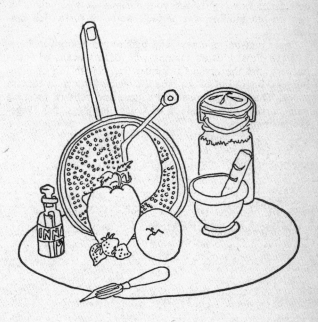

A SWITCH to natural foods does not necessarily mean that you must give up such luxuries as jellies and jams, pickles, relishes and other condiments. Make them yourself. Here are three bread spreads—a carrot marmalade, apricot jam and peach honey. Sweetened with honey, they are good on whole wheat toast, pancakes or fresh bread, and make novel gifts for your friends. A marmalade or jam on hot muffins is a perfect substitute for a rich dessert.

Some unusual chutneys and pickles are also given here. Try the Pink Pickled Onions with baked beans or hamburgers, and the Fresh Cucumber Relish with fish or hamburgers. Instead of catsup, use the recipe for a spicy tomato sauce. There are also several sauces and relishes to serve with curries, plus a galaxy of sauces for eggs, fish, vegetables or meats.

EGG SAUCE
(1¼ cups)

2 T butter or margarine
2 T rye or whole wheat
    flour
1 cup milk

½ t salt
⅛ t pepper
1 hard-cooked egg,
    chopped

Melt butter in a small saucepan. Add flour and stir until bubbly. Add milk and cook and stir until smooth and thickened. Add salt and pepper, then lightly stir in egg. Serve hot on poached fish or vegetables.

SAUCE SOUBISE
(2½ cups)

2 cups chopped onions
¼ t salt
3 T butter or margarine
2 T rye flour

2 cups milk or half milk
    and half broth
Salt, pepper

Add onions and salt to hot butter in a saucepan and cook slowly for *20 to 30 minutes,* stirring often. Onions should be almost pureed when cooked. Stir in flour until smooth, then add milk and cook and stir until smooth and thickened. Season to taste with salt and pepper. Use on hard-cooked eggs, vegetables or in casseroles.

FRESH MUSHROOM SAUCE
(2 cups)

⅓ cup oil
½ lb. mushrooms, sliced
1 clove garlic, minced, or
    2 t minced shallot
¼ cup flour (rye, whole
    wheat or unbleached
    white)

½ t salt
Dash cayenne
2 cups milk

Heat oil in a saucepan, add mushrooms and cook and stir until lightly browned. Add garlic or shallot and stir a minute or so. Stir in flour, salt and cayenne. Add milk and cook and stir until thickened.

CHEESE SAUCE
(2 cups)

¼ cup butter or margarine
¼ cup whole wheat or rye
    flour
1 t dry mustard
⅛ t cayenne

½ t salt
2 cups rich milk
2 cups (½ lb.) shredded
    natural sharp Cheddar
    cheese

Melt butter in a saucepan and stir in flour, making sure it is smooth. Stir in mustard, cayenne and salt. Add milk and cook and stir until smooth and thickened. Add cheese and heat, stirring now and then, until melted.

LEMON BUTTER
(1¼ cups)

¼ cup lemon juice
½ lb. butter or margarine, melted

Stir lemon juice into melted butter. Pour into a small pitcher or sauceboat and serve hot over Barbecued Salmon, other fish or hot cooked vegetables.

MUSTARD SAUCE
(6 tablespoons)

2 T dry mustard
¼ t salt
1 T vinegar
1 T melted butter or mar-
    garine or oil

¼ cup boiling water
1 t honey

Blend mustard and salt in a small bowl. Stir in vinegar, butter, boiling water and honey. Mix well and serve warm with hamburgers or other meats or chill and serve with cold meats or on sandwiches.

PARSLEY BUTTER
(4 to 6 servings)

3 T butter or margarine
1 to 2 t lemon juice
1 T minced parsley
½ t salt (if sweet butter is
 used)

Melt butter and stir in lemon juice, parsley and salt. Pour over broiled fish, grilled hamburgers or boiled new potatoes.

DELUXE TOMATO SAUCE
(2½ cups)

¼ cup oil
1 onion, sliced
1 carrot, sliced
1 rib celery with leaves,
 sliced
2 T minced parsley
1 T minced fresh or 1 t
 dried marjoram
2 or 3 cloves garlic,
 crushed

¼ cup mushrooms, chopped
 (optional)
½ t honey
½ cup dry red or white
 wine
3½ cups chopped peeled,
 seeded and drained
 tomatoes
1 t salt
¼ t pepper

Heat oil in large saucepan. Add onion, carrot, celery, parsley, marjoram, garlic, mushrooms and honey. Sauté just until vegetables are turning pale golden. Add wine and boil uncovered until most of wine is evaporated. Add tomatoes, salt and pepper. Cover and simmer *1 hour,* adding hot water from time to time if sauce becomes too thick. Puree through a food mill or press through a fine sieve and reheat. If too thin, which can happen with watery tomatoes, simmer uncovered until thick as desired. Serve over pasta or meats or use in recipes which call for canned tomato sauce.

HORSERADISH MAYONNAISE
(2½ cups)

¼ cup lemon juice
¾ t salt
½ t honey
1 egg
1 cup oil

3 T freshly grated
  horseradish
1 cup sour cream or
  whipped cream

Combine lemon juice, salt, honey and egg in a blender and blend at high speed. With motor running, add oil in a very fine stream and continue blending until all oil is incorporated into sauce. Stop motor and scrape down sides of container with rubber scraper now and then. Stir in horseradish. Pour sauce from blender into a bowl and fold in sour cream or whipped cream. Serve cold as a sauce for Barbecued Salmon, other broiled or poached fish.

CUCUMBER CREAM
(2½ cups)

2 T lemon juice
1 T honey
1 cup well-drained diced
  cucumber

1 cup heavy cream,
  whipped
Salt, pepper

Mix lemon juice, honey and cucumber. Whip cream and fold in the cucumber mixture. Season to taste with salt and pepper. Serve cold with broiled fish, cold poached fish, shrimp salads or sliced tomato.

NOTE: Use 2 cups plain yogurt instead of whipped cream for a low-calorie sauce. Do not stir yogurt vigorously or it will break down.

LAURIE'S TOMATO SAUCE
(4 to 5 pints)

1 qt. chopped peeled
    tomatoes
4 green peppers, diced
4 onions, diced
2 cups brown sugar,
    packed

2 cups vinegar
1 T salt
¼ t crushed red chiles
1 t cinnamon
½ t cloves

Combine tomatoes, green peppers, onions, sugar, vinegar, salt, chiles, cinnamon and cloves in a large kettle. Simmer, stirring often to prevent sticking, until thick. Pour into hot sterilized jars and seal at once. Serve as a condiment sauce with meats.

SAUCE MEUNIÈRE FOR FISH
(4 to 6 servings)

3 T butter or margarine
½ t tarragon

1 T minced parsley
1 T lemon juice

Melt butter and cook until golden, being careful not to let butter turn brown. Stir in tarragon, parsley and lemon juice. Pour over hot broiled, baked and sautéed fish.

LEMON SAUCE FOR FISH
(4 to 6 servings)

¼ cup minced parsley
1 small onion, minced
¼ cup lemon juice

Combine parsley, onion and lemon juice in a small saucepan. Heat but do not boil. Serve hot over hot fried, broiled, baked or poached fish.

FRESH CUCUMBER RELISH
(3 cups)

2 cucumbers
½ cup honey
⅔ cup white vinegar

2 t coarsely ground pepper
1 small onion, minced

Peel cucumbers and slice very thinly. Place in bowl and add honey, vinegar, pepper and onion. Cover and chill several hours or overnight. Serve as a relish with meats, especially with hamburgers or roast beef sandwiches.

RANCH SALSA
(10 to 12 servings)

2 cups chopped peeled
  tomatoes
1 rib celery, diced
1 onion, diced
1 green pepper, diced
1½ t salt

1 T vinegar
1 T honey or brown
  sugar
1 hot green chile, peeled
  and diced

Combine tomatoes, celery, onion, green pepper, salt, vinegar, honey and chile. Blend well. If a finer texture is wanted, salsa may be ground in a food grinder, using fine blade. Cover tightly and chill overnight to blend flavors. Serve cold as a relish with meats or sandwiches.

OLD SOUR
(1 pint)

2 cups strained freshly
  squeezed lime juice,
  preferably small yellow
  limes

1 T salt
1 small red chile (optional)

Mix lime juice and salt until salt is thoroughly dissolved. Pour into a pint bottle, cap and let stand in a cool dark place at least 3 months before using. Old Sour turns an amber to brown color while aging. Some connoisseurs claim the older it is the better, boasting of batches 2 or 3 years old. Sprinkle on greens, seafood or salads at the table.

PEPPER VINEGAR
(1 pint)

Small red, green or yellow chiles
1 clove garlic, optional
Cider or wine vinegar

Wash chiles and drain well. Pack into a pint bottle (preferably with a shaker top) but do not crush chiles. Add peeled garlic and fill bottle with vinegar. Cap and let stand 2 or 3 days before using. Vinegar may be replenished as the spiced vinegar is poured off. Sprinkle on cooked greens, dry bean dishes or salads at the table.

HERBED ONIONS
(6 servings)

2 large sweet onions
6 fresh mint leaves
1 T minced parsley
¼ t crumbled thyme

Salt, coarsely ground
pepper
½ cup oil
¼ cup vinegar

Peel onions and cut into ¼-in. slices. Mix mint, parsley and thyme in a bowl or mortar and crush to blend well. Arrange onion in layers in a small shallow dish, sprinkling each layer with some of the herb mixture, salt and pepper. Mix oil and vinegar. Spoon carefully over onions. Cover and chill at least an hour, spooning dressing over onions now and then. Serve cold with roast lamb or in sandwiches. Dressing may be drained off and used on salads.

PINK PICKLED ONIONS
(about 2 quarts)

2 lb. small boiling onions
1 cup beet liquid (from
    cooking beets)
1 cup white vinegar

1 T mixed pickling spice
3 T honey
4 to 6 whole dried chiles

Cut off stem and root ends of unpeeled onions and cook
the onions in boiling salted water *5 minutes* or until skins
slip off easily. Onions should still be crisp. Slip off skins.

Combine beet liquid, vinegar, pickling spice and honey.
Bring to a boil. Pack peeled onions in jars and put two
or three chiles in each. Pour hot liquid over onions.
Cover tightly and let stand two or three days before serving.

SNAPPY PICKLED BEETS
(about 1 quart)

1 bunch beets
¼ cup freshly grated horseradish (about)
Cider vinegar to cover beets

Wash beets and cut off tops, leaving a 1-in. stub of the stem
attached to the beet. Place beets in a greased shallow baking
pan. Bake at 375° until easily pierced with a fork, *25 to 45
minutes,* depending on size of beets. Cool until beets can be
handled, peel and slice. Alternate thin layers of beets and
horseradish in a jar or deep bowl. Bring vinegar to a
boil and pour over beets. Cover and refrigerate overnight
or longer.

FRESH TURNIP PICKLE
(2 to 2½ cups)

1 lb. white turnips
1½ cups lemon juice
2 t salt

Peel turnips and cut into thin strips or slices. Place turnips
in a glass or earthenware container. Pour lemon juice

over turnips and sprinkle with salt. Mix lightly with a fork, cover and let marinate 3 to 4 hours. Drain well and store in a bowl or jar in refrigerator. Serve cold with sandwiches or salads.

DOWN HOME APPLESAUCE

Firm tart apples   Lemon juice, optional
Water, salt   Honey, optional

Whole apples or trimmings left from Sesame Apple Rings, salads or other recipes may be used. This is a cinch if you have a food mill or cone sieve. These gadgets puree the cooked apple and remove the seeds, peeling and pithy portions at the same time. If you do not have a food mill or sieve, peel apples and cut out all the core, seeds, stem portions and pithy portions surrounding seeds. Cut apples into chunks if they are to be pressed through a sieve or food mill.

Place apples in a saucepan with just enough water to prevent sticking. Simmer until apples are tender, stirring often and adding more water if needed. Puree apples through a food mill or sieve, or drain off excess liquid and mash apples until smooth with a potato masher or fork. Stir in salt, lemon juice and honey to taste. Applesauce may be reheated, packed into hot jars; adjust caps as manufacturer directs and process 10 minutes in a boiling water bath. Or applesauce may be stored in a covered container in the refrigerator.

Red Applesauce. Cook a few raspberries or red plums with apples. This applesauce may be seasoned with cinnamon or, to serve with meats, horseradish.

OLD-FASHIONED APPLESAUCE
(about 2 quarts)

4 qt. sweet cider, preferably fresh
2 qt. pared, cored and quartered firm apples
Cinnamon, honey, optional

Pour cider into a large pot with wide cooking surface and boil uncovered until reduced to about 2 qt. Add apples and simmer uncovered *2 or 3 hours*, stirring occasionally. When of sauce consistency, season with cinnamon and honey, if wished; however, sauce made this way usually requires no additional sweetening. If you have a food mill or sieve, apples need not be peeled and cored, only washed and quartered. When apples are tender, force through the food mill.

SPICED ORANGES
(12 servings)

3 small oranges
¾ cup honey
¼ cup water

10 whole allspice
8 whole cloves

Cover washed unpeeled oranges with boiling water and boil *10 minutes*. Drain and cut each orange, including skin, into 8 wedges. Combine honey, water, allspice and cloves. Bring to a boil, add orange pieces and boil *10 minutes*. Cool, cover and chill several days. Remove whole allspice and cloves after two or three days. Serve as a relish with meats or curries.

SESAME APPLE RINGS
(6 servings)

3 large red apples
¼ cup butter or margarine, melted
½ cup fine dry rye or whole wheat bread crumbs

1 T brown sugar
2 T sesame seeds

Core apples but do not peel. Cut two ½-in. slices from center of each apple, saving remainder for salads or applesauce. Brush apple slices on both sides with melted butter and coat with crumbs. Arrange in a greased shallow baking dish. Sprinkle with brown sugar and sesame seeds. Bake at 400° *20 minutes* or until tender. Serve hot with meats or poultry.

CRANBERRY ORANGE RELISH
(makes 2½ cups)

1 small orange
2 cups fresh cranberries
⅔ to ¾ cup honey

Wash orange and cranberries and drain. Cut orange into quarters, discarding seeds but leaving skin intact. Put orange and cranberries through food grinder, using coarse blade. Mix with honey. Cover and chill several hours before servings. Serve with poultry, meats or curries.

MINT CHUTNEY
(about 1¼ cups)

2 cups mint leaves, packed
1 small onion, minced
¼ cup pomegranate juice
    or apple juice

¼ cup lemon juice
½ t salt

Wash mint leaves thoroughly and drain well. Pick off any stem portions and discard. Combine onion, pomegranate juice, lemon juice and salt in blender and blend until smooth. Add mint leaves and blend until smooth. Serve with curries or meats.

NOTE: To extract pomegranate juice, break apart fruit into halves (they do not have to be absolutely equal in size or regular in shape). Twist on an orange juice extractor.

CRISP ONION FLAKES

Onions
Oil

Peel, wash and cut onions into paper-thin slices. Pour about 1 in. of oil into a large heavy skillet. Add onions. The oil should cover the onions, so add more oil, if needed. Cook and stir over moderate heat until onions become translucent in appearance, then turn heat very low and cook, turning often and taking care not to burn, until onions are a deep tan color throughout. If they begin to burn, remove the pan from heat and turn the onions with a spatula until scorching stops. When uniformly browned throughout, pour onions and oil quickly into a strainer. The oil may be saved for cooking onions again. Draining promptly prevents some of the onions from becoming too brown from stored heat.

Turn onions out onto a towel and drain thoroughly. When cool, store in covered jars until needed. Sprinkle over soups, stews, salads, curries or meat and poultry dishes.

OLD-FASHIONED PEACH HONEY
(1 cup)

3 cups chopped peeled peaches
2 cups honey
Cinnamon, optional

Combine peaches and honey in a large wide saucepan. Season lightly with cinnamon, if wished. Simmer uncovered *2 hours* or longer, stirring occasionally to prevent scorching. Store in refrigerator and use as spread for bread or waffles and pancakes.

TAWNY APRICOT JAM
(about 3 cups)

1½ cups dried apricots
1 cup water
1 unpeeled lemon, sliced

3 cups brown sugar,
firmly packed

Put apricots in bowl, add water and let soak 2 or 3 hours, until they are softened. Place apricots and soaking water in blender with lemon. Blend until mixture is pureed, turning motor off now and then and scaping unblended portions into center with rubber spatula. Scrape into a wide saucepan. Add brown sugar and mix well. Bring to a boil over moderate heat. Cook uncovered, stirring often, until mixture drops off spoon in thick blobs or sheets. Pour into jars, cover and refrigerate or seal with paraffin for long term storage. This makes a dark reddish brown jam which may be used as a spread for bread, topping for pancakes or sauce for desserts. Makes about 3 cups.

HONEY-CARROT MARMALADE
(about 1½ cups)

½ cup water
1 cup peeled and thinly
   sliced carrots, 3 or 4
1 unpeeled lemon, sliced

1 2-inch piece fresh ginger
   root, peeled and
   sliced, optional
1½ cups honey

Pour water in blender container. Add carrots and lemon. If ginger is used, add it at this time. Blend until carrots and lemon are finely chopped. Scrape into a wide saucepan. Add honey and mix well. Bring to a boil over moderately high heat. Cook uncovered, stirring often until consistency is as thick as applesauce. Pour into jars and cover and refrigerate, or seal with paraffin for long term storage. This makes a dark amber colored spread which may be used on bread or as a dessert sauce.

Breads

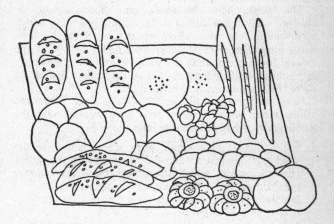

FRAGRANT homemade breads, full of ingredients that nurture body and soul, are the supreme triumph of fine home cooking. But with a little practice, anybody can make a good loaf of bread.

The recipes here use whole grain flours almost exclusively. Bolting or sifting is the milling operation which removes the bran from whole wheat flour. Since this bran is the nourishing part of flours most highly valued by the natural foods cook, don't sift whole grain flours. However, soy flour is another matter. It is so dense that it must be stirred before measuring to break it up.

After much experimenting with whole grain flours and asking other baking experts who have worked with the whole grains, we found these points:

1. For a mixed grain bread, work wheat flour into the yeast mixture first to allow development of the gluten (the component which strengthens the yeast action), then add the rye, buckwheat, soy or other flours.
2. Soy flour is quite dense, so use no more than one part to four parts of wheat flour.
3. In working with whole wheat and mixed grain doughs, use as little flour as possible. These breads are heavy by nature, and only as much flour as is necessary to make the dough workable should be used.
4. Vigorous kneading helps to prevent many of the problems inherent in these whole grain breads. This means 10 to 15 minutes kneading for a person with average strength and vigor in his or her hands. Don't make double recipes of these heavier breads, as the dough will be almost impossible to manage.
5. Whole wheat breads should rise three times. Let the bread rise, then punch it down and pull the edges of the dough to the center. Let rise again, which will take about half the time of the first rising. Then shape the bread and let it rise again.

Keep in mind that these are rather solid breads, substantial in texture and flavor. Some of us appreciate this. If you want a fluffy, cotton-ball texture, you won't get it with whole grain flours.

Quick whole grain breads do not present quite the problem as yeast breads. Though they, too, have a substantial texture and may not rise so high and be as light and fluffy as their white flour counterparts.

These dark, full-flavored breads become a major part of a meal, rather than just an accessory. A slice with soup or salad and cheese or fruit makes a meal. A sandwich made with one of these breads is truly nourishing.

CHAPPATIES
(6 to 8 servings)

2 cups whole wheat flour
½ t salt

3 T butter or margarine
¾ to 1 cup cold water

Mix flour and salt in a bowl. Clarify butter according to directions on page 87. Mix into the flour mixture until it is crumbly. Work in enough water to make a stiff but workable dough. Knead it thoroughly and round up into a ball. Cover and let stand at room temperature 2 or 3 hours. Knead vigorously again. Divide into six or eight portions, shape each into a ball, then roll out paper thin. Bake on a lightly greased griddle until browned on one side, turn and brown the other. Serve at once.

NOTE: Chappaties and Puris, which follows, are unleavened breads which are typical of Indian cookery. These breads usually are served with curries, but are good with soups, salads and as a substitute for crackers with snack spreads. Some Americans like them with molasses or honey, as pancakes.

PURIS
(10 or 12 servings)

3 cups whole wheat flour
1 t salt
½ cup butter or margarine

1½ cups yogurt, about
Oil for frying

Combine flour and salt in a bowl. Clarify butter according to directions on p. 87. Mix into the flour mixture until crumbly. Work in enough yogurt with a fork, to make a stiff but workable dough. Knead on a lightly floured surface until dough clings together and is no longer sticky, about 5 minutes of vigorous kneading. Round up into a ball, cover and let stand at room temperature 30 minutes. Divide dough into 10 or 12 portions, roll each into a ball, then roll out to a thin circle. Fry in hot deep fat until lightly browned. Puris will puff up within a few seconds after they hit the hot fat and then will brown. Drain on absorbent paper and serve at once.

BASIC WHOLE WHEAT PANCAKES
(6 to 8 servings)

2 cups buttermilk	2 t soda
3 or 4 eggs	1 t salt
2 T honey	2 T oil
2 cups whole wheat flour	Honey or molasses
2 T wheat germ	

Beat together buttermilk, eggs and honey until smooth. Blend in whole wheat flour, wheat germ, soda, salt and oil. Pour batter by large spoonfuls onto hot lightly greased griddle. Bake until bubbles form on top and bubbles at edges pop. Turn and brown other side. Serve hot with honey or molasses and butter.

Blueberry Pancakes. Immediately after pancakes are poured onto griddle, sprinkle a small spoonful of washed and drained fresh blueberries over pancakes.

Banana Pancakes. Immediately after pancakes are poured onto griddle, place two or three thin banana slices on each pancake.

Coconut Pancakes. Immediately after pancakes are poured onto griddle, sprinkle lightly with shredded coconut.

OATMEAL PANCAKES
(4 to 5 servings)

2 cups milk	2½ t baking powder
1½ cups uncooked oatmeal	1 t salt
½ cup sifted unbleached white flour	2 eggs, beaten
½ cup whole wheat flour	1 T honey
	⅓ cup oil

Pour milk over oatmeal and let stand 5 minutes. Mix white and whole wheat flours, baking powder and salt and add to oatmeal mixture. Beat in eggs, honey and oil until well mixed but not necessarily smooth. For each pancake, pour ¼ cup batter onto a hot lightly greased or seasoned griddle. Bake until bubbles form on top and bubbles begin to pop at edges, turn and bake until other side is browned. Serve hot with butter or margarine, honey or syrup.

NORWEGIAN PANCAKES
(6 to 8 servings)

1 cup cottage cheese	¾ cup whole wheat flour
1 cup sour cream	1 T honey
4 eggs	1 t salt

Combine cottage cheese, sour cream and eggs. Beat together until well blended, but some of the cottage cheese curds will remain. Beat in flour, honey and salt. Bake on a hot griddle, greased, if necessary. Turn when top is bubbly and dry, then bake second side until browned. Serve hot with butter and honey or molasses.

GIANT POTATO PANCAKES
(4 to 6 servings)

2 eggs	¼ t nutmeg, optional
4 medium potatoes	2 to 3 T rye or whole wheat
1 medium onion	flour
1 t salt	Oil for frying
⅛ t pepper	Applesauce

Beat eggs slightly in a large bowl. Peel and grate potatoes into bowl with eggs. Stir occasionally while grating to coat potatoes with eggs to prevent darkening. Grate onion into bowl with potato mixture, then stir in salt, pepper, nutmeg and enough flour to make batter hold together. Heat 2 tablespoons oil in a shallow 10-in. skillet until almost sizzling. Pour in half the batter, about 2 cups, and spread quickly to the sides of the pan. Cook over moderate heat until well-browned on the underside. Lift carefully with spatula to check brownness. Slide pancake onto a large plate, cover with another plate and flip over so the cooked side is uppermost. Slide back into the pan and brown other side. Turn out onto plate. Cool the pancake. Cut pancakes into wedges and serve with applesauce. This batter also can be used for smaller pancakes. Drop batter by large spoonfuls into hot oil and brown well on each side.

RAISED BUCKWHEAT CAKES
(30 3-in. cakes)

½ cup warm water	½ t salt
1 T dry yeast	1 t molasses
1½ cups milk, scalded	½ t soda
1½ cups buckwheat flour	2 eggs or ¼ cup oil

Pour warm water into a warm bowl, sprinkle in yeast and stir until dissolved. Cool milk to lukewarm, add yeast mixture and mix well. Beat in buckwheat flour and salt, cover for 3 or 4 hours and let stand in a warm place until bubbly and doubled in bulk. Beat in molasses, soda and oil. If not to be used at once, refrigerate.

Pour by spoonfuls onto a hot greased or well-seasoned griddle. Bake until bubbles which form on top break and look slightly dry. Turn and brown other side. Serve hot with butter or margarine and syrup or honey.

NOTE: If thicker buckwheat cakes are wanted, beat in 2 or 3 tablespoons additional flour. If thinner cakes are wanted, beat in about 1 tablespoon warm water, though buckwheat cakes generally are preferred with some substance to them.

WHOLE WHEAT WAFFLES
(3 large waffles, 6 servings)

1 cup unbleached white flour	2 t honey
1 cup whole wheat flour	2 cups buttermilk
1 t soda	2 eggs
½ t salt	¼ cup oil

Mix the flours, soda and salt in a bowl. Stir in honey and buttermilk, then beat in eggs, then oil. Spoon onto hot waffle iron until batter runs to within about ½ in. of the edge of the grids on all sides. Close waffle iron and bake until steaming stops, usually about 4 minutes for each waffle. Serve hot with butter, honey or syrup.

RYE POPOVERS
(6 to 8 popovers)

2 eggs
1 cup milk
1 T oil

½ t salt
1 cup rye flour

Break eggs into a bowl or blender and beat or blend until frothy throughout. Stir in milk and oil. Combine salt and flour and add to liquids all at once. Beat with a rotary beater or blend until smooth. Pour into well-greased heated popover cups or custard cups, filling about three-quarters full. Bake at 500° *10 minutes*. Reduce heat to 350° and bake *20 minutes* or longer until brown and puffed. Serve hot with butter or any preferred spread.

AIRY WHOLE WHEAT PUFFS
(12 to 14 puffs)

1 egg, separated
½ cup light cream
1 cup milk
2 t salt

1⅓ cups unbleached white
flour
⅔ cup whole wheat flour

Beat egg yolk until light and lemon colored. Add the cream, milk and salt. Gradually stir in the flours and beat vigorously after each addition. Continue beating 4 or 5 minutes longer. Beat egg whites until stiff and fold into batter. Turn into hot buttered muffin cups, filling cups level with top. Bake at 350° *20 minutes* or until browned and puffed.

SOUR CREAM CORN MUFFINS
(12 medium muffins)

1¼ cups cornmeal
¾ cup whole wheat flour
3 t baking powder
½ t salt
1 egg

¾ cup milk
2 T honey
½ cup sour cream
¾ cup raisins

Mix cornmeal, whole wheat flour, baking powder and salt in a bowl. Beat egg and combine with milk and honey. Add to cornmeal mixture and mix well. Stir in sour cream, then raisins. Turn batter into well-greased or paper-lined muffin cups and bake at 400° *15 to 20 minutes*. Serve hot with butter or margarine.

APPLESAUCE WHEAT MUFFINS
(18 medium muffins)

1½ cups sifted unbleached
　　 white flour
3 t baking powder
1 t cinnamon
½ t nutmeg
½ t salt
½ cup brown sugar,
　　 packed

¾ cup wheat germ
2 eggs, lightly beaten
1 cup thick applesauce
½ cup milk
¼ cup oil

Sift together flour, baking powder, cinnamon, nutmeg and salt into a bowl. Stir in brown sugar, making sure all lumps are broken up, and wheat germ. Mix eggs, applesauce, milk and oil. Add to dry ingredients and stir just to moisten thoroughly. Spoon batter into greased or paper-lined muffin cups, filling no more than ⅔ full. Bake at 400° *18 minutes* or until a wooden pick inserted in center of a muffin comes out clean. Serve hot with butter, margarine or preferred spread.

WHOLE WHEAT MUFFINS
(18 medium muffins)

1½ cups whole wheat flour	1 cup buttermilk
1 t soda	3 T oil
1 t salt	¼ cup molasses
1 egg	½ cup raisins

Combine whole wheat flour, soda and salt in a bowl. Mix well. Combine egg, buttermilk, oil, molasses and raisins in a blender. Blend until mixed and raisins are coarsely chopped. Add to dry ingredients and mix just until flour mixture is moistened. Do not overmix. (If blender is not available, mix liquids in a bowl, chop raisins and add to liquid.)

Turn batter into well-greased or paper-lined muffin cups. Bake at 375° *20 minutes* or until muffins are browned. Serve immediately with butter. Any leftovers can be frozen and reheated.

WHEAT GERM MUFFINS √
(12 medium muffins)

1 cup buttermilk	½ t baking soda
½ cup water	1 t salt
1 egg	2 T oil
1 cup wheat germ	2 T honey
1 cup whole wheat flour	

Mix buttermilk and water in a bowl, then beat in egg thoroughly. Stir in wheat germ and let stand two or three minutes to absorb moisture. Mix whole wheat flour, soda and salt on a square of waxed paper. Add to wheat germ mixture and mix just until flour mixture is moistened. Stir in oil and honey. Spoon into greased or paper-lined muffin cups, filling no more than two-thirds full. Bake at 400° *20 to 25 minutes*, until browned and done. Serve hot with butter and honey or jam.

DARK MOIST BRAN MUFFINS
(24 muffins)

2 cups whole wheat flour	2 cups buttermilk
1½ cups pure bran	1 egg
2 T brown sugar	½ cup dark molasses
¼ t salt	2 T melted butter or
1¼ t soda	margarine or oil

Combine flour, bran, brown sugar, salt and soda and mix well. Combine buttermilk, egg, molasses and butter. Add all at once to dry ingredients and stir just to moisten flour mixture. Spoon into well-greased muffin cups, filling two-thirds full. Bake at 350°*20 to 25 mintues.*

NOTE: The pure bran which produces the typical moist texture and dark color of these muffins can be purchased in health food stores or markets which stock specialty grains. Ordinary bran cereals do not produce identical results, but make good muffins.

WHOLE WHEAT BANANA LOAF
(1 loaf)

2 eggs	2 cups whole wheat flour
3 medium bananas (1½ cups mashed)	1 t soda
	½ t salt
¼ cup oil	1 cup chopped nuts,
½ cup honey	optional
Juice of ½ lemon (1 T)	

Break eggs into blender container and blend until mixed. Add peeled bananas and blend until mashed. Add oil, honey and lemon juice and blend thoroughly. (If no blender is available, beat eggs in a bowl, add bananas and mash with a fork until smooth, then beat in oil, honey and lemon juice.) Mix whole wheat flour, soda and salt in a bowl. Add liquid mixture and mix just until dry ingredients are moistened. Be careful not to overmix. Stir in nuts. Turn batter into a well-greased 9 x 5-in. loaf pan, spreading into corners of pan. Bake at 350° *45 to 55 minutes,* until a wooden pick inserted in center comes out clean. If bread should brown too rapidly on top, cover with aluminum foil. Let cool in pan 10 minutes, then turn onto wire rack to cool. Wrap and store overnight before slicing.

HONEY NUT BREAD
(1 loaf)

2 cups whole wheat flour　　　1 egg
½ cup wheat germ　　　　　　1 cup buttermilk
½ t soda　　　　　　　　　　½ cup honey
½ t salt
½ to ¾ cup chopped
　　walnuts or pecans

Mix together flour, wheat germ, soda and salt in a mixing bowl. Stir in nuts. Beat egg lightly and combine with buttermilk and honey. Stir egg mixture into dry ingredients just until mixture is blended. Dough will be lumpy. Be careful not to overmix. Turn dough into a well-greased 9 x 5-in. loaf pan. Bake at 375° *35 to 40 minutes*, until a wooden pick inserted in center comes out clean. Cool 10 minutes in pan, then turn out onto rack to cool completely. Wrap in waxed paper or foil and store overnight before slicing. Slice thin and spread with butter, cream cheese, cottage cheese or peanut butter.

WHOLE WHEAT HONEY FRUIT BREAD
(1 loaf)

1½ cups sifted unbleached　　1 cup chopped nuts
　　white flour　　　　　　　1 egg
1½ t baking powder　　　　　1¼ cups buttermilk
½ t soda　　　　　　　　　　¾ cup honey
½ t salt　　　　　　　　　　2 T oil
1 cup whole wheat flour
1 cup raisins or chopped
　　dates

Sift together white flour, baking powder, soda and salt into a bowl. Stir in whole wheat flour, raisins and nuts.

Beat egg lightly, add buttermilk, honey and oil and add to dry ingredients. Stir just until dry ingredients are moistened. Turn into a well-greased 9 x 5-in. loaf pan or two 1-lb. fruit cans. Bake at 375° *35 to 40 minutes* or until a wooden pick inserted in center comes out clean. Cool 10 minutes in pan, turn out and cool thoroughly on a wire rack. Refrigerate or store overnight for easier slicing.

BRAN-MOLASSES BREAD
(2 loaves)

2 cups bran
1 cup whole wheat flour
1 cup unbleached white
    flour
2 t baking powder
1 t salt

1 t soda
1 egg
1¾ cups buttermilk
½ cup molasses
1 cup raisins or chopped
    nuts

Combine bran and whole wheat flour in a bowl. Sift together white flour, baking powder, salt and soda into bran mixture. Beat egg, then stir in buttermilk and molasses. Add to flour mixture along with raisins and mix just until dry ingredients are moistened. Overmixing will produce a loaf with tunnels in it.

Pour batter into two greased 8 x 4-in. loaf pans. Let stand 20 minutes at room temperature, then bake at 375° *1 hour* or until a cake tester inserted in center comes out clean. If using glass loaf pans, reduce over temperature to 350°. Turn bread out onto wire rack to cool. Wrap tightly and store overnight before slicing.

SUGAR PLUM NUT BREAD
(1 loaf)

1 egg
1 cup brown sugar,
    packed
1 cup buttermilk
2 t grated lemon peel
1 t salt

1¼ t soda
1 cup moisturized or
    soaked pitted prunes,
    cut up
1 cup chopped nuts
2 cups whole wheat flour

Combine egg, brown sugar and buttermilk in bowl. Mix well, then stir in lemon peel, salt and soda. Add prunes and nuts and stir well. Add whole wheat flour and stir just until flour is moistened throughout. Some lumps will remain in batter. Turn batter into a well-greased 9 x 5-in. loaf pan. Bake at 350° *40 to 50 minutes*, until a cake tester inserted in center comes out clean. This is a very moist loaf, so make sure it is done before removing from oven. Cool in pan 10 minutes, then turn out onto wire rack and cool completely to prevent sogginess. Store overnight before slicing.

HUSHPUPPIES
(6 to 8 servings)

2 cups cornmeal	1½ cups buttermilk, about
1 t soda	1 egg
1 t salt	Fat for frying
1 large onion, minced	

Mix cornmeal, soda and salt in a bowl. Add onion, then buttermilk and beaten egg. Let stand 10 or 15 minutes, then drop by spoonfuls into about 1 in. hot fat in a heavy skillet. If batter spreads too much, add more cornmeal or a tablespoonful or two of whole wheat flour. However, batter should not remain in a compact mound or Hushpuppies will be heavy. Cook until browned on one side, turn and brown on the other side. Drain on absorbent paper and serve hot. This Florida backwoods bread traditionally is fried in fat left from frying fish and is served with fish. However, lacking the panfish, Hushpuppies are excellent with greens or other simple dishes.

DIXIE CORNBREAD
(8 to 10 servings)

Oil, bacon drippings or lard	1 t soda
2 cups cornmeal	2 cups buttermilk
1 t salt	3 or 4 eggs

Pour about ¼ in. fat into a 10-in. heavy iron skillet or use it to oil cornstick pans or muffin pans. Heat skillet or pans while oven is preheating and while mixing batter. Mix cornmeal, salt and soda in a large bowl. Add buttermilk and eggs and mix well. Pour into skillet or hot pans. Bake at 450° *20 to 25 minutes* for cornsticks or muffins, *25 to 30 minutes* for skillet. Serve hot with butter or margarine. Leftover cornbread can be split, toasted, and buttered.

BLUEBERRY CORNBREAD RING
(10 to 12 servings)

1¾ cups cornmeal
1¼ cups sifted unbleached
    all-purpose flour
    (may use half whole
    wheat)
3 t baking powder
1 t salt

1½ cups fresh blueberries,
    washed and drained
2 eggs, beaten
¼ cup oil
⅓ cup honey
1½ cups milk

Combine cornmeal, flour, baking powder and salt in a bowl. Reserve 2 tablespoons flour for mixing with berries. Mix the flour with the berries and add to dry ingredients. Beat eggs and beat in oil, honey and milk. Add to dry ingredients and mix lightly but thoroughly. Turn into two well-greased 9-in. ring molds. Bake at 425° *25 minutes* or until a skewer inserted in center comes out clean. Cool about 5 minutes and turn out onto plates. Serve hot with butter or margarine. This bread is especially good for brunch with scrambled eggs and mushrooms. This bread may be baked in one 9 x 13-in. baking pan if more convenient.

CAROLINA BATTER BREAD
(4 to 6 servings)

1 cup cornmeal
1 t salt
2 t baking powder
2 cups milk

2 eggs
1 cup boiling water
2 T melted butter or
    margarine

Mix cornmeal, salt and baking powder in a well-greased 1½-quart baking dish. Stir in milk, then beat in eggs with a wire whisk. Add boiling water and butter and mix well. Bake at 375° *35 minutes* or until puffed and golden brown on top. Serve with butter or gravy.

BOSTON BROWN BREAD
(10 to 12 servings)

1 cup rye flour	¾ cup dark molasses
1 cup cornmeal	2 cups buttermilk
1 cup whole wheat flour	½ cup raisins or chopped
1 t soda	prunes, optional
1 t salt	

Mix the rye flour, cornmeal, whole wheat flour, soda and salt. Add molasses and buttermilk and beat with a wooden spoon until smooth. Stir in raisins.

Generously grease two 1-lb. coffee cans or three 1-lb. tomato or fruit cans (No. 303 cans) or a 7-in. ring mold. Spoon batter into prepared pans. Pans should be filled no more than ⅔ full. Cover with two thicknesses of waxed paper and tie in place tightly with clean string. Place mold(s) on trivet in a large kettle and pour in boiling water to reach half way up the sides of the mold(s). Cover kettle and steam bread 3 hours, adding more boiling water if it boils away. Using a thick pot holder, remove mold(s) to a rack and cool 5 or 10 minutes. Loosen bread at sides with a slender spatula, open bottoms of cans and push out bread. Slice thin, sawing with a tightly stretched string or serrated knife, and serve hot with butter. This is the traditional accompaniment to Boston Baked Beans (page 82).

BASQUE SHEPHERD'S BREAD
(1 large loaf)

3½ cups warm water	8 cups unbleached white
3 T honey	flour, or more
3 T dry yeast	1 T salt

Mix ½ cup warm water, honey and yeast in a small bowl. Stir and let stand in a warm place until bubbly, 10 to 15 minutes. Mix flour and salt, then add yeast mixture and remaining 3 cups warm water. Mix thoroughly, then knead on a lightly floured surface until smooth, satiny and elastic, about 10 minutes. (Knead in enough more flour to make a stiff dough.)

Round up dough and place in a greased bowl and turn to grease top. Cover and let rise in a warm place until doubled, about 1 hour. A Dutch oven 10 in. in diameter and 3 in. deep with a flange lid is used for this recipe, though a casserole of similar dimensions can be used. Grease inside of Dutch oven and lid thoroughly.

Punch down dough and let rest 10 minutes. Shape into a round loaf and place in greased Dutch oven. Cover with lid and let rise in a warm place until dough just begins to lift lid, 20 to 25 minutes. (If using casserole, let rise until doubled.) Bake at 350° *1 hour 5 minutes.* Check several times while baking to see that lid has not tilted off bread. Remove lid and bake *10 minutes* longer to allow top to brown. Turn out of Dutch oven and cool completely.

WHITE SOY BREAD
(2 loaves and 12 rolls)

2 T dry yeast	½ cup soy flour, stirred
3 cups warm water	before measuring
2 T honey	¾ cup nonfat dry milk
6 to 7 cups unbleached	3 t salt
or all-purpose flour	2 T oil
3 T wheat germ	

Sprinkle yeast into warm water in large warm bowl and let stand until dissolved. Stir in honey. Mix 3 cups white flour, wheat germ, soy flour, dry milk and salt. Add to yeast mixture and stir until blended. Add oil and 2 or 3 more cups of flour or enough to make a stiff dough. Turn out onto floured surface and knead until smooth and elastic, about 10 minutes. Shape into a ball.

Place in a greased warm bowl, turn to grease top, cover and let rise in warm place until doubled, about 1 hour. Punch down and let dough rest about 10 minutes. Turn out onto floured surface and divide into three portions. Shape two portions into loaves and the other into 12 balls. Place loaves in greased 8 x 4-in. loaf pans and the rolls side by side in a greased 8-in. layer cake pan. Brush tops with oil, cover and let rise in warm place until puffed above edges of pans, about 45 minutes. Bake at 350° *40 minutes* for rolls or *50 minutes* for loaves. Turn out onto wire racks to cool.

WHOLE WHEAT SOY BREAD
(2 loaves)

2 T dry yeast
3 cups warm water
½ cup molasses
6 to 7 cups whole wheat
   flour
½ cup soy flour, stirred
   before measuring

¾ cup nonfat dry milk
3 T wheat germ
4 t salt
3 T oil

Sprinkle yeast over warm water in large warm bowl and stir until dissolved. Stir in molasses and let stand 5 minutes. Stir in 2 cups whole wheat flour and beat until strands of gluten begin to develop. This will take about 1 minute. Stir in soy flour, dry milk, wheat germ and 3 more cups whole wheat flour. Beat or stir until well blended. Work in salt and oil, then enough more whole wheat flour to make a soft dough.

Turn out onto a well floured surface and knead until smooth and elastic, about 10 minutes. Round up into a ball and place in greased bowl and turn to grease all sides. Cover with a greased square of waxed paper and a towel and let rise in a warm place until doubled, about 1 hour. Punch dough down and let rise again until doubled, about 30 minutes. Turn out onto floured board and divide dough in halves. Shape each half into a loaf and place in a well-greased 9 x 5-in. loaf pan. Cover and let rise in a warm place until loaves rise slightly above tops of pans. Bake at 375° *50 minutes* or until loaves sound hollow when thumped. Turn out onto wire racks to cool.

WHOLE WHEAT RYE BREAD
(2 loaves)

2 T dry yeast	3 T molasses
3 cups warm water	3 T oil
4½ cups whole wheat flour, about	1 T salt
	3 cups rye flour, about

Sprinkle yeast over 1 cup warm water in a large bowl. Stir until dissolved, then beat in 1½ cups whole wheat flour. Cover and let rise in a warm place until puffed and foamy, about 15 minutes. Beat in molasses, oil, salt, remaining 2 cups warm water, 3 more cups whole wheat flour and 3 cups rye flour or enough of both to make a soft dough. Turn out onto a floured surface and knead until smooth and elastic, about 10 minutes.

Round up, place in a greased bowl and turn to grease top. Cover and let rise in a warm place until doubled, about 1 hour. Punch down and let rise again until doubled, about 20 minutes. Turn out onto floured surface and divide dough in halves. Shape each half into a loaf and place in a greased 8 x 4-in. loaf pan. Cover and let rise until loaves reach above edges of pans. Bake at 375° about *50 minutes,* until loaves sound hollow when thumped. Turn out onto a wire rack to cool.

WHOLE WHEAT OATMEAL LOAF
(1 loaf)

3½ cups whole wheat flour, about	¾ cup milk
1½ cups uncooked oatmeal	¼ cup oil
1½ t salt	3 T honey
2 T dry yeast	2 eggs
¼ cup water	1 cup currants, chopped dates, nuts or raisins

Mix 1 cup flour, ½ cup oatmeal, salt and the yeast in a large bowl. Combine water, milk, oil and honey in a saucepan. Heat until very warm (about 140°). Gradually add liquid mixture to dry ingredients, mixing well, and beat at medium speed of electric mixer 2 minutes, scraping bowl now and then. Add eggs, currants and ½ cup more flour. Beat at high speed 2 minutes, scraping bowl now and then. Stir in remaining oatmeal and enough more flour to make a soft dough. Turn out onto a lightly floured board and knead until smooth and elastic, about 10 minutes of vigorous kneading.

Place in a greased bowl and turn to grease top of dough ball. Cover and let rise in a warm place until doubled in bulk, about 1½ hours. Turn out onto board and knead lightly, return to bowl and let rise again until doubled. Punch down and let dough rest on board 10 minutes. Shape into a loaf or slightly flattened ball and place in a greased 9 x 5-in. loaf pan or on a greased baking sheet. If desired, brush top with water and sprinkle with oatmeal. Cover and let rise until doubled in bulk. Bake at 350° about *50 minutes* or until loaf sounds hollow when thumped. Turn out of tin and cool on wire rack.

OATMEAL SOY BREAD
(2 loaves)

2 T dry yeast	3 T oil
¾ cup warm water	4 t salt
¼ cup honey	5 to 6 cups whole wheat
2 cups uncooked oatmeal, quick or old fashioned	flour
	½ cup stirred soy flour
	¼ cup wheat germ
2¼ cups boiling water	¾ cup nonfat dry milk

Sprinkle yeast over warm water to soften and stir in honey. Measure oatmeal into a large bowl, and add boiling water. Cool to warm and stir in oil and salt. Mix 2½ cups whole wheat flour with the soy flour, wheat germ and dry milk. Add yeast mixture to oatmeal mixture, then stir in the flour mixture. Beat until smooth. Stir in enough more whole wheat flour to make a dough which pulls away from the bowl. Turn out onto floured surface and knead until smooth and dough does not stick to the board, about 10 minutes. Round up into a ball. Place in a warm greased bowl and turn to grease top. Cover with waxed paper, then a damp towel. Let rise in a warm place until doubled in bulk, about 45 minutes to 1 hour. Punch dough down with fist and pull edges to center. Cover and let rise until doubled, about 20 minutes.

Turn out onto floured surface and cut into two portions. Shape each into a loaf. Place in well-greased 8 x 4-in. loaf pans. Brush tops with oil. Cover and let rise in warm place until dough is risen well over tops of pans, about 30 minutes. Bake at 350° *1 hour* or until loaves sound hollow when thumped. Turn out onto racks to cool.

RAISIN PUMPERNICKEL BREAD
(2 loaves)

2¼ cups cold water	¼ cup warm water
¾ cup cornmeal	1 t honey
2 t salt	3 to 3½ cups whole
½ cup molasses	wheat flour
2 T butter or margarine	3 to 3½ cups rye flour
2 T dry yeast	1 cup raisins

Stir water into cornmeal in saucepan and cook over medium heat, stirring often, until thickened and just boiling. Remove from heat and stir in salt, molasses and butter. Cool to lukewarm. Sprinkle yeast over warm water in a small cup. Add honey and stir until dissolved. Add yeast to cornmeal mush and stir in 2 cups each whole wheat and rye flour. Sprinkle some of the remaining flour on a board and knead dough on the board, working in flour as needed to form a dough that does not stick. Continue to knead until smooth and elastic, about 10 minutes. Knead in raisins.

Round up dough into a ball and place in a large well-greased bowl. Turn to grease top. Cover and let rise in a warm place until doubled in bulk, about 1 hour. Punch dough down and let rise again until doubled, about 20 minutes. Turn out onto floured board and divide into halves. Shape each portion into a well-rounded ball and place on a greased baking sheet. Brush tops with milk or melted butter. Cover with waxed paper, then a damp towel and let rise in a warm place until doubled, about 45 minutes. Bake at 375° *45 minutes* or until loaves sound hollow when thumped. Remove from oven and brush crusts with butter or margarine. Turn out onto wire racks to cool.

3-TO-1 ENGLISH MUFFINS
(16 to 18 muffins)

1 cup milk
2 T honey
1 t salt
3 T butter or margarine
1 cup warm water
2 T dry yeast or yeast cakes

1½ cups unbleached white flour
4 to 4½ cups whole wheat flour
Cornmeal

Heat milk in saucepan until tiny bubbles form at edge. Stir in honey, salt and butter. Cool to lukewarm. Measure warm water (using lukewarm or just barely warm to the touch if using cake yeast) into a large warm bowl. Sprinkle or crumble in yeast and stir until dissolved. Stir in lukewarm milk mixture, the white flour and 1 cup whole wheat flour. Beat until smooth. Stir in enough whole wheat and white flour more to make a stiff dough. Turn out on a board sprinkled with whole wheat flour and knead, working in as much more whole wheat flour to make a very stiff dough. Knead until smooth and elastic, about 10 minutes.

Round up dough into a ball and place in warm greased bowl. Turn to grease top. Cover and let rise in a warm place until doubled, about 1 hour. Punch dough down and divide in halves. Sprinkle board with cornmeal and place dough on it. Pat out each half ½ in. thick. Cut with 3-in. round cutters which are well floured.

Place cornmeal side down on lightly greased griddle heated to 350° (not quite as hot as for pancakes) and bake *10 minutes* or until lightly browned. Turn and bake other side. Cool on wire racks. Store in a covered container or wrapped airtight. To serve, split with a fork and gently tear apart. Toast and serve hot with butter, margarine or desired spread.

Desserts

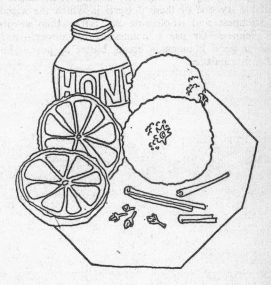

THE MOST natural dessert possible is a piece of luscious fresh fruit, juicy and naturally sweet. When this is not available try one of these desserts in which the accent is on freshness and wholesomeness, rather than sweetness and richness. Or use a nondessert for dessert—a fruit salad or good homemade bread, butter or peanut butter and a marmalade.

GINGER DIP WITH FRUIT
(1 cup)

1 cup dairy sour cream　　3 T diced crystallized ginger
1 T honey　　　　　　　　Fresh fruit

Blend sour cream, honey and ginger. Serve as a dip with
fruit. Especially good with the ginger are orange sections,
pear wedges or persimmon, though any fruits or berries
may be served.

HONEY BLUEBERRY COMPOTE
(4 servings)

¼ cup honey　　　　　　3 whole cloves
¼ cup water　　　　　　⅛ t salt
　1 t lemon juice　　　　1 pt. blueberries
　1 cinnamon stick, broken

Combine honey, water, lemon juice, broken cinnamon,
whole cloves and salt in a small saucepan. Boil uncovered
3 or 4 minutes. Remove spices and cool honey syrup.
Wash blueberries and drain thoroughly. Place in small
bowl and add syrup. Mix lightly and refrigerate for *3 or 4
hours*. Serve in sherbet glasses with sour cream or whipped
cream.

HONEYED MELON COMPOTE
(8 to 10 servings)

　1 cup honey　　　　　½ cantaloupe
¾ cup muscatel or Madeira　⅛ watermelon
　　wine　　　　　　　　2 oranges
¼ cup lemon juice　　　1 grapefruit
　6 whole cloves　　　　2 red apples
½ pineapple　　　　　　Strawberries

Combine honey, wine, lemon juice and cloves in a saucepan. Simmer *10 minutes,* stirring now and then. Remove
cloves and chill syrup several hours or overnight. Peel and
cut pineapple into crosswise slices, discarding core. Cut
cantaloupe and watermelon into balls, using ball cutter
or ½-teaspoon measure. Peel and section oranges and
grapefruit. Wash unpeeled apples and cut into thin wedges.
Add fruits to chilled honey syrup, mix lightly and spoon
into dessert dishes with some of the syrup in each serving.
Garnish with strawberries.

SUNSHINE COMPOTE
(4 servings)

⅓ cup honey	1 cup fresh melon balls,
¼ cup orange juice **or**	mixed for color
water	Finely chopped mint,
1 T lemon juice	optional
1 cup diced fresh	
pineapple	

Combine honey, water and lemon juice in a saucepan.
Bring to a boil. Add pineapple and melon balls, mix well
and immediately remove from heat. Chill well. Spoon into
stemmed dessert glasses. Sprinkle with mint, if wished.

DRIED-APPLE COMPOTE
(4 servings)

½ lb. dried apple rings	4 to 6 pods cardamom
½ cup orange juice, about	Honey, optional

Snip any bits of core from apple rings and place rings
in a small bowl. Add orange juice to almost cover and
turn apples carefully to coat with juice. Break open
cardamom pods and push out seeds into the fruit mixture.
Cover and refrigerate overnight or until apples are softened.
Sweeten to taste with honey, though we think this compote

tastes fresher if only the natural sweetness of the orange juice prevails. Serve cold.

AVOCADO CREAM
(3 to 4 servings)

2 large avocados | ½ cup honey
Juice of 1 lime or lemon | Lime or lemon wedges

Peel avocados and remove seeds. Force pulp through a sieve or mash with a fork. Beat in lime juice and honey. Pile into dessert glasses and chill 1 hour or longer. Garnish with lime wedges.

CAROB YOGURT MOUSSE
(3 to 4 servings)

2 T carob powder | 1 t vanilla
2 T honey or to taste | 1 cup yogurt

Blend carob and honey in a small bowl until carob forms a dark brown paste. Blend in vanilla. Add yogurt and mix lightly but thoroughly. Pile into dessert glasses and serve as is, with whipped cream or a dab of plain yogurt sweetened with honey. Or serve as a sauce on fresh pear halves.

HOT COCONUT BANANA COMPOTE
(6 servings)

5 bananas | 3 T lemon juice
½ cup halved seeded red | ¼ cup honey
grapes or diced | ¼ cup shredded coconut
pineapple | Orange slices for garnish
⅓ cup orange juice |

Cut bananas into ½-in. slices. Combine in a greased 1-qt. casserole with grapes or pineapple and mix lightly. Mix

orange and lemon juices with honey. Pour over fruit.
Bake at 400° *10 minutes* or until heated through. Sprinkle
with coconut and bake *5 minutes* longer or until coconut
is lightly browned. Garnish with orange slices. Serve warm.

NUTTY BANANAS
(6 servings)

6 bananas
1 egg
1 T milk

½ cup finely chopped nuts
or fine whole wheat
bread crumbs

Peel bananas and remove strings which cling to fruit. Beat
egg with milk. Roll bananas in egg, then in nuts or bread
crumbs. Place in a greased shallow baking pan and bake
at 350° *30 minutes* or until a skewer pierces a banana
easily. Serve warm with whipped cream and brown sugar
or mashed strawberries sweetened with honey.

BANANA POUF
(4 servings)

4 ripe bananas
1 T lemon juice
1 T honey

½ cup heavy cream,
whipped

Peel bananas and remove any strings which cling to fruit.
Mash bananas until smooth or puree in blender with
lemon juice. Beat in honey. Pile into dessert dishes and
top with whipped cream.

BANANAS CARIBBEAN
(6 servings)

6 green-tipped bananas
¼ cup butter or margarine,
    melted
½ cup molasses
¼ t salt

2 t grated lemon peel
¼ cup lemon juice
½ t cinnamon
½ cup grated coconut

Peel bananas and cut in halves lengthwise. Place in a shallow baking pan. Combine butter, molasses, salt, lemon peel and juice and cinnamon. Heat and stir until well blended, then pour over bananas and sprinkle with coconut. Bake at 375° *15 minutes,* basting occasionally.

CARROT CHEESE WITH YOGURT
(6 servings)

1½ cups carrot puree,
    about 4 large carrots
8 oz. cream cheese,
    softened

3 T honey
Grated peel of 1 lemon
1 cup yogurt

Peel carrots, cut in chunks and steam or cook in a small amount of salted water until tender. Drain fhoroughly, and puree by forcing through a food mill or in a blender.

Beat cream cheese until fluffy and beat in honey, lemon peel and yogurt. Fold in pureed carrot. Turn into a dessert bowl and chill 2 or 3 hours.

HONEY-BAKED APPLES
(6 servings)

6 firm apples
3 T raisins

3 T chopped walnuts
¼ cup honey

Core apples and peel about halfway down from the top. Place in a greased baking dish with about ½ in. water. Place some raisins and walnuts in core cavity of each apple. Drizzle honey into core cavities, then over tops. Cover and bake at 350° *40 minutes* or until pierced easily with a skewer. Baste several times with pan juices. Serve warm or cold.

Orange-Baked Apples. Mix 1 T grated orange peel with honey for baked apples and pour ¼ cup orange juice over apples just before baking.

MAPLE APPLES
(6 servings)

6 tart firm apples
4 T shaved maple sugar

3 T butter or margarine
1 cup boiling water

Peel, quarter and core the apples. Arrange one layer deep in a greased pie pan. Mix the maple sugar, butter and boiling water in a saucepan. Boil uncovered *5 minutes,* until syrupy. Pour syrup over apples and baked at 375° until apples are soft, but still hold their shape. Baste occasionally with syrup. Serve warm or chilled with cream, yogurt or sour cream. Sprinkle with a dash of cinnamon, if wished.

HONEYED-BAKED FRUIT
(6 to 8 servings)

1 pineapple
1 pt. strawberries
3 pears
⅓ cup orange juice
⅓ cup honey

1 T grated orange peel
Boiled-Honey Custard
(page 290), whipped
cream or sour cream

Cut off top and bottom of pineapple, then stand upright on a board and cut off rind, using long cuts with a sharp knife. Cut pineapple into fingers or cubes, discarding the core. Wash and cap the strawberries and drain well. Just before assembling compote, peel and cut pears into wedges. Arrange fruits in a greased shallow baking dish in which the fruits fit rather snugly. Mix together orange juice, honey and grated peel. Drizzle over fruits. Bake at 350° *20 to 25 minutes,* basting occasionally with syrup in dish. Cool a few minutes before serving. Serve with custard, whipped or sour cream.

HONEY APPLE CRISP
(8 to 10 servings)

½ cup butter or margarine	½ cup honey
1 cup brown sugar, packed	2 T lemon juice
¼ cup whole wheat flour	12 whole cloves
¼ cup wheat germ	
6 large tart apples, peeled and sliced	

Blend butter with brown sugar, flour and wheat germ until well mixed and a soft sticky dough is formed. Combine apples, honey, lemon juice and cloves in a saucepan. Cook over low heat until apples are soft but not mushy. No water is needed unless apples are very dry, in which case add a tablespoonful or two. Fish out whole cloves or, if preferred, let them remain in apples. Turn into a greased deep 9-in. pie pan. Drop brown sugar topping in large blobs over apple mixture. Bake at 350° *35 minutes* or until topping is lightly browned. Serve warm with sour cream, yogurt or whipped cream.

BAREFOOT APPLE PIE
(4 to 6 servings)

6 to 8 firm tart apples	3 to 4 T honey
½ t cinnamon	Water, optional

Peel apples or use with peels on. Cut into thin wedges, cutting out core and seeds. Arrange in overlapping circles in a well-greased 8-in. pie pan. Sprinkle with cinnamon and drizzle with honey. Bake at 350° *30 to 40 minutes* or until apples are tender. If apples become very dry, sprinkle with a little hot water, but they should not be swimming in juice when done. Very hard apples, however, may need added water. Serve warm with cream, plain yogurt or sour cream.

MOLASSES SWEET POTATO PUDDING
(6 servings)

2 eggs
1 cup molasses
½ cup milk
½ cup butter or margarine,
    melted

½ t salt
4 large sweet potatoes
Lemon Honey Sauce
    (page 298)

Beat eggs well, then stir in molasses, milk, melted butter
and salt. Peel sweet potatoes with a swivel blade peeler
and grate into egg mixture. Mix well and turn into a
greased 2-qt. casserole. Bake at 350° *2 hours* or until
pudding is a dark caramel color. Serve warm with Lemon
Honey Sauce or cream.

HUGUENOT TORTE AU NATUREL
(4 to 5 servings)

1 egg
¾ cup brown sugar, packed
2 t whole wheat flour
2 t baking powder
½ t salt
1 cup diced peeled apple,
    not too tart

¾ to 1 cup chopped pecans
    or walnuts
½ t nutmeg
Cream or milk, optional

Beat egg, then blend in sugar and beat until creamy.
Beat in flour, baking powder and salt. Fold in apples,
pecans or walnuts and nutmeg. Spread in a well-greased
1-qt. baking dish or 8-in. square baking pan. Bake at 350°
30 minutes or until set and lightly browned. Cool a few
minutes and serve warm with cream or milk.

WHEAT GERM BETTY
(4 to 6 servings)

¼ cup butter or margarine
1 cup wheat germ
2 cups thinly sliced peeled
    apples
1 t cinnamon

¼ t nutmeg
½ t salt
½ cup honey
2 T water, optional
1 T lemon juice, optional

Melt butter in a large skillet. Add wheat germ and stir over low heat until it is lightly toasted. Spread about a third of the wheat germ mixture in a greased 1-qt. baking dish. Add about half the apples and sprinkle with half the cinnamon, nutmeg and salt. Drizzle half the honey over apples. Repeat layers, ending with wheat germ mixture. If apples are quite firm, sprinkle with water. If apples are not tart, sprinkle with lemon juice. Cover and bake at 350° *30 minutes* or until apples are tender. Uncover and bake at 400° *15 minutes* longer, until lightly browned. Serve with cream, custard sauce or ice cream.

CHERRY CRISP
(6 servings)

3 cups pitted sour red
    cherries
½ t almond extract
⅓ cup whole wheat flour
1 cup uncooked oatmeal,
    quick or old fashioned

½ cup brown sugar, packed
½ t salt
⅓ cup butter or margarine,
    melted

Combine cherries and almond extract and turn into a greased 2-qt. baking dish. Blend whole wheat flour, oatmeal, brown sugar and salt. Add melted butter and mix until crumbly. Sprinkle over cherries. Bake at 375° *25 minutes* or until cherries are tender and juices bubble. Serve warm with cream or sour cream.

INDIAN PUDDING I
(6 servings)

¼ cup yellow cornmeal
½ cup cold water
1 t salt
3 cups milk, scalded
2 eggs, beaten
¼ cup honey or brown
    sugar

½ cup light molasses
1 T butter or margarine
1 t cinnamon
½ t ginger

Mix cornmeal with water and salt in a saucepan. Stir into the scalded milk and cook over low heat 10 minutes, stirring constantly. Beat together eggs, honey, molasses, butter and spices. Blend into cornmeal mixture. Turn into a greased 8-in. square baking dish. Set in a pan of hot water and bake at 325° until done, about *45 minutes*. Serve warm or cold with cream or ice cream.

INDIAN PUDDING II
(6 to 8 servings)

4 cups milk	½ cup molasses
½ cup cornmeal	½ t salt
1 T butter, margarine or oil	½ t ginger

Pour 2½ cups milk into top of double boiler and heat over boiling water until tiny bubbles form at edge. Mix cornmeal with ½ cup milk and stir into scalded milk. Cook *25 minutes* or until the consistency of a thick gruel, stirring every 4 or 5 minutes. Stir in butter, molasses, salt and ginger. Pour into a greased 1½-qt. baking dish. Pour the remaining 1 cup cold milk over pudding, cover and set in a pan of hot water. Bake at 300° *2 hours*. Uncover and bake *1 hour* longer. Serve warm or cold with cream.

APPLE BREAD PUDDING
(8 servings)

8 slices whole wheat bread, toasted	½ t cinnamon
	⅛ t salt
1½ cups milk	2 cups diced peeled tart apple
¼ cup butter	
6 eggs	¾ cup wheat germ
¾ cup honey	1 T butter
1 T lemon juice	

Trim crusts from toast and cut toast into small cubes. Place in a greased 1½-qt. baking dish. Heat milk and butter in a saucepan until tiny bubbles form at edge. Pour over toast cubes, stir and let stand until toast absorbs most of the milk. Beat eggs lightly, gradually beat in honey, then add lemon juice, cinnamon, salt and apple. Mix well, add to bread mixture and mix thoroughly. Sprinkle with wheat germ and dot lightly with 1 T butter. Place in pan of hot water and bake at 350° *45 to 50 minutes,* until a knife inserted near center comes out clean. Serve warm with milk or cream.

STEAMED CAROB PUDDING
(5 to 6 servings)

¼ cup butter	¼ cup whole wheat flour
3 eggs	1 t vanilla
½ cup honey	½ cup chopped walnuts
¼ cup carob powder	

Cream butter until fluffy and beat in eggs one at a time. Gradually beat in honey. Thoroughly blend in carob powder, whole wheat flour and vanilla. Stir in nuts. Turn batter into greased custard cups. Set in a large skillet or saucepan containing boiling water to reach about half-way up sides of custard cups. Cover and steam *30 to 35 minutes,* until a skewer inserted in center of a pudding comes out clean. Check once or twice while puddings are steaming and add more boiling water if needed. Serve warm or cooled with milk or cream, if wanted.

HONEY CARROT PUFF
(6 to 8 servings)

8 to 10 large carrots	5 T whole wheat flour
Boiling water	1 cup orange juice
1½ t salt	½ cup honey
½ t nutmeg	4 eggs, separated
4 T butter or margarine	⅛ t cream of tartar

Peel and slice carrots and place in a saucepan. Add boiling water to a depth of 1 in. and salt. Cover and cook until carrots are tender. Drain well, saving liquid for soups or broths. Mash carrots with a fork and mix in nutmeg. Set aside.

Melt butter in a saucepan and carefully stir in whole wheat flour. Make sure flour is well blended. Stir in orange juice a little at a time and continue to stir and cook until thickened. Stir in honey. Add egg yolks to orange juice mixture one at a time and beat in thoroughly. Stir in carrot mixture and remove from heat. Beat egg whites until foamy throughout. Add cream of tartar and beat until stiff peaks form. Fold half the egg whites into carrot mixture thoroughly, then fold in remaining egg whites lightly. Turn into an ungreased 1½-qt. soufflé dish or casserole. Place in a pan of hot water on lower shelf of preheated oven and bake at 375° *40 to 45 minutes* until a knife inserted in center comes out clean. Serve warm or cold with whipped cream or sour cream drizzled with honey.

For a vegetable dish to accompany meats, reduce honey to ¼ cup and serve warm.

OLD-FASHIONED DATE TORTE
(6 to 9 servings)

½ cup chopped dates	2 T whole wheat flour
½ cup chopped pecans or walnuts	1 t baking powder
	⅓ cup honey
1 t vanilla or grated lemon peel	3 eggs

Combine dates, nuts, vanilla, flour and baking powder in bowl and mix well. Stir in honey. Beat in eggs one at a time. Turn batter into a well-greased 8-in. square or 7 x 9-in. baking pan. Bake at 350° *25 to 30 minutes*. Cut into squares and serve warm with sour cream or whipped cream sweetened lightly with honey, or ice cream.

GRAHAM CHRISTMAS PUDDING
(8 to 10 servings)

2 cups graham or whole wheat flour	4 t baking powder
½ t nutmeg	1 egg
½ t salt	1 cup dark molasses
1 t soda	1 cup milk
	1 cup raisins

Blend flour, nutmeg, salt, soda and baking powder. Set aside ¼ cup of the mixture for dredging raisins. Beat egg, then beat in molasses and milk. Stir into the molasses mixture. Toss raisins with reserved flour mixture. Stir into pudding batter. Turn into a well-greased pudding mold, cover tightly. Place on trivet in large pot, add boiling water half the depth of mold and steam *3 or 4 hours*. Turn out of pudding mold and serve with hard sauce.

REFRIGERATOR RICE PUDDING
(6 servings)

2 cups cooked brown rice, preferably hot	¼ cup honey
1 to 1½ cups milk	3 T carob powder

Spoon rice onto a deep platter or shallow bowl. Add milk, using enough so rice is well moistened but not drenched. Blend honey with carob powder, add to rice and milk mixture and mix well. Chill at least 2 hours.

HEIRLOOM RICE MERINGUE PUDDING
(6 servings)

2 cups milk	½ cup raisins, optional
2 cups cooked brown rice	½ t cinnamon
3 egg yolks	Honey Meringue (page 323)
¼ cup honey	
¼ t salt	

Heat milk in double boiler over boiling water until tiny bubbles form at edges. Add rice. Beat egg yolks well, then beat in honey and salt. Gradually stir hot rice mixture into the egg yolk mixture. Return to double boiler and cook over simmering water until thick, stirring now and then. This will take *30 to 35 minutes*. Fold in raisins and cinnamon. Turn into a greased 1½-qt. baking dish. Spread meringue over pudding and bake at 350° *12 to 15 minutes* or until meringue is lightly browned.

ORANGE CHARLOTTE
(4 servings)

1 envelope unflavored gelatin	2 T honey
½ cup cold water	Grated peel of 1 orange
1 cup heavy cream	(about 1½ t)

Sprinkle gelatin over cold water in cup. When softened set cup in boiling water in saucepan and heat until gelatin is thoroughly dissolved. Cool to room temperature. Whip cream until stiff, then gradually beat in honey·and orange peel. Carefully stir in cooled dissolved gelatin. Chill in bowl or turn into dessert dishes and chill until set. Garnish with sliced oranges, if wished.

BOILED HONEY CUSTARD
(4 to 6 servings)

3 eggs	2 cups milk
¼ cup honey	1 t vanilla
⅛ t salt	

Beat eggs with honey and salt in top of double boiler until blended, then stir in milk. Place over hot, not boiling, water and cook and stir until custard coats a metal spoon. Cool promptly by placing pan in a larger pan of cold water. Stir in vanilla and chill well. Serve alone as dessert or serve as sauce on fruit.

BAKED HONEY CUSTARD
(4 servings)

2 eggs
¼ cup honey
¼ t salt

2 cups milk, scalded
1 t vanilla
Grated nutmeg

Beat eggs until well mixed and beat in honey, salt, vanilla and scalded milk. Pour into custard cups. Sprinkle a few flecks of nutmeg on top of each custard. Set cups in a pan of hot water and bake at 350° *50 minutes* or until the tip of a knife inserted into centers comes out clean. Cool, then refrigerate.

Jason

FRUIT CUSTARD
(6 servings)

1½ cups hot milk
2 T honey
⅔ cup diced or sliced
    apple, peach or
    soaked dried apricots
    or prunes

2 eggs

Combine hot milk, honey and fruit in blender and blend until almost smooth, about 1 minute. Add eggs and blend a few seconds, just until egg is mixed in. Pour into greased custard cups. Place in a pan of hot water and bake at 350° for *50 minutes* or until a knife inserted in center comes out clean.

FRESH FRUIT PARFAIT
(8 to 10 servings)

2 envelopes unflavored
    gelatin
½ cup cold water
2½ cups buttermilk
2 T lemon juice

¾ cup honey
6 peaches or persimmons
    or equivalent apricots
    or berries

Sprinkle gelatin over cold water in saucepan. Stir over low heat until gelatin is dissolved. Remove from heat and beat in buttermilk, lemon juice and honey. Chill until mixture mounds when dropped from a spoon. Peel and dice fruit or wash and cap berries and drain well. Layer gelatin mixture and fruit into tall glasses, beginning and ending with gelatin mixture. Chill until firm.

PUMPKIN NUT MOLD
(6 to 8 servings)

1 envelope unflavored gelatin	1 cup milk
	½ t cinnamon
¼ cup cold water	½ t salt
1 cup mashed cooked pumpkin	¼ t ginger
	¼ t nutmeg
3 eggs, separated	1 cup chopped walnuts or pecans
¾ cup honey	

Sprinkle gelatin over cold water in small cup. Combine pumpkin, egg yolks, honey, milk, cinnamon, salt, ginger and nutmeg in top of double boiler. Cook over boiling water, stirring constantly, until slightly thickened. Add gelatin and stir until dissolved. Remove from heat and refrigerate until mixture mounds when dropped from a spoon. Beat egg whites until stiff but not dry. Fold into pumpkin mixture along with nuts. Pile into dessert glasses or individual molds which have been rinsed in cold water. Chill until firm. Unmold or serve in dessert glasses. Garnish with whipped cream or sour cream, if wanted.

HONEY ICE CREAM
(1 gallon)

1 qt. milk	1¾ cups honey
1 qt. heavy cream	1 T vanilla
¼ t salt	6 eggs

Beat together milk, cream, salt and honey until well blended in a saucepan. Heat to lukewarm and add vanilla. Chill thoroughly. Beat egg whites until stiff but not dry.

Without washing beaters, beat egg yolks until thick and light colored. Fold egg yolks, then egg whites into chilled mixture.

Pour mixture into a 1-gallon freezer can, making sure it fills can no more than two-thirds full to allow for expansion. Insert dasher and cover with lid. Place in freezer tub and surround with coarsely crushed ice and rock salt, using four to six parts ice to one part rock salt. The smaller proportion of rock salt produces finer textured ice cream but prolongs freezing somewhat. Engage freezer crank.

Turn slowly until mixture begins to pull slightly, the point at which the ice cream begins to thicken noticeably. This takes about *30 to 45 minutes,* with constant turning and several ice cream lovers to spell each other at the crank. Increase speed to whip ice cream for *5 or 10 minutes.* Ice cream can be frozen until firm, but has better texture if frozen to a soft-whipped consistency, then packed and allowed to ripen.

To pack, remove dasher, being careful not to let salty water get into the ice cream. Pack ice cream solidly in can with a spoon. Replace lid and plug hole in the lid with a cork. Put ice cream can in a home freezer for 2 hours or longer or repack in freezer tub with ice and salt, using a four-to-one ratio if ice cream is to ripen less than 2 hours, six-to-one if to ripen longer. Wrap freezer tub in several layers of newspaper, heavy towels or other covering while ice cream ripens.

To use an automatic refrigerator freezer, pour ice cream into ice cube trays (without dividers) or other shallow trays and freeze until mushy, stirring two or three times. Chill a bowl, turn ice cream into bowl and whip vigorously until fluffy. Return to freezer trays, then to freezer and freeze until firm. Refrigerator freezer should be set at the coldest setting while ice cream is freezing, but should be turned to moderate after ice cream is frozen.

Peach, Strawberry or Pineapple Ice Cream. Add 2 to 3 cups mashed or finely chopped fresh fruit sweetened to taste with honey to ice cream mixture just before pouring into freezer can. Reduce vanilla to 1 teaspoon if using peaches and add a few drops of lemon juice or almond extract, if wished.

Philadelphia Ice Cream. Omit eggs from recipe for Honey Ice Cream. For added richness milk may be reduced to 1 pt. and heavy cream increased to 1½ qt.

FROZEN HONEY LEMON DESSERT
(6 servings)

3 eggs, separated	¼ t salt
1 T grated lemon peel	1 cup heavy cream
½ cup honey	¼ t vanilla
¼ cup lemon juice	⅔ cup granola

Mix egg yolks with lemon peel and ¼ cup honey in saucepan. Gradually stir in lemon juice. Stir over low heat until thickened. Beat egg whites with salt until they hold firm peaks when beaters are lifted. Continue beating, adding remaining ¼ cup honey in a fine stream, until egg whites are very stiff. Fold gently into warm egg yolk mixture. Cool. Whip cream until stiff and whip in vanilla. Fold into cooled egg mixture. Sprinkle half the granola over bottom of an 8-in. pie pan. Spread lemon filling over crumbs. Sprinkle remaining crumbs around edges of pie. Freeze until firm. Cut into wedges while frozen. Let stand at room temperature 5 to 10 minutes before serving.

BANANA NUT POPS

Bananas
Honey
Finely chopped toasted walnuts

Peel bananas and insert a wooden skewer into one end of each banana. Brush with honey, then roll in nuts, pressing in nuts lightly to make as many as possible adhere. Carefully place bananas on a foil-lined tray and freeze until firm. Carefully wrap in foil and keep frozen until ready to eat. Bananas will have texture of rich ice cream. They are eaten off skewers as if they were an ice cream pop.

PEANUT COCONUT DROPS
(about 3 dozen candies)

1 cup peanut butter
¼ cup honey
1½ cup raisins

1 t grated orange peel
1 to 1½ cups shredded
    coconut

Blend peanut butter and honey until smooth. Stir in raisins. Mixture will be rather soft. Blend in orange peel. Spread coconut on a flat dish or tray. Drop peanut butter mixture by teaspoonfuls onto coconut and roll in coconut to coat completely. Cover and chill or let stand at room temperature until dry.

APRICOT SNOWBALLS
(about 2 dozen candies)

½ lb. dried apricots
  Water
2 T honey

2 cups shredded coconut,
  about

Cook apricots in a small amount of water until barely tender. Drain, reserving liquid in case it is needed to moisten candy. Chop apricots in chopping bowl or on a board with a chef's knife. Work in honey and about 1 cup coconut. Add a few drops of the reserved apricot liquid, if needed to moisten. Shape apricot mixture into small balls, and roll in remaining coconut. Arrange in one layer on a plate and let dry for 24 hours.

STUFFED APRICOTS
(6 servings)

6 large or 12 small fresh
    apricots
3 oz. cream cheese, softened
2 T finely chopped nuts or
    shredded coconut

1 T honey
6 mint sprigs

Peel, pit and halve apricots. Beat cheese until fluffy, then beat in nuts or coconut and honey. Stuff into apricot cavities and press halves together. Garnish with mint.

APRICOT CANDY
(about 24 pieces)

3 oz. cream cheese
1 T lemon juice
1 t grated lemon peel
1 t grated orange peel
¾ cup dried apricots, finely
    chopped
½ cup chopped nuts
¾ cup shredded coconut
Milk or cream

Soften cream cheese at room temperature. Add lemon juice, lemon and orange peels, and mix thoroughly. Gradually blend in apricots, nuts and coconut. Work in a small amount of milk or cream if needed to moisten. Shape into small balls, and if wished, roll in additional shredded coconut or chopped nuts.

FRUIT SAUSAGE
(1¼ lb.)

½ cup pitted dates
½ cup raisins
½ cup snipped dried figs
¼ cup candied cherries
¼ cup candied pineapple
½ cup pecans
⅓ cup shredded coconut
¼ t salt
¼ cup orange juice
Finely chopped nuts or
    additional coconut

Grind dates, raisins, figs, cherries, pineapple, pecans and ⅓ cup coconut, using coarse blade of food grinder. Add salt and orange juice and knead until well mixed. Taste and add a little honey, if needed. Shape mixture into rolls 1 in. in diameter and about 3 in. long or into small balls, and coat rolls with finely chopped nuts or additional coconut. Wrap individually in waxed paper and store in a tightly covered container.

FIG CONFECTIONS
(1 lb. candies)

12 oz. dried figs
½ cup walnut or pecan pieces, about

Steam figs in a steamer or place in a colander which will fit over boiling water in a kettle, cover and steam until tender. The figs will be soft and moist when done. Calmyrna figs take about *20 minutes* to reach this stage, Black Mission figs, *25 to 30 minutes.* Turn figs out of steamer and cool to room temperature. Slit the side of each and push in a piece of nut. Pinch fig around nut to enclose it. Serve as a confection. A plate of part Calmyrna and part Black Mission figs is especially attractive.

BUTTER CRUNCH DESSERT TOPPING
(5 cups)

4 cups uncooked oatmeal, quick or old-fashioned
1 cup brown sugar, packed
⅔ cup butter or margarine, melted

Mix oatmeal, brown sugar and butter together until crumbly. Spread in a shallow pan. Bake at 350° *10 minutes,* shaking pan occasionally. Cool 15 minutes, then toss lightly with a fork to form crumbs. Store in a covered container in the refrigerator. Serve as a topping for baked custard, ice cream or sour cream or whipped cream served on fruit for dessert.

THIN COCONUT CREAM
(4 cups)

1 coconut
Hot water

Remove coconut meat from shell (see page 29). Cut it into small slices or cubes. It is not necessary to remove brown skin of coconut. Put half of it in blender and add 2 cups hot water. Turn on blender until coconut is grated and water has turned milky. Strain through a clean cloth and press hard to extract as much cream as possible. Repeat with remaining coconut, adding 2 more cups of hot water. This Coconut Cream is used in cooking curries and meats or as a flavoring for beverages or on fruits, though Thick

Coconut Cream is more commonly used as a sauce for fruits.

Thick Coconut Cream (2 cups). Prepare as for Thin Coconut Cream, but use only 1 cup hot water with each batch of coconut. This will make a rich sauce, similar in texture to light cream. Use it on fruits, puddings or any desserts instead of cream.

Coconut Cream Without a Blender. If no blender is available, coconut cream can be made by shredding the fresh coconut, covering it with boiling water, letting it stand for 30 minutes to an hour, then extracting the cream by pressing through a clean piece of cheesecloth.

LEMON HONEY SAUCE
(1½ cups)

½ cup honey
1 T arrowroot
⅛ t salt
1 cup boiling water

Dash nutmeg
2 T butter or margarine
2 T lemon juice

Mix honey, arrowroot and salt in small saucepan. Gradually add boiling water and cook over low heat, stirring constantly, until thick and translucent. Add nutmeg, butter and lemon juice. Mix well. Serve warm.

CREAM FOR FRUIT
(2 cups)

1 cup heavy cream
2 T honey
1 t unflavored gelatin

1 cup sour cream
1 t vanilla or lemon juice

Combine heavy cream, honey and gelatin. Heat, stirring constantly, until honey and gelatin are dissolved and blended with cream. Chill until thickened. Fold in sour cream and vanilla. Chill well and serve as a sauce over fresh fruits for dessert.

CHANTILLY CREAM
(2 cups)

½ cup heavy cream
½ cup sour cream
2 T honey

½ t vanilla or grated lemon
  peel

Whip heavy cream with chilled beater in chilled bowl until stiff. Fold in sour cream, honey and vanilla. Chill well. Stir to blend and serve over fruit for dessert or salads.

BANANA HONEY SAUCE
(3 cups)

3 medium bananas
3 T honey
2 t lemon or lime juice

1 cup heavy cream
⅓ cup chopped nuts,
  optional

Mash bananas until smooth, working in honey and lemon juice. Whip cream until stiff, fold in banana mixture and nuts. Serve as a sauce for fruits for dessert or salad.

MOLASSES SAUCE
(1 cup)

1 cup molasses
1 T butter or margarine
1 T vinegar

Combine molasses and butter in a small saucepan. Bring to a boil over medium heat and boil about *5 minutes,* stirring often. Remove from heat and slowly stir in vinegar. Serve warm over Brown Betty or Indian pudding.

HONEY SAUCE
(1½ cups)

1 egg
½ cup honey
1 cup hot water

1 T butter or margarine
Juice and grated peel of
  ½ lemon

Beat the egg in top of a double boiler and stir in honey, hot water, butter and lemon juice and peel. Cook over hot, not boiling, water *15 minutes,* stirring constantly.

BLUEBERRY DESSERT SAUCE
(2 cups)

1 pt. blueberries
¼ cup honey
1 T lemon juice

¼ t salt
¼ t nutmeg
½ t cinnamon

Wash blueberries and drain well. Crush slightly in a saucepan and add honey. Bring to a boil and boil *1 minute.* Remove from heat and stir in lemon juice, salt, nutmeg and cinnamon. Chill and serve over ice cream, baked custard, sliced peaches or melon balls.

Cakes, Cookies
and Pies

IF YOU'VE never had it, try a slice of Famous Oatmeal Cake. It is made without a touch of white flour, only whole wheat flour and oatmeal, and no white sugar, only brown. These 40-plus recipes demonstrate the fine baked goods which can be made with whole grain flours and cereals and honey or brown sugar as sweetening. Follow carefully the instructions on beating as honey must be added very slowly to fats or eggs and beaten in thoroughly. Whole wheat cakes and cookies tend to be somewhat heavier than those made with white flour, so make sure measurements are level to assure accuracy. Carob, a chocolate flavor from the tropical tree—St. John's bread—is used in a few recipes. Carob powder is quite dense, so when substituting it in one of your own recipes reduce flour measure for measure of the carob powder.

FAMOUS OATMEAL CAKE

2½ cup boiling water
  2 cups oatmeal, quick or
    old fashioned
  1 cup soft butter or
    margarine
  2 cups brown sugar,
    packed
  1 cup honey

4 eggs
2½ cups whole wheat flour
  1 t salt
  2 t soda
  2 t cinnamon
  2 t nutmeg
  2 t vanilla

Pour boiling water over oatmeal and let stand while preparing pans and starting to mix the cake. Cream together butter and brown sugar until fluffy. Add honey in a thin stream, continuing to beat rapidly. Beat in eggs one at a time. Stir in whole wheat flour, salt, soda, cinnamon, nutmeg and vanilla. Stir in oatmeal mixture.

Turn batter into a well-greased 12-cup bundt or tube pan or a 9-cup bundt pan and 8-in.-square baking pan. Bake at 350° *1 hour and 10 minutes* for the large bundt pan or *35 to 50 minutes* for small bundt pan and shallow baking pan. Cool cake in pan 10 minutes, then turn out on wire rack and cool completely.

CAROB NUT CAKE

1 cup whole wheat flour
½ cup carob powder
  1 t baking powder
  1 t soda
½ t salt
  1 cup milk
  1 cup honey

3 T oil
2 eggs
¾ cup chopped walnuts or
  pecans
Honey Frosting (page
  315)

Combine whole wheat flour, carob powder, baking powder, soda and salt in a large bowl. Add milk, honey, oil and eggs. Beat at high speed of an automatic mixer for *3 minutes* or by hand for 150 strokes for each minute. Add nuts and mix well. Turn into a greased and lightly floured

8-in.-square baking pan. Bake at 350° *1 hour* or until a long skewer inserted in center comes out clean. Cool in pan 10 minutes, turn out onto rack and cool completely. Spread with Honey Frosting or serve with whipped cream. Cut in squares or slices to serve.

HONEY BANANA CAKE

3 or 4 bananas, depending on size
1 T lemon juice
1 cup honey
½ cup oil
2 eggs
2 cups whole wheat flour
½ t salt
1 t soda
1 t vanilla
1 cup chopped pecans or walnuts
1 cup raisins

Peel bananas and mash with a fork, or place in large bowl of mixer, add lemon juice and beat until bananas are pureed. Beat in honey and oil, then eggs. Add whole wheat flour, salt, soda and vanilla and blend well. Stir in nuts and raisins.

Turn into a greased and lightly flour 9 x 12-in. baking pan. Bake at 350° *35 minutes* or until a wooden pick inserted in center comes out clean. Cool in pan 10 minutes, loosen carefully with a spatula and turn out onto rack to cool. Frost or cut into squares and serve with sour cream and brown sugar.

WHOLE-WHEAT CARROT CAKE

1¾ cups whole wheat flour
2 cups brown sugar, packed
2 t soda
1 t cinnamon
½ t nutmeg
¼ t cloves
1 t salt
1 cup oil
4 eggs
3 cups grated carrots, lightly packed (almost 1 lb.)
1 t vanilla
Brown Sugar Frosting (page 315)

Combine flour, brown sugar, soda, cinnamon, nutmeg, cloves and salt in a bowl. Mix well, then blend in oil. Add eggs one at a time, beating well after each addition. Stir in carrots and vanilla.

Turn into two greased and lightly floured 9-in. layer pans. Bake at 350° *35 to 40 minutes* or until tops of layers spring back when touched lightly. Let cool in pans on wire rack 10 minutes, turn out and cool completely. Frost with Brown Sugar Frosting.

Variation. Carrot Cake can be baked in a 11 x 7-in. shallow pan and will take *40 to 45 minutes* baking time in this pan. The cake can be frosted in the pan or served warm, cut into squares and topped with a dessert sauce or whipped cream or ice cream.

PUMPKIN SPICECAKE

1⅔ cups whole wheat flour
1¼ t soda
1 t baking powder
1 t salt
1 t cinnamon
½ t nutmeg
¼ t ginger
¼ t cloves

1 cup brown sugar, packed
1 cup mashed stewed pumpkin
½ cup buttermilk
⅓ cup oil
2 eggs

Combine whole wheat flour, soda, baking powder, salt, cinnamon, nutmeg, ginger, cloves and brown sugar in a large bowl. Mix well. Add pumpkin, buttermilk and oil. Beat at medium speed 2 minutes or 300 strokes by hand. Add eggs and beat 2 minutes longer. Turn into a greased and lightly floured 10-in. tube pan. Bake at 350° *40 minutes to 1 hour,* until a skewer inserted near center comes out clean. Cool 10 minutes in pan, then turn out onto rack to cool completely. Frost, if wished.

HONEY SPICECAKE

1½ cups sifted unbleached white flour
¼ t salt
½ t soda
1 t baking powder
½ t ginger
½ t cinnamon
⅛ t cloves

½ cup butter or margarine
¾ cup honey
¼ cup brown sugar, packed
1 egg
½ cup buttermilk
Honey Frosting (page 315)

Sift flour with salt, soda, baking powder, ginger, cinnamon and cloves. Cream butter until fluffy. Add honey slowly, beating in well, then beat in brown sugar and egg thoroughly. Add buttermilk to creamed mixture alternately with flour mixture, mixing after each addition. Turn into a well-greased and floured 11 x 7-in. baking pan. Bake at 375° *25 to 30 minutes* or until top springs back when touched lightly. Cool in pan and spread with Honey Frosting. Cut into squares to serve.

FARM STYLE GINGERBREAD
(6 to 9 servings)

2½ cups whole wheat flour
1½ t ginger
1 t soda
½ t salt

½ cup oil
½ cup boiling water
1¼ cups molasses

Mix flour with ginger, soda and salt in a bowl. Mix oil, boiling water and molasses. Add to dry ingredients and mix until smooth. Turn into a well-greased 8- or 9-in. square pan. Bake at 350° *55 minutes to 1 hour*. Serve warm with Lemon Honey Sauce (page 298), butter or margarine or soft cheese.

This is a mildly spiced not-too-sweet gingerbread which is also suitable as bread with the main course.

ALMOND TORTE

6 oz. unblanched almonds (1⅛ cups)	1 T lemon juice
	½ t ginger or cinnamon
6 eggs, separated	½ cup fine dry bread
⅛ t salt	crumbs (whole wheat,
¾ cup honey	pumpernickel or rye
1 t grated lemon peel	are good)

Grease bottom but not sides of an 11 x 7-in. baking pan or three 8- or 9-in. layer cake pans. Line bottom with waxed paper and grease again.

Put almonds through food grinder, using fine blade, or grate in blender, a few at a time. Add salt to egg whites and beat until stiff peaks form when beater blades are lifted. Add honey in a fine stream, beating rapidly and constantly, then continue to beat until egg whites are stiff. Without washing beater, beat egg yolks with lemon peel and juice and ginger or cinnamon until well blended. Fold about a quarter of the egg whites into yolks, then fold yolk mixture into whites. Sprinkle almonds and bread crumbs over batter and fold in gently but thoroughly.

Turn into prepared pan or pans and bake at 325° *40 to 45 minutes* or until top springs back when lightly touched. Cool in pan. Run spatula around edges and turn out onto wire racks. Carefully peel off waxed paper. Serve with ice cream or sliced peaches and whipped cream.

CAROB ROLL
(8 servings)

6 eggs	⅛ t cream of tartar
½ cup honey	Orange Charlotte (page
6 T carob powder	290)
1 t vanilla	

Separate eggs and let warm to room temperature if time allows. Preheat oven to 350°. Grease a 15 x 10-in. jelly roll pan, line with waxed paper and grease again.

Beat egg yolks vigorously, preferably with an electric mixer, until thick and creamy colored. Add honey in a fine stream and continue beating. Beat in carob powder a tablespoonful at a time, then beat in vanilla. Wash and dry beaters thoroughly, then beat egg whites until foamy throughout. Add cream of tartar and beat until stiff but not dry. Fold egg whites into carob mixture.

Spread batter in prepared pan. Bake at 350° *20 to 25 minutes*, until top springs back when lightly touched. Meanwhile, dust a sheet of aluminum foil or a towel with more carob powder. Carefully invert cake over prepared foil and remove pan. Very gently peel off paper. (This cake is extremely tender, so care must be taken not to break it.) Lifting carefully with foil, roll cake from narrow end. Wrap in foil, when cool, unroll to fill.

Beat Orange Charlotte which has set until smooth and spread some of it on roll. Reroll, place seam side down on a tray and spoon remainder over roll. Chill until ready to serve.

HONEY NUT ROLL
(6 to 8 servings)

7 eggs, separated	1 cup ground walnuts or
5 T honey	pecans
½ t cream of tartar	Filling (p. 316)

Grease a 15 x 10-in. jelly roll pan well, line with waxed paper, folding the paper smooth at corners, and grease the paper thoroughly. Beat egg yolks at high speed of mixer or with a whisk until very light colored and thick. This will take about 10 minutes with a high speed mixer. Add honey in a fine stream while continuing to beat. Wash beaters thoroughly and dry them, then beat egg whites until foamy throughout. Add cream of tartar and continue to beat until stiff but not dry. Gently but thoroughly fold in egg yolk mixture. Fold in ¾ cup nuts, mixing well. Spread batter in prepared pan. Bake at 325° *35 to 40 minutes* or until top springs back when touched lightly and cake pulls away from sides of pan.

Meanwhile, spread remaining ¼ cup ground nuts on aluminum foil or a clean towel. Invert pan over the nuts on foil and lift off pan. Remove pan and very carefully peel paper off cake. Roll warm cake, starting with narrow end. Foil or towel should be used to push the cake into a roll. Wrap the roll in waxed paper and cool. When cool, unroll and fill. Roll up again, place on serving tray and garnish as wished—with more of the filling, whipped cream, custard sauce or mashed and honeyed fresh fruit. Slice to serve.

TAWNY SPONGE CAKE

12 eggs, separated
2 t cream of tartar
1 cup brown sugar, packed

¾ cup whole wheat flour
¼ cup honey
1½ t vanilla

Separate eggs and let come to room temperature. Beat egg whites until foamy throughout. Add cream of tartar and continue to beat until stiff but not dry. Add brown sugar 2 T at a time and beat in each addition until thoroughly dissolved. (If brown sugar is lumpy it must be sifted before adding to egg whites.) Sprinkle about ¼ cup flour at a time over egg whites and fold in gently but thoroughly. Beat egg yolks until thick and lemon colored, then beat in honey and vanilla. Fold carefully but thoroughly into egg white mixture.

Turn into an ungreased 10-in. tube pan. Bake at 325° *50 to 60 minutes,* until top springs back when touched lightly. If top of cake should brown too rapidly, cover with a loose sheet of foil or brown paper. When cake is done invert pan on a cake rack or by inverting funnel over a bottle. When cake is thoroughly cooled, loosen at edges and around funnel with thin-bladed spatula. Turn out. Serve plain with crushed fruit or frost, if desired.

CHEWY WALNUT COOKIES
(makes 2½ dozen)

2 cups quick cooking
  oatmeal
1 cup brown sugar, packed
½ cup oil
½ t salt

1 t vanilla or grated orange
  peel
2 eggs, lightly beaten
¾ cup chopped walnuts
1 cup shredded coconut

Mix oatmeal, brown sugar and oil in a large bowl. Let stand in the refrigerator several hours. Add salt, vanilla, eggs, walnuts and coconut. Mix well. Drop from a teaspoon onto a well-greased cooky sheet. Pat out with a greased spatula or spoon to make 2 in. round. Bake at 350° *8 to 10 minutes* or until golden brown. Remove to wire racks to cool. These crunchy cookies are especially good as an accompaniment to fruit for dessert.

BUTTER ALMOND WAFERS
(about 1½ dozen)

½ cup butter or margarine
¾ cup blanched almonds

¼ cup honey
2 T whole wheat flour

Melt butter in a large skillet. Grind almonds, using fine blade of food grinder, or about half at a time in the blender. Stir almonds and honey into melted butter and cook and stir until well blended. Stir in whole wheat flour. Remove from heat.

Grease and lightly flour cooky sheet. Drop almond batter by heaping teaspoonfuls onto prepared cooky sheet, allowing 2 to 3 in. between each cookie for spreading. Bake at 350° *5 to 6 minutes,* just until edges begin to brown. Remove from oven and loosen cookies from pan with a spatula. Let set in pan until partially cooled, then remove to wire racks to cool completely. These cookies are especially good with strawberries, peaches or other fresh fruit.

INCREDIBLE FRUITCAKE COOKIES
(10 or 12 dozen)

2 to 2½ cups chopped candied or dried fruit
1 cup sherry, white grape juice or orange juice
2 cups chopped pecans or walnuts
3 cups whole wheat flour
1 t powdered cloves
2 t cinnamon
1 t soda
3 eggs
1 cup honey
½ cup oil
1½ t vanilla

Any assortment of fruits you prefer may be used. We like about 1 cup raisins with the balance made up of about equal parts candied cherries, pineapple, citron and orange or lemon peel. Add sherry or fruit juice to fruit, mix well, cover bowl and let stand at room temperature several hours or overnight. Add nuts to fruit before mixing dough.

Mix whole wheat flour, cloves, cinnamon and soda. Beat eggs, then beat in honey and oil. Add flour and mix well. Stir in fruit and nuts, then vanilla. This will make a heavy dough.

Drop by teaspoonfuls onto greased cooky sheets, shaping cookies into mounds since they do not spread much. Bake at 325° *10 minutes* or until just barely tinged with brown.

PEANUT COOKIES
(about 2 dozen)

½ cup butter or margarine
¾ cup brown sugar, packed
1 egg
1 cup whole wheat flour
1 t baking powder
1 to 1½ T milk
½ cup salted peanuts
½ cup oatmeal, uncooked

Soften butter at room temperature. Beat until fluffy, then beat in brown sugar until creamy. Beat in egg thoroughly. Add flour and baking powder. Mix well but lightly. Blend in enough milk to make a soft dough, then blend in peanuts and oatmeal. Drop by teaspoonfuls onto greased cooky sheets. Bake at 375° *12 to 15 minutes,* until lightly browned. Cool on wire racks.

HONEY MOLASSES COOKIES
(6 to 7 dozen 3-in. cookies)

1 cup butter or margarine	1 t cinnamon
2 eggs	3¼ cups whole wheat flour
¾ cup honey	1 t salt
1 cup molasses	2 t soda dissolved in 2 T
½ t ginger	water
½ t dry mustard	

Soften butter at room temperature, then cream until fluffy. Beat in eggs thoroughly, then beat in honey and molasses until smooth. Beat in ginger, mustard and cinnamon. Add a cupful of flour and blend well. Add the salt and another cupful of the flour and blend well. Add remaining flour and blend well. Stir in the soda dissolved in water.

Drop by teaspoonfuls onto a greased cooky sheet. Allow plenty of space since this cooky spreads a great deal. Bake at 375° until lightly browned, *8 to 10 minutes.*

CAROB WHEAT GERM WAFERS
(3½ to 4 dozen)

½ cup butter	½ t soda
¾ cup brown sugar, packed	½ t salt
1 egg	½ cup whole wheat flour
1 cup wheat germ	1 t vanilla
¼ cup carob powder	

Cream together butter and sugar until fluffy. Beat in egg. Stir in wheat germ ¼ cup at a time. Mix in the carob powder, soda, salt, whole wheat flour and vanilla. Drop by teaspoonfuls onto an ungreased baking sheet, spacing cookies at least 2 inches apart. Bake at 375° for *8 to 10 minutes.* Cool on wire racks.

MAGIC PEANUT BUTTER DROPS
(about 4 dozen)

1½ cups peanut butter
¾ cup honey
2 egg whites, unbeaten

Blend peanut butter and honey until smooth. (Use a rubber spatula or sturdy wooden spoon for blending as the peanut butter is too sticky for use of an automatic mixer.) Gradually blend in egg whites. Drop by teaspoonfuls onto ungreased cooky sheets. Bake at 350° *10 to 12 minutes*, until lightly browned and firm when touched lightly. Let cool a minute or two before removing from baking sheets. Cool on wire racks.

BROWN SUGAR OAT CRISPS
(about 3½ dozen)

2 eggs	2 t baking powder
1 cup brown sugar,	¼ t salt
1 T oil	2 cups oatmeal
1 t vanilla	

Beat eggs in bowl until foamy, then beat in sugar and continue to beat until mixture ribbons off beater when lifted. Beat in oil and vanilla. Mix baking powder, salt and oatmeal. Add to egg mixture and mix well. Drop by teaspoonfuls 3 in. apart onto cooky sheets which have been greased and floured. Bake at 375° *9 to 10 minutes*, until edges brown lightly. Remove to wire racks to cool.

PECAN KISSES
(about 3 dozen)

1 egg white	1½ cups coarsely chopped
⅛ t salt	pecans
1 cup brown sugar, packed	½ t nutmeg

Beat egg white until soft peaks form. Add salt and gradually add sugar, beating constantly, and continue to beat until very stiff and glossy. Fold in pecans and nutmeg. Drop by teaspoonfuls 3 in. apart on well-greased baking sheets. Bake at 250° *30 minutes*, until tops of kisses are dry. Remove from baking sheets at once and cool on wire racks.

HONEY PEANUT MACAROONS
(about 4 dozen)

3 egg whites
1 cup honey
1 cup toasted wheat germ

1 cup salted peanuts,
chopped

Let egg whites warm to room temperature. Beat until stiff but not dry. Add honey in a fine stream, continuing to beat constantly. Beat about 2 minutes longer after honey is added. Fold in wheat germ, then peanuts. Drop by teaspoonfuls 2 in. apart onto well-greased cooky sheets. Bake at 325° *18 to 20 minutes*. Immediately remove from cooky sheets and cool on wire rack. Cookies will be sticky when removed from oven, so be careful not to pile them on top of each other. They will become more firm as they cool.

OATMEAL MACAROONS
(about 4 dozen)

3 egg whites
½ t vinegar
½ t vanilla

1 cup brown sugar, packed
½ cup oatmeal

Beat egg whites until frothy and add vinegar and vanilla. Add brown sugar a tablespoonful at a time, continuing to beat until whites are stiff and glossy. Fold in oatmeal. Drop by teaspoonfuls 2 in. apart onto a greased cooky sheet. Bake at 300° *20 to 25 minutes*. Remove from cooky sheets when cool.

WALNUT DREAMS
(about 3 dozen)

3 egg whites
¼ t cream of tartar
⅛ t salt
1 t vanilla

1 cup brown sugar,
packed
1½ cups finely chopped
walnuts

Beat egg whites until foamy throughout. They will beat up faster and with higher volume if warmed to room temperature before beating. Add cream of tartar and salt and beat until stiff but not dry. Beat in vanilla, then beat in brown sugar 2 tablespoons at a time. (If brown sugar has any lumps in it, sift before adding to egg whites, as it is essential that the brown sugar be thoroughly dissolved in beating.) Continue to beat until very stiff, then fold in walnuts. Drop by heaping teaspoonfuls onto well-greased and lightly floured baking sheets. Bake at 250° *30 minutes* or until pale tan in color. Immediately remove from baking sheets and cool on wire rack.

HONEY FROSTING

4 egg whites
Dash salt
1 cup honey

Beat egg whites with salt until soft peaks form when beater is lifted. Pour honey in a fine stream over egg whites, continuing to beat rapidly. Beat *10 or 15 minutes* longer, until frosting stands in stiff peaks. Grated orange or lemon peel may be added to frosting or beat in a teaspoonful of lemon juice with the honey. Makes about 4 cups, enough for two layers or top of an 11 x 7- or 13 x 9-in. baking pan.

BROWN SUGAR FROSTING

8 oz. cream cheese
½ cup butter or margarine
1 cup brown sugar, packed

1 t vanilla
1 cup chopped walnuts or pecans

Let cream cheese and butter stand in bowl for an hour or so to soften. Cream together at high speed of mixer or by hand. Gradually beat in brown sugar and vanilla. Fold in half the nuts. Use to frost Whole Wheat Carrot Cake and sprinkle remaining nuts in circle around edge of top or in other decorative pattern on cake.

STRAWBERRY HONEY FILLING

1 pt strawberries
2 T honey (or to taste)
1 cup sour cream

Wash strawberries, drain thoroughly and cut or pick off caps. Slice into a bowl and drizzle with honey. Cover and chill *several hours*. Just before using, carefully fold sour cream into strawberries. Spread on Honey Nut Roll or Cake Roll. Roll up cake again and garnish with any remaining filling or additional whole berries.

STREUSEL TOPPING

½ cup brown sugar, packed
¼ cup whole wheat flour
¼ t cinnamon
¼ t nutmeg
¼ cup butter or margarine, softened
¼ cup chopped nuts
¼ cup wheat germ

Combine all ingredients in a small bowl and blend until crumbly and well mixed. Sprinkle over cakes before baking, or use as a topping on fruit pies instead of a top crust.

SWEET POTATO PIE

2½ lb. red sweet potatoes
½ cup honey
½ t nutmeg
⅛ t cinnamon
1 t salt
¼ cup butter or margarine
3 eggs
¼ cup milk
1 unbaked 9-in. whole wheat pie shell
Whipped cream, optional

Use the dark-red-skinned sweet potatoes with dark orange flesh which often are labeled yams in market. Boil the unpeeled sweet potatoes in water to almost cover until tender. Drain, cool until sweet potatoes can be handled, peel and mash well. Blend in honey, nutmeg, cinnamon, salt and butter. (If potatoes are still warm, they will melt butter. Otherwise melt butter before adding.) Beat in eggs and milk. Turn into unbaked pie shell. Filling will be rather stiff, so spread it in smoothly. Bake at 350° *1 hour to 1 hour and 10 minutes,* until a skewer inserted half way between edge and center comes out clean. Serve warm or cold with whipped cream, if desired.

NOTE: This recipe makes a very full filling, so pie shell should be fluted with high sides. Any leftover filling can be baked separately in custard cups to serve as pudding.

PUMPKIN CHIFFON PIE

1 envelope unflavored
    gelatin
¼ cup cold water
3 eggs, separated
1 cup mashed cooked
    pumpkin
¾ cup honey
1 T butter or margarine

1 t cinnamon
½ t salt
½ t ginger
¼ t nutmeg
1 9-in. Granola or Oatmeal
    Nut Pie Shell (pages
    321, 322)

Soften gelatin in cold water. Beat egg yolks in top of double boiler, add pumpkin, honey, butter, cinnamon, salt, ginger and nutmeg. Cook over boiling water, stirring constantly, until slightly thickened. Stir in gelatin and cook and stir until dissolved. Cool mixture well. Beat egg whites until stiff and fold into pumpkin mixture. Pile into pie shell. Chill until firm.

MOLASSES PECAN PIE

2 eggs
1 T whole wheat or all-
    purpose flour
1 cup molasses
2 T butter or margarine,
    melted
½ t salt

1 t vanilla
1½ cups coarsely chopped
    pecans
1 unbaked 9-in. Whole
    Wheat Pie Shell
    (pages 322, 323)

Beat eggs until well mixed, then blend in flour until smooth. Add molasses, butter, salt and vanilla and mix well. Spread pecans in pie shell. Pour filling over pecans.

Bake at 325° *45 minutes* or until filling is firm and lightly browned. Cool and serve with sour cream or whipped cream.

BUTTERMILK RAISIN PIE

3 eggs	1 cup buttermilk
⅔ cup honey	1 cup raisins
¼ t salt	1 unbaked 9-in. Whole
1 t cinnamon	Wheat Pie Shell (pages
½ t nutmeg	322, 323)
¼ t cloves	

Beat eggs lightly, then slowly beat in honey. Add salt, cinnamon, nutmeg, cloves and buttermilk and beat until well mixed. Spread raisins in pie shell. Pour filling over raisins. Bake at 450° *10 minutes*. Reduce heat to 350° and bake *25 minutes* longer or until a skewer inserted in center comes out clean. Serve warm or cooled.

COLONIAL MOLASSES PIE

4 eggs	½ t salt
1 T whole wheat or rye flour	1 t vanilla
2 cups molasses	1 unbaked 9-in. Whole
2 T butter or margarine, melted	Wheat Pie Shell (pages 322, 323)

Beat eggs until mixed then beat in flour until smooth. Beat in molasses, butter, salt and vanilla. Turn into pie shell and bake at 325° *1 hour* or until filling is firm. Cool slightly and serve plain or with whipped cream.

PRUNE CHEESE PIE

8 oz. cream cheese
2 T honey
½ t vanilla
1 cup plain yogurt

1½ cup chopped prunes
1 9-in. Granola Pie Shell
(pages 321, 322)

Soften cream cheese at room temperature. Beat with electric mixer or cream with a sturdy wooden spoon until fluffy. Beat in honey and vanilla, then gradually beat in yogurt. Spread half the cream cheese mixture in pie shell. Top with about half the prunes, then spread remaining cream cheese mixture over prunes, smoothing the top. Carefully sprinkle remaining prunes in a circle near edges of pie filling. Chill *6 hours or overnight*.

FRESH CHERRY PIE

Pastry for a two-crust
Whole Wheat 9-in. pie
(pages 322, 323)
1 qt. sour or dark sweet
cherries, firm ripe

⅔ to ¾ cup honey
¼ cup whole wheat flour
2 T lemon juice
1 T butter or margarine

Line a 9-in. pie pan with half the pastry rolled out thin. Refrigerate until ready to fill. Wash and pit cherries. There should be 3 cups. Mix with honey (the smaller amount for sweet cherries, the larger amount for sour cherries), whole wheat flour and lemon juice. Turn into pie shell and dot with butter. Roll out remaining pastry, cut into strips and weave lattice fashion over top of pie. Bake at 400° *40 to 45 minutes*, until juice boils in large heavy bubbles and crust is lightly browned. If edge of crust begins to brown too rapidly, cover with aluminum foil. Serve warm or cooled.

APRICOT SOUR CREAM PIE

1½ cups dried apricots
   Boiling water
1 egg
½ cup sour cream
3 T whole wheat flour

1 t salt
⅔ cup honey
1 unbaked 9-in. Whole
   Wheat Pie Shell
   (pages 322, 323)

Put apricots in a bowl, cover with boiling water and let stand 5 or 10 minutes. Drain well and snip apricot pieces into quarters. Beat egg and stir in sour cream, flour and salt. Beat well, then beat in honey. Spread apricot pieces evenly in the pie shell. Pour egg mixture over fruit. Bake at 400° *35 to 40 minutes* or until almost set in center. Remove from oven and cool before cutting.

HONEY GRAPEFRUIT PIE

1 envelope unflavored
   gelatin
¾ cup grapefruit juice
1 t grated grapefruit peel
½ cup honey
½ t salt
3 eggs, separated

2 cups drained fresh grapefruit sections
1 Granola or baked 9-in.
   Whole Wheat Pie
   Shell (pages 321, 322,
   323)

Sprinkle gelatin over grapefruit juice in saucepan and let stand until gelatin is moistened throughout. Stir in grapefruit peel, ¼ cup honey and salt. Cook and stir over low heat until gelatin is dissolved. Beat egg yolks, then stir in a spoonful or two of the gelatin mixture. Stir egg yolk mixture into gelatin and cook and stir over low heat until thickened. Remove from heat and chill until mixture mounds on a spoon. Fold in the grapefruit sections. Beat egg whites until stiff peaks form. Add remaining ¼ cup honey in a fine stream, continuing to beat until stiff peaks form. Fold lightly but thoroughly into grapefruit mixture. Turn into pie shell and chill until firm. Garnish with additional grapefruit sections, if wanted.

CRUNCHY BANANA PIE

6 or 7 bananas
1 9-in. Granola Pie Shell
  (pages 322, 323)
2 T lemon juice

¼ cup granola
¼ cup chopped almonds
2 T shredded coconut
2 T honey

Peel bananas and slice half of them thinly into pie shell, arranging in overlapping circles. Sprinkle with half the lemon juice, half the granola, half the almonds and half the coconut. Drizzle with half the honey. Slice remaining bananas over first layer, arranging carefully in overlapping circles. Sprinkle with remaining lemon juice, then remaining granola, almonds, coconut and honey. Cover and chill 2 or 3 hours.

GREEK YOGURT PIE
(8 servings)

8 oz. cream cheese
1 cup plain yogurt
¼ cup honey
2 t vanilla

1 8-in. Granola Pie Shell
  (below or page 322)
Fresh fruit, optional

Soften cream cheese at room temperature. Beat until fluffy with an electric mixer or wooden spoon. Blend in yogurt. Beat in honey and vanilla. Turn into pie shell, spreading evenly. Chill overnight. Garnish with sliced fresh fruit, sweetened with honey, if wanted.

GRANOLA PIE SHELL I

1½ cups granola
¼ cup brown sugar, packed
⅓ cup butter or margarine, melted

If granola is very coarse, grind to medium-fine crumbs in a blender, grinding a half cupful at a time. Blend granola, brown sugar and butter. Press onto bottom and sides of a 9-in. pie pan. If wished, ¼ cup of the mixture can be reserved for topping for the pie. Chill well before filling.

GRANOLA PIE SHELL II

1⅔ cups granola
¼ cup butter or margarine, melted

Grind granola to fine crumbs in blender at medium speed. Pour into medium-size bowl. Pour melted butter gradually over granola and blend until crumbly throughout. Press mixture to bottom and sides of an 8- or 9-in. pie pan. Chill well before filling.

OATMEAL NUT PIE SHELL

1 cup rolled oats
½ cup chopped walnuts or
    slivered almonds
½ cup brown sugar, packed
⅓ cup butter or margarine,
    melted

Spread oats in a shallow pan and bake at 350° *5 minutes.* Add nuts and toast *5 minutes* longer. Combine toasted oats and nuts with brown sugar and butter. Mix thoroughly. Press onto bottom and sides of a 9-in. pie pan. If wished, ½ cup of the mixture can be reserved for topping for the pie. Chill well before filling.

WHOLE WHEAT PASTRY I

3 cups whole wheat flour
1 t salt
1 cup lard or hydrogenated
    shortening
½ cup cold water, about

Mix flour and salt, then cut in lard or shortening with a pastry blender or two knives until mixture resembles coarse meal. Sprinkle with 1 tablespoon water and work in with a fork. Continue adding water and working with a fork until pastry clings together in a ball. Gather up in two parts with fingers and shape into balls. Roll half the pastry out thin on a pastry cloth or floured board to a circle about 2 in. larger in diameter than pie pan. Carefully transfer to pie pan and fit in loosely. Be careful not to stretch pastry. Fill and top with second half of pastry also rolled out thin.

Flute edges, sealing top crust to bottom crust, and slit top to allow steam to escape. Bake as directed for pie.

Baked Pie Shell. Use half the recipe for Whole Wheat Pastry. Roll out and fit into the pie pan. Prick bottom and sides well with a fork. Shell can be filled with uncooked dry beans or rice to help prevent puffing, but if not stretched and if carefully pricked it should not puff. Bake at 450° *10 to 12 minutes,* until lightly browned.

WHOLE WHEAT PASTRY II

1¾ cups whole wheat flour   ½ cup oil
   1 t salt   3 to 4 T cold water

Mix whole wheat flour and salt in a bowl. Beat together oil and 3 tablespoons water until foamy, then pour over flour mixture and mix in quickly with a fork. Add remaining water in drops if needed to make pastry cling together. Round up pastry into a ball on a 12-in. square of waxed paper. Place another square of waxed paper over pastry and roll out to a round about 12 in. in diameter. To keep edges of circle from breaking, round up the pastry with cupped hands several times while rolling. Very carefully lift top sheet of waxed paper off rolled out pastry. Invert the pastry with bottom sheet of waxed paper over 8- or 9-in. pie pan and gently push pastry into pie pan. Peel off waxed paper and fit pastry into pie pan, being careful not to stretch or break it. Flute edges. Fill and bake as directed for pie, or for a baked shell bake at 450° *12 to 15 minutes.* Makes 1 8- or 9-in. pie shell.

HONEY MERINGUE
(Enough for topping an 8- or 9-in. pie)

3 egg whites
⅛ t cream of tartar
6 T honey

Beat egg whites until foamy throughout. They will have better volume if at room temperature. Add cream of tartar and beat rapidly until egg whites hold soft peaks when beaters are lifted. Add honey in a fine stream, continuing to beat. Honey must be blended completely into egg whites or meringue will break down. Continue to beat until very stiff. Pile onto cream or other pie fillings, or puddings. Make sure meringue is sealed completely to edge of dish or pie shell. Bake as directed for the dessert or at 350° *10 to 15 minutes,* until lightly browned. Meringues are best served the day they are made. This is especially important with honey meringues, which tend to "weep" more rapidly than meringues made with sugar.

BROWN SUGAR MERINGUE
(Enough for topping an 8- or 9-in. pie)

3 egg whites
⅛ t cream of tartar
6 T sifted brown sugar

Beat egg whites until foamy throughout. Add cream of tartar and beat until the egg whites stand in soft peaks when beaters are lifted. Add brown sugar a teaspoonful at a time and beat each addition until thoroughly dissolved. Pile on pies and puddings and bake as for Honey Meringue.

Naturally
Refreshing
Beverages

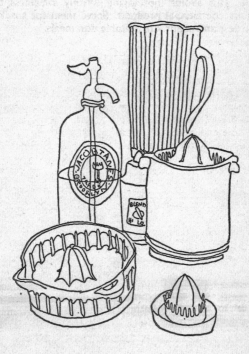

Recent converts to natural foods invariably are impressed by their flavor and freshness. For a test, in case you need proof, taste the difference between canned grapefruit juice and freshly squeezed grapefruit juice. The flavor of a freshly made drink as compared with a bottled drink is unbelievable to one who hasn't tried it. Many of the drinks given here are unsweetened or sweetened just lightly. This avoids the cloying, syrupy sweetness typical of many commercial products. Serve them for snacks and at parties; and many are suitable for meals.

FRESH TOMATO JUICE COCKTAIL
(4 servings)

1½ cups peeled and seeded
    chopped tomato
1 large stalk celery with
    leaves

1 small onion, sliced
1 small carrot, diced
1 or 2 sprigs parsley
Salt, pepper, dill

Prepare tomatoes as directed for peppers on page 195. Put about a half cupful in blender and turn on motor until pureed. Add remaining tomatoes and celery which has been cut in chunks, sliced onion, carrot and parsley. Put cover on blender and run motor until vegetables are pureed. Turn off motor and push vegetables into center of mixture two or three times, if necessary. Chill thoroughly in blender container. If mixture separates, blend a few seconds just before serrving. Season with salt, pepper and dill.

FRESH MINTADE
(4 tall or 6 punch cup servings)

2 bunches or handfuls
    fresh mint
3 cups water
¼ cup honey

¼ cup lemon juice
1 cup freshly squeezed
    grapefruit juice

Wash mint and place in saucepan. Add 1 cup water and the honey. Bring to a boil and simmer uncovered 10 minutes. Chill, then strain mint syrup. Add lemon and grapefruit juices and remaining water to mint syrup. Pour over ice in tall glasses and, if wished, garnish with mint sprigs and lemon slices.

HONEY LEMONADE
(1 serving)

Juice of 1 lemon   Ice
1 T honey   Mint sprig
Water or club soda

Combine lemon juice and honey in a tall glass. Stir until dissolved. Add water or club soda to fill about half full, then fill glass with ice. Garnish with a mint sprig.

PARTY HONEY LEMONADE
(8 servings)

Peel of 1 lemon, cut in   Dash salt
   thin strips   ½ cup lemon juice
¾ cup honey   Cold water
½ cup water

Combine lemon peel, honey, water and salt in a saucepan. Boil 5 minutes. Strain out peel or remove with a slotted spoon, cool syrup and add lemon juice. Pour into a 2-qt. pitcher or punch bowl and add 6 cups cold water. Pour over ice in tall glasses and, if wished, garnish with mint sprigs or maraschino cherries.

Syrup for lemonade can be refrigerated for several days. To make lemonade by the glassful, pour 3 tablespoons lemonade syrup into each tall glass and fill with ice and cold water.

TROPICAL FRUIT JULEP
(4 to 6 servings)

2 cups diced ripe papaya   Cracked ice
2½ cups diced pineapple   Mint sprigs
¼ cup lemon juice   Pineapple spears
¼ to ⅓ cup honey   Papaya cubes

Combine papaya, pineapple, lemon juice and honey in blender. Puree at high speed until liquefied. Pour over cracked ice in tall glasses. Garnish with mint, pineapple spears and papaya cubes speared on bamboo skewers.

COOL GRAPEFRUIT
(2 servings)

1 cup freshly squeezed grapefruit juice
1 cup celery leaves, packed
¼ t salt

Combine grapefruit juice, celery and salt in blender and blend until celery leaves are pureed fine. Pour over ice cubes in tall glasses and serve.

CRANBERRY COCKTAIL
(2 to 3 servings)

2 cups raw cranberries
2 cups water and cracked ice

⅓ cup honey
2 thin slices orange peel

Wash and drain cranberries. Combine in blender with water, honey and orange peel, processing half at a time if blender will not hold entire amount. Blend until orange peel is chopped to tiny bits. Pour into tall glasses and garnish with orange slices, if wanted.

THICK STRAWBERRY SHAKE
(1 serving)

5 or 6 strawberries
½ cup cottage cheese
2 T honey

⅓ cup cold milk
Mint sprigs or strawberries for garnish

Wash and cap strawberries and put in blender with cottage cheese. Blend until strawberries are pureed. Add honey and milk and blend until smooth. Pour into a tall glass and garnish with mint or a whole strawberry.

Thick Vanilla Shake. Omit strawberries in recipe and blend 1 T carob powder with cottage cheese. Dust lightly with cinnamon, if wished.

Thick Vanilla Shake. Omit strawberries in recipe and blend 1 t vanilla with cottage cheese. Dust lightly with nutmeg, if wished.

Thick Banana Shake. Omit strawberries in recipe and slice a peeled banana into blender before adding cottage cheese. If too thick, thin with milk as desired.

HONEY AND ALMOND MILK
(1 serving)

½ cup unblanched almonds   2 T nonfat dry milk
¾ cup milk   1 T honey

Grind almonds a few at a time in blender. Add milk a little at a time and then nonfat milk. Blend until smooth, then blend in honey. Serve at once.

DATE SHAKE
(2 servings)

(This refreshing drink is sold at roadside stands near Indio, California, center of the only commercial date-growing region in the United States.)

½ cup coarsely chopped fresh dates
2 cups cold milk
Honey, optional

Snip dates into blender and add ½ cup milk. Turn on blender and run until dates are almost pureed. Add remaining milk and honey to taste. Blend until well mixed, pour into tall glasses and serve at once.

Orange Date Shake. Add two or three small slivers of orange peel to dates for Date Shake and blend until very finely chopped.

Vanilla Date Shake. Add ½ t vanilla to pureed dates along with milk.

Cinnamon Date Shake. Add ½ t powdered cinnamon to dates before adding remaining milk. A long cinnamon stick may be used as stirrer in the glass or mug.

PINEAPPLE SHAKE DELUXE
(1 serving)

1 1-in. wedge fresh pine-
  apple
1 T honey or to taste

¾ cup milk
2 T nonfat dry milk

Place pineapple in blender. Add honey, milk and dry nonfat milk. Turn on blender and blend until frothy and pineapple is liquefied. Pour into a tall glass and serve at once.

Pineapple Coconut Shake. Substitute Thin Coconut Cream (page 297) for half or all the fluid milk in recipe for Pineapple Shake Deluxe.

NATURAL INSTANT BREAKFAST
(1 serving)

2 T honey
½ cup orange juice
1 egg

1 banana
1 t lemon juice

Combine honey and orange juice in blender and blend until well mixed. Wash egg and break into blender. Add banana, which has been peeled and cut into chunks, and the lemon juice. Blend until smooth. Pour into a large chilled glass.

NOTE: It is advisable to wash eggs which are to be used raw to prevent danger of contamination from harmful organisms which might be on the shell.

HONEY EGGNOG
(4 servings)

2 eggs
2 cups milk
2 T honey

1 t vanilla
Nutmeg, optional

Have eggs and milk very cold. Wash eggs and break into blender. Add milk, honey and vanilla. Blend until smooth and foamy. Pour into punch cups. Dust a little nutmeg over each.

HONEY MINT PUNCH
(30 servings)

3 cups honey, preferably
orange blossom or
clover
3 cups water
1 cup mint leaves, packed

1 cup orange juice
1 cup lemon juice
8 cups water
Block of ice
Sliced lemon and orange

Combine honey and water in a saucepan and stir over medium heat until dissolved. Bring to a boil, add mint and simmer 5 minutes. Cool and stir. Combine with orange and lemon juices and water. Chill thoroughly. Pour punch over ice in a punch bowl and garnish with lemon and orange slices.

Pineapple Mint Punch. Substitute 1 cup pineapple which has been pureed in a blender for ½ cup orange juice and ½ cup lemon juice in Honey Mint Punch.

HERBAL TEAS

A WIDE variety of herbal teas are available in health food stores and herbalists' shops. But an adventurous tea fancier can concoct his own from fresh or dried herbs and spices in the kitchen.

Possibly the best known is mint tea. Simply crush fresh or dried mint leaves, cover with boiling water and let steep for 10 minutes. The pot should be rinsed in hot water first. Pour the tea into cups and drink plain or sweetened with honey.

Bay leaf, sage, whole cloves, or a slice of fresh ginger make interesting teas. Home dried orange or lemon peel also make an unusual hot drink. Rose hips make one of the most popular teas because of their high vitamin C content. If you have old-fashioned roses which produce hips, dry hips by spreading on a cloth or screen for several days as the undried rose hips have a very thin flavor.

HOT SPICED TOMATO JUICE
(4 to 5 punch cup servings)

2 cups tomato juice
2 T honey
6 whole cloves
Cinnamon sticks
1 stalk celery with leaves,
    sliced

Salt, pepper
3 T lemon juice
Sliced lemon, optional

Combine tomato juice, honey, cloves, a small cinnamon stick broken and celery in a saucepan. Cover and simmer *15 minutes*. Strain and return to saucepan. Season to taste with salt and pepper and add lemon juice. Reheat but do not boil. Garnish with a cinnamon stick in each cupful or a slice of lemon studded with a whole clove floating on each serving.

HOT APPLE TEA
(6 servings)

1 qt. apple juice
4 t tea
Apple slices, lemon slices

Bring apple juice to a boil. Pour over tea leaves in a tea pot, cover and brew *2 or 3 minutes*. Serve with apple slices and lemon slices in each cup or mug.

Feeding
Young
Gourmets
Naturally

FEEDING baby with natural foods is no trouble at all if you have the equipment to puree and mash family foods. With few exceptions, a baby can eat almost anything you can if you prepare it according to his tastes and less well-developed digestive system, although you will want to check with your doctor about what foods to introduce when. Home-processed foods are considerably less expensive than commercial baby foods, especially for a fussy eater whose whims may have Mom opening a shelf full of cans and jars to tempt his finicky appetite.

And there will be a word or two later on how to deal with finicky toddlers.

Orange juice usually is the first nonmilk food in an infant's diet. Some infants have iron-clad stomachs and can drink freshly squeezed orange juice. But for the baby with a more fragile digestion the orange juice should be strained and diluted with water. Gradually reduce the dilution and as the baby's tolerance for the juice is built up, he soon will drink straight orange juice.

Cereal is another early food adventure. Whole grain cereals generally are too coarse for the young baby, so serve him cooked grits, corn meal mush or farina. Try the coarser cereals a spoonful at a time as the baby grows older and, hopefully, better able to handle adult foods.

The next step on baby's gastronomic odyssey is usually egg yolk. Simply break the egg and separate the white into a small jar and carefully drop the yolk into a small skillet of boiling water. It will be poached to perfection in 2 or 3 minutes. There are several recipes for meringues and other egg white cookies in this book to make delicious use of the leftover egg whites, which should be refrigerated in an airtight jar until you accumulate enough for the recipe you want to use for the rest of the family.

Soon vegetables, fruits and meats are introduced to a budding gourmet's diet. An inventive mother who works a blender, food mill or cone sieve with a tamper can prepare any of these foods.

First, try applesauce, which is usually a baby favorite. (See page 245 for a sound recipe.) You will want to puree it even finer than for adult consumption to remove any coarse pieces of cellulose, the indigestible component of fruits and vegetables which can cause discomfort to an immature digestive system. Then try cooked fresh or dried peaches, apricots or prunes.

Any vegetable which is not too highly seasoned can be pureed for babies. Put a spoonful in the blender, food mill or sieve and puree it until smooth. With foods to be pureed for the whole family, most mothers remove baby's portion before salt, pepper or heavy seasonings are added. Remember, baby's taste buds are more lively than adult taste buds, so his foods need less seasoning than you might expect.

Meats also can be pureed in a blender or chopped in a food grinder for baby. For instance, a couple of tablespoons of pureed liver is filled with nourishment and goodness.

Few healthy infants are problem eaters, though many have definite tastes. The trick is to find which foods baby prefers and make sure he gets these at least occasionally.

However, as baby becomes a toddler and his rate of growth slows down, his appetite and actual need for calories lessens accordingly. If he has acquired a taste for unnecessary foods, Mother may find herself with a real eating problem in the high chair. As his appetite slows down, cut his milk consumption to about a half pint a day. Continue to offer a variety of foods, but don't make a fetish of having him clean his plate. He just isn't as hungry as when he was tripling his weight from birth to one year.

And keep a step ahead of him. Don't keep appetite-stealing foods within reach. If he likes lots of milk, get some of his other foods in his milk. (See the basic milk punch recipe below.) If he nibbles toast, spread it with peanut butter or cheese occasionally. If he likes to eat with his fingers, give him a half dozen tidbits of meat, a raw carrot stick and a tiny wedge of peach or banana that he can handle.

TODDLER'S MILK PUNCH
(1 serving)

½ cup milk
½ cup chopped fruit
Molasses or honey, to taste

Combine milk, fruit and sweetening in blender. Blend until smooth and serve at once. Stewed apricots, prunes, pineapple or uncooked strawberries, banana or cantaloupe may be used.

FRESH APRICOT PUREE
(2 servings)

1 T orange juice
½ cup peeled pitted apricot halves
2 t honey

Combine orange juice, apricots and honey in blender and blend until smooth. Or force apricots through a sieve or food mill and mix with orange juice and honey.

BANANA FRUIT PUREE
(2 servings)

2 T pineapple or orange juice
1 small banana, peeled

Combine pineapple or orange juice and banana in blender. Blend until smooth. Or mash banana with a fork and beat in fruit juice.

BABY PRUNES
(2 servings)

½ cup pitted cooked prunes   1 or 2 T prune juice
1 t lemon juice   Honey to taste

Combine prunes, lemon juice and 1 tablespoon prune
juice in a blender. Blend until smooth. Stir in honey to
taste. Or force prunes through a food mill or sieve and
mix with prune juice, lemon juice and honey.

BABY'S OATMEAL SOUP
(1 serving)

⅓ cup beef, chicken or   3 or 4 slices raw carrot
    vegetable broth   1 T cooked green peas
1 spray celery leaves   2 T cooked oatmeal (can
1 thin slice raw onion   use leftover)

Combine broth, celery leaves, onion, carrot, green peas
and oatmeal in blender. Blend until smooth. Turn into a
small saucepan and warm, but do not serve too hot.

BABY CREAM SOUP
(1 serving)

½ cup milk   ¼ or ½ cup chopped or
 2 t whole wheat flour or   diced vegetable
    wheat germ   (cooked carrot, aspar-
 1 t butter or margarine   agus, spinach, mush-
    Dash salt   rooms, peas, winter
                         squash, pumpkin or
                         potato)

Combine milk, flour, butter, salt and vegetable in blender.
Blend until smooth. Pour into a small saucepan and heat
and stir until thickened slightly. Cool if too warm.

BABY LAMB AND VEGETABLES
(2 to 3 servings)

½ cup Fresh Tomato Juice
    Cocktail (page 327)
4 T diced raw lamb
½ cup shelled peas

¼ cup sliced raw carrot
1 sprig parsley
1 spray celery leaves
Salt, optional

Combine tomato juice, lamb, peas, carrot, parsley and celery in blender. Blend until smooth. Pour into a small saucepan and bring to a boil. Sprinkle lightly with salt if infant likes salt.

Extras of any of these foods can be frozen in ice cube trays, the blocks transferred to a freezer bag, sealed and stored in the freezer for as long as four or five weeks. Each block will make a tiny serving. Reheat it to serve.

And leftovers of family vegetables and meats can be pureed and frozen for baby's future use.

Communal
Cooking

COOKING for a crowd poses problems that are more tactical than technical. The communal cook needs a good head for arithmetic (how many oranges make 30 servings if 6 oranges make 6 servings, for one simple exercise).

The communal cook also needs a knowledge of how recipes multiply or divide and which ones just don't. Salads and soups, for example, generally can be done in double or triple recipes with little or no adjustment beyond the multiplication of ingredients. As for seasoning, simply taste as you go along and add more as needed.

Remember that a large pot of beans, especially if the texture is rather dense, takes longer to cook than a small pot. One grave danger of quantity cooking is contamination. It is better to heat a casserole dish in several shallow baking pans than one deep pot, which may hold the food at a treacherously low temperature for hours. Shallow pans also speed up cooking, important in holding to a mealtime schedule.

Numerous recipes in other chapters are adaptable to communal cooking—30 servings or more. Soups, salads and stews are most easily adapted. Bread and cakes should be made in recipes as given, as adjustments may be disastrous. Great masses of yeast dough are difficult to knead sufficiently.

However, most cakes or breads will provide multiple servings since they generally are planned for use for several family-size meals.

Fish, chicken and meats cooked in one layer in pans for baking are ideal for large quantity cooking. Simply multiply pans and ingredients.

When cooking rice, spaghetti and other grains in large amounts, make sure the water is boiling vigorously before adding the grain. And add it very slowly, so boiling does not stop. Otherwise, you may have a sticky mass of rice or pasta. It often is more simple to make grains and pasta in several batches.

Vegetables are best cooked in smaller quantities, too, since they tend to steam too long and have a steam table taste when cooked in huge quantities.

For recipes which have been tested for 30 people, try the following:

VEGETARIAN LENTIL SOUP
(30 servings)

3 lb. lentils
2 gallons water
6 onions
3 or 4 stalks celery
3 green peppers

6 cloves garlic
2 T salt
1 t freshly ground pepper
1 cup oil

Wash lentils, put in large kettle with water and bring to a boil over moderate heat. Stir occasionally to prevent burning—especially important with a large quantity. Chop 3 onions, the celery, 2 green peppers and 3 cloves of garlic. Add to lentils along with salt and pepper. Cover and simmer *2 hours*, or until lentils are tender. Heat oil in a large skillet, add remaining 3 onions and green pepper, which have been chopped, and the remaining garlic, which has been minced. Sauté until onion is tender. Add to soup. Taste and add more salt and pepper, if needed. Simmer *1 hour* longer or until lentils are quite soft. If soup is too thick, add boiling water from time to time. Stir often to make sure soup does not stick to bottom of kettle. Serve in warm bowls, sprinkled with grated cheese, minced parsley or green onion tops, if wished.

DAHL
(30 servings)

3 lb. lentils
5 qt. water
2 T salt
20 bay leaves, crumbled
2 cups diced celery
4 cups chopped onion
3 or 4 green peppers, chopped
6 tomatoes, peeled and chopped
12 sticks cinnamon, broken

1 T turmeric
1 T coriander
1½ t ground cumin
1 t crushed red chiles
1 t coarsely ground black pepper
2 T dark colored hot curry powder
1 cup butter or margarine
Whole wheat flour, if needed

Combine lentils and water in a large kettle or two or three kettles. Bring to a boil, cover and simmer *1 hour.* Add salt, bay leaves, celery, onion, green peppers, tomatoes, cinnamon, turmeric, coriander, cumin, chiles, pepper, curry powder and butter. Cover and simmer *1 hour* longer or until lentils and vegetables are soft and consistency is like thick soup. Skim out pieces of cinnamon and most of the bay leaf. If not thick enough, stir a few tablespoons whole wheat flour to a paste with cold water, stir into soup and boil and stir for *2 or 3 minutes.* Ladle into hot bowls. Top each serving with a spoonful of yogurt and minced green onion, if wanted.

PRUNE CEREAL
(3 lbs.)

12 oz. pitted prunes
1 lb. old fashioned oatmeal, uncooked
1 cup shredded unsweetened coconut
1 cup chopped unblanched almonds

1 cup hulled sunflower seeds
1 cup wheat germ
½ cup sesame seeds
½ cup honey
½ cup oil

If prunes are hard, cover with boiling water, let stand about 10 minutes to moisten slightly, then drain on towels. Moisturized prunes do not need blanching. Snip prunes into small pieces with kitchen shears. Combine oatmeal, coconut, almonds, sunflower seeds, wheat germ and sesame seeds in a large bowl. Combine honey and oil in a saucepan and heat until almost boiling. Stir into oatmeal mixture. Mix well. Spread a third to a half of the mixture in a large shallow baking pan. Bake at 325° *25 minutes,* stirring occasionally. Repeat with remaining mixture. When all cereal is baked, stir in the snipped prunes. Cool and store in refrigerator in tightly covered containers. Serve as a snack or breakfast cereal with milk.

MOLASSES-BAKED SOY BEANS
(30 servings)

4 lb. dried soy beans	¼ cup dry mustard
Water	3 T salt
1 lb. sweet butter or	2 or three dried red chiles
margarine	6 cups chopped peeled
6 onions, diced	tomatoes
¾ cup molasses	

Cover beans generously with water, using several large bowls or pans if one pan will not accomodate them. Let soak overnight. Simmer beans in the soaking water about *1 hour,* or until almost tender. Add water if needed, but most of water should be evaporated when beans are done. Add butter, onion, molasses, dry mustard which has been mixed with salt and chiles. Distribute beans among shallow baking dishes. Cover and bake at 300° *2 hours.* Stir in tomato, taste and add more salt, pepper and mustard, if needed, cover and bake *30 minutes* longer.

CHEESE-BAKED EGGS
(30 servings)

1½ qt. milk	¾ t cayenne
3 dozen eggs	3 cups shredded Cheddar
3 t salt	or Swiss cheese

Grease three 9-in.-square baking pans well. For each pan, beat together 2 cups (½ qt.) milk, 1 dozen eggs, 1 teaspoon salt and ¼ teaspoon cayenne. And sprinkle 1 cup cheese in each pan. Pour in egg mixture slowly. Bake at 350° *45 minutes to 1 hour,* until eggs are set. Serve hot.

FISH STEAKS FOR A CROWD
(30 servings)

10 lb. halibut, sea bass or other fish steaks or fillets
Water, white wine or fish stock

¾ lb. butter or margarine
Salt, white pepper
Paprika

Grease enough shallow baking pans to hold fish without stacking or overlapping. Arrange fish in pans. Pour water, wine or fish stock around fish to a depth of ½ in. Dot with half the butter and sprinkle lightly with salt and pepper. Bake at 400° *35 to 40 minutes,* until fish flakes easily when tested with a fork. Dot with remaining butter and sprinkle with paprika. Broil for *4 to 5 minutes,* until lightly browned. Serve at once with lemon or lime wedges or tartar sauce.

DIXIE BRUNSWICK STEW
(30 servings)

2 large stewing chickens, 3 to 4 lb. each
4 lb. lean boneless pork (boned pork butt is a good choice)
15 potatoes, about 5 lb.
12 onions, about 4 lb.
4 unpeeled lemons, sliced
3 qt. peeled chopped tomatoes

3 qt. corn cut off cob
¼ cup dry mustard
1 t pepper
2 T salt
2 cups Laurie's Tomato Sauce (page 241)
1 to 2 cups fine dry whole wheat bread crumbs
½ lb. butter or margarine
Hot cooked brown rice

Cut up chicken and cut pork into 1½-in. cubes. Cover with water and cook until very tender, about *1½ hours.*

Remove chicken from broth, strip meat off bones and discard bones. Return meat to stew and add potatoes, which have been peeled and diced, onions, which have been peeled and chopped, and the lemons. Cook until potatoes are tender. Add tomatoes, corn, mustard, pepper, salt, and tomato sauce. Cover and simmer about 30 minutes. Stir in bread crumbs and butter or margarine to thicken. Taste and add more salt and pepper, if needed. If not lemony enough, squeeze in a little extra lemon juice. Serve hot over rice in large soup plates.

LEMON CHICKEN
(30 servings)

6 or 7 broiler-fryers
Salt, coarsely ground
  pepper

Oil
1 cup lemon juice

Cut chicken into serving pieces and season with salt and pepper. Brush a shallow pan generously with oil and arrange chicken one layer deep in pan, doing one or two chickens at a time. Brush chicken with oil and broil close to heat until browned, about *10 minutes* in a preheated broiler, turn and brown other side. Transfer chicken to a large pan (roasting pan, casserole or other large pan which is ovenproof) and continue browning remaining chicken. After all chicken is browned and in roasting pan, pour lemon juice evenly over it. Cover pan and bake chicken at 400° *30 minutes* or until tender. Uncover and bake *10 minutes* longer to crisp the surface slightly.

GLAZED CHICKEN WINGS
(30 servings)

5 dozen chicken wings
½ cup butter or margarine
½ cup oil
1 T salt
1 t pepper

4 cups chopped peeled
  tomatoes
2 cups honey
¼ cup soy sauce
1 cup minced onion

Arrange chicken wings in three or four shallow baking pans. Heat butter and oil until butter is melted. Brush over chicken wings and sprinkle with salt and pepper. Bake at 350° *30 minutes*. Mix tomatoes, honey, soy sauce and onion. Pour over chicken wings. Bake *30 minutes* longer, basting two or three times with pan drippings. Serve hot with brown rice.

CHAMPION CHILI
(30 servings)

3 lb. beef (chuck or round)	2 cloves garlic, minced
5 lb. pork chops	4 t ground oregano
2 qt. peeled and quartered tomatoes	4 t ground cumin
	3 t pepper
¼ cup diced celery	1 cup chopped green pepper
½ cup diced onion	2 cups tomato juice
½ t salt	1 lb. Jack cheese, shredded
½ t pepper	
10 small green chiles	
1 qt. homemade chicken broth	

Trim fat from beef and cut meat into ¾-in. cubes. Trim fat from pork, remove bone and cut meat into ¾-in. cubes. Combine meats, tomatoes, celery, onion, salt and pepper in a large kettle. Cover with water and simmer *3 hours*. Stir occasionally and add boiling water if mixture becomes too dry. Skin chiles as directed on page 195, place in a saucepan, cover with water and boil *15 minutes*. Drain and remove seeds, then cut chiles into ¼-in. squares.

Combine the meat mixture, chicken broth, chiles, garlic, oregano, cumin, pepper, green pepper and tomato juice in a large kettle. Bring to a boil, turn heat low, cover and simmer *2 hours*. The last 5 minutes add cheese. Taste and add salt, if needed. Serve with pinto beans and brown rice, if wished.

COFFEE CAN SUPPER
(1 serving)

1 thick slice tomato	1 T diced green pepper
1 thick slice onion	½ cup diced raw potatoes
1 thick ground beef patty	1 t soy sauce
or ½ cup drained	¼ t salt
cooked dry beans	⅛ t pepper
1 T minced parsley	

Use a 1-lb. shortening can with lid or 1-lb. coffee can for each serving. Turn cans upside down and shape heavy duty aluminum foil over each. Turn cans right side up and fit foil into them as liners. The food is easier to manage if foil ends are left long enough to lift out after cooking. Place tomato in bottom of can, then onion, then meat or dry beans. Sprinkle with parsley, and green pepper, then finish with potatoes. Sprinkle with soy sauce, salt and pepper. Cover can, using additional aluminum foil, if necessary. Place cans in campfire which has burned down to hot coal and cook *30 or 40 minutes,* turning can occasionally to cook evenly. Or bake at 350° *30 to 40 minutes.* To eat, remove covers of can and lift food out by foil ends.

These individual suppers can be assembled before a picnic and kept refrigerated until time to cook or each person can assemble his own.

SQUASH SQUARES
(30 large servings)

8 lb. yellow crook-neck	4 onions, minced
squash	4 cups fine dry whole wheat
Salt, pepper	bread crumbs
6 eggs, beaten	2 or 3 T butter or margarine
3 to 4 cups shredded	
Cheddar cheese	

Wash and slice squash and cook in a small amount of boiling salted water until tender. Cook uncovered rapidly to evaporate as much liquid as possible, and drain off any excess liquid. Season squash well with salt and pepper, keeping in mind that it will be mixed with unseasoned eggs.

Beat in the eggs. Layer squash into greased 2-in. deep baking dishes with cheese, onions, and bread crumbs. Finish layers with crumbs and dot with butter. Bake at 350° until firm, about *30 minutes*. Cut into squares to serve. May be served with a mushroom sauce, if wanted.

TURKEY FRUIT SALAD
(30 servings)

10 cups cubed cooked turkey or chicken	3 cups diced dates
2½ cups slivered blanched almonds	3 cups mayonnaise
	½ cup chicken broth
3 cups pineapple chunks	2 t soy sauce
2½ cups seedless grapes	2 t curry powder, optional
3 cups thinly sliced celery	Salt, pepper

Combine turkey, almonds, pineapple, grapes, celery and dates. Toss lightly to mix. Blend mayonnaise with chicken broth, soy sauce and curry powder. Add to salad and toss to mix well. Taste and add salt and pepper if needed and toss again.

INDEX